RECENT RELEASES

The Bible in the Modern World, 15

RECENT RELEASES

THE BIBLE IN CONTEMPORARY CINEMA

edited by

Geert Hallbäck
and
Annika Hvithamar

SHEFFIELD PHOENIX PRESS

2008

RELIGION IN THE 21ST CENTURY
UNIVERSITY OF COPENHAGEN

Published with support from Religion in the 21st Century,
University of Copenhagen,
www.ku.dk/satsning/religion

Published by Sheffield Phoenix Press
Department of Biblical Studies, University of Sheffield
Sheffield S10 2TN

www.sheffieldphoenix.com

A CIP catalogue record for this book
is available from the British Library

Typeset by Forthcoming Publications
Printed by Lightning Source

Hardback ISBN 978-1-906055-36-3

ISSN 1747-9630

CONTENTS

INTRODUCTION

Geert Hallbäck and Annika Hvithamar

In January 2007, an international seminar on the Bible, religion and cinema (*Biblical Variations in Contemporary Cinema*) was held in Copenhagen, Denmark. The goal of this seminar was to bring together European scholars working in this area of research, each with their own approach and perspective: researchers in theology, who are focusing on the reception of the Bible and Christian religion in popular culture; researchers studying religion, who are focusing on the relationship between religion and society; and researchers in the media-sciences, who are focusing on religious themes and figures as components of contemporary movie-making. The seminar was arranged by the editors of this book. Geert Hallbäck is Associate Professor of New Testament Studies at the University of Copenhagen and Annika Hvithamar is Assistant Professor of the Religious Studies at the University of Southern Denmark. Thus, as a team, we combine two approaches, and we hope that this volume will also contribute to the interdisciplinary exchange between these differing, but interwoven approaches to the Bible in contemporary cinema. The transdisciplinary outlook of the book is true for the authors as well, who represent Biblical Exegesis, Systematic Theology, Media Studies and the History of Religion.

We invited scholars from Great Britain, Germany, the Netherlands, Iceland and Denmark. A strong contingent of participants is from Iceland. This is due to the fact that a scholarly circle has been established around the Theological Faculty at the University of Iceland, studying the multifaceted interface of religion and film and maintaining a database that includes religious themes and motifs in a large number of registered films. The Icelandic scholars call their project *Deus ex Cinema*; from the start, the database has been in Icelandic, but a translation into English is underway. When the translation is eventually finished, the *Deus ex Cinema* database will be an invaluable tool for any scholarly work on religion and cinema.

In the manifesto of the seminar, we stated that contemporary cinema represents one of the most influential media for religious signification.

According to popular theories of secularization, it is astounding how biblical elements remain a significant theme in contemporary fiction. Biblical narratives are transformed to the screen and biblical themes are incorporated into the universe of cinema both explicitly and on a more latent scale, in psychological melodrama, fantasy and horror movies and romantic comedy. There is no doubt that these biblical elements often communicate a religious worldview. On the other hand, this exposure does not automatically result in a religious worldview among the viewers. Therefore, the study of these films could be central to an understanding of the multi-facetted religiosity, which is communicated by popular culture.

We invited the participants in the seminar to consider the following topics and questions:

1. *Contemporary history of religion.* Cinema is often mentioned as one of the most important media for communication of belief and religious significance. In what way does the occurrence of biblical references in contemporary movies contribute to the formation of religious life in modern society?

2. *Ambiguousness.* Biblical themes in contemporary movies are often coupled with themes from other religious traditions. What does the occurrence of biblical references side by side with references to other religious traditions in modern movies reveal about contemporary religious syncretism?

3. *Formal and stylistic features.* Religion in cinema is communicated through various filmic methods. Is it possible to characterize specific formal or stylistic features which are characteristic of religious movies?

We did not expect any of the participants to engage these questions directly in their papers; but, nevertheless, the chapters in this book reflect one or more of these topics and contribute to the ongoing effort to understand how religious life in contemporary society is mediated through the media and not least through the cinema.

The seminar as well as this book were sponsored by the research priority area 'Religion in the 21st Century', which covers research within all of the six faculties at the University of Copenhagen, in order to combine the study of separate themes into an overall picture of religion in the twenty-first century. In a statement on the research area and why it was established, the University of Copenhagen maintains that the last two decades have made it obvious that religion is, and will continue to be, influential in many areas and in all types of societies. Religion influences both the lives of individuals and the construction of collective norms.

Thus, there is a need for a comprehensive picture of the development and significance of religion in the twenty-first century. The work in this research priority area has been categorized in terms of four fields of research:
1. Religion, society and law
2. Religion between conflict and reconciliation
3. Religion in transformation
4. Religious knowledge and knowledge about religion

More than 70 projects—seminars, study groups, book-projects, conferences—have been organized within this framework. Our work on the Bible in contemporary cinema is only a tiny contribution to the study of *Religion in the Public Sphere*, which forms a subgroup under the heading 'Religion in Transformation'. But we are very grateful to the research area for its financial support and great interest in our work. Without their support, the seminar would probably never have taken place and the present volume would not have appeared.

However, the conceptual focus of the seminar originated in a more limited research project within the Biblical Studies Section at the University of Copenhagen, called the Centre of the Study of the Bible in Theology and Culture. The purpose of the Centre is to initiate and coordinate scholarly research, academic teaching and popular presentation within two interconnected areas. The first one is the study of the history of interpretation of the Bible—that is, the 'professional' interpretation of the Bible in the context of the Church or the University. Instead of the well-known linear study of the history of interpretation, where one sees every new generation of scholars as followers of the former generation—either in opposition to or in continuation with their teachers—we want to study the differing periods of interpretation in the context of broader cultural and social currents in the relevant epochs. The idea is that interests in certain aspects of the Bible are felt to be relevant in one period but not in another, and that these trends coincide with similar trends within other areas of culture and society without any traceable connection. One example might be the upcoming interest in apocalyptical texts and worldview in the late nineteenth century, which coincides with the focus on death and perishableness found in symbolistic art and literature of the time. Another example is the period after the First World War, when all the arts were redefined: theatre was to be theatrical, painting was to be forms and colours, literature was to be sounds and words—and theology was to be *theo*-logical.

Because the 'professional' interpretation of the Bible is in some way or another connected to broader currents in culture and society, the study of the reception of the Bible in art and culture, in education and in religious life will illustrate the same connectedness from the other side, so to speak. Therefore, the study of the reception of the Bible in the arts and culture is the other main area of focus for the Centre of the Study of the Bible in Theology and Culture. This study has a historical dimension, but it also, and foremost, has a contemporary dimension. The study of how the Bible is received in contemporary art, music, literature, cinema, theatre and so on is of great importance both for the student of modern culture and for the student of the Bible.

Within theology and biblical studies, it is often felt that the Bible has vanished from modern society. As a consequence of the ongoing secularization, a fatal loss of tradition has occurred and knowledge of the Bible has diminished or even disappeared completely from the consciousness of modern people. In this context, the biblical scholar faces an enormous didactical task. He or she is to re-establish knowledge of the Bible. This is not primarily seen as a theological or religious task, but as a cultural necessity, since anyone who cannot recognize biblical references will be estranged from most of European culture. However, the very preliminary studies of the reception of the Bible in contemporary art and culture conducted by the Centre do not confirm this gloomy picture.

We find that the Bible is alive and well—out there. I would even maintain that there is a growing interest in the Bible among contemporary artists. And biblical references in popular culture form part of the vast reservoir of cultural identity markers and figures of recognition that facilitate communication with the public. We also find that the Bible is received and understood in ways quite distant from the orthodoxies of the scholarly world and the Church. The Bible, first and foremost, is not seen as a historical document or an authoritative canon; rather, it is part of the cultural intertext, where it appears together with popular figures from cartoons and the 'classics' of literature and film. Or it is seen as referring to deep religious experiences that might inspire modern artists in their search for authentic spirituality.

At the Centre, we think that it is paramount for biblical scholars to get in touch with these 'unauthorized' ways of understanding and making use of the Bible. We tend to live in an isolated world of scholarly concern, which is not only legitimate, but also necessary for the continuation, progression and education of academic works on the Bible. But we must realize that there are other and perhaps more vital ways of living with the Bible or making the Bible alive outside the university. For three reasons it would be profitable for the biblical scholar to obtain more comprehensive knowledge and understanding of the Bible's latent or evident life in contemporary culture. First, if the scholar wants to promote the academic understanding of the Bible to a broader public, he/she should know how that public relates to the Bible as part of normal cultural behaviour, instead of presupposing that the public has no relation to the Bible from the start. That presupposition will almost certainly be wrong and his/her didactic strategy might fail. Second, the study of the reception of the Bible is, in any case, part of the scholarly work on the Bible and that evidently includes contemporary cultural reception as well. The scholar might even understand his/her own academic concerns better when he/she sees them in the perspective of the broader cultural reception of the Bible. Third, the non-academic understanding of the Bible that is manifested in artistic practices might open up eyes the eyes to the semantic possibilities of the texts that have been covered up by the normal academic reading practice. It is sound for any reader of the Bible to be reminded of the fact that no reading or understanding of it can exhaust the texts' semantic possibilities.

Among the many ways of cultural and artistic receptions, the cinematic reception of the Bible is of special interest. Movies have an exceptionally strong impact on audiences due to the fact that they combine different artistic disciplines—such as imagery, narrative, sound, acting—and are shown in a dark hall where sensorial competition is reduced to a minimum. The audience is in some way absorbed by the action on the screen. Also, film is a popular and commercial art. The production of a film is costly compared to other disciplines and the filmmakers—or rather the investors—would like it to make money. In addition, the circulation of a film is relatively swift; it will be shown in the cinema for a couple of months at the most—and that is only if it is a success. The filmmakers therefore will try to secure the attention of a vast public for a short time, and in order to do that they will stimulate cultural stereotypes and figures of identification, but they will also have to present something surprising and remarkable. They will attempt to create something at the leading edge of the public's interest, to try to guess where the public's attention is moving. This makes movies a privileged place to study the most recent movements of the collective consciousness. If you are interested in cultural reception of any kind, and certainly also the cultural reception of the Bible, contemporary cinema should be first place for you to look.

Seen from a sociology of religion approach, as well, religious elements in films are here to stay. And in recent releases, they seem to be increasing. But from a science of religion perspective, the focus for examining religion in film does not stop with the Bible. The religious topics of the films are relevant whether they refer to the Bible, the Mahabharata, the Koran or any other religious source that is the basis of inspiration. The overall question from this perspective is, therefore, how the religious texts are used and how this use reflects developments in society—for instance, how religious texts are mixed and matched in contemporary cinema. In this respect, the focus is more on the relation between religion and society than on how the plots of the films relate to the sacred sources. An example of this kind of approach is an analysis of the way religious elements in films can be differentiated. Religion may be present in many films, but there is a difference between films in which the religious element is only present in the form of set pieces, like a religious building in the background of a scene, and films in which the plot directly or indirectly is built upon religious themes (Mikkel Eskjær's contribution deals with this theme). Thus, it is relevant for the analysis to consider that religious effects sometimes are present just as props to indicate a geographical location (e.g. monks in orange robes or medicine men), a historical period (e.g. crusaders or Greek temples) or to describe a quality (e.g. a someone wearing a cross, showing the pious, or hypocrite, or spiritually inclined personality of a certain character).

Therefore, the study of religion also raises the question of whether it is always legitimate to interpret certain filmic topics as religious, or with a religious significance—let alone biblical. Does the impact of the Bible on Western civilization imply that Christian scripture inevitably inspires contemporary artists when they address philosophical questions? To pick one example, when is it possible to talk about a Christ figure? When Robert Duvall in *The Apostle* (Robert Duvall 1997), in spite of his evident sins, is a model for his congregation? When Keanu Reeves in *The Matrix* (Andrew Wachowski 1999–2003) reveals himself as the Chosen One? When Emily Watson in *Breaking the Waves* (Lars von Trier 1996) sacrifices her life for her husband's sake? From the perspective of the study of religion, the question is whether the Christian myth of the sinless life, passion and miraculous resurrection is the myth upon which all other stories treating those themes is built—or whether the cosmic fight of good against evil, the ultimate sacrifice and the victory of the weak and poor over scrupulous powers are primordial themes that the Christian myths have incorporated. Britt Istoft's chapter in this book is one example of how primordial themes that are used in biblical films serve the same functions when they are transferred to another religious universe like the *Star Trek* universe.

The intentions of the scriptwriter or director of a particular film does not necessarily restrict the analysis of the film in relation to the question of religious influence. However, in a culture which on the one hand is secularized and on the other hand is multireligious, it is necessary to keep in mind this context.

One interesting theme in contemporary cinema, seen from the perspective of religious studies, is the individualization of religion—e.g. films that question the validity of religious institutions and their dogmas. The vigorous debate that was raised when the book (and later the film) *The Da Vinci Code* (Ron Howard 2006) was released is an example of a theme that questions the interpretation of Christianity. But it is worth noting that the popular religious understanding of Jesus as an extraordinary being, with superhuman features, was not questioned. *The Matrix* trilogy with its mix of Christian and Gnostic ideas of salvation with Buddhist teaching of the illusion of the ego and the Platonic allegory of the cave is another example of how individualization of religion is revealed in contemporary cinema. In the present volume, this perspective is incorporated in Caroline Vander Stichele's contribution, which analyzes how the directors' views of Mary Magdalene are decisive for their portrayal of her character. As such, it is not the institution, the Church, which decides how Mary could be interpreted, but the artistic taste of individual directors. Further, Thorkell Ottarsson's contribution, which analyzes both traditional and eclectic uses of the Eden theme, exemplifies the theme of individualization.

Another appealing topic is the role of religion in popular culture. Popular cinema is filled with religious elements that are not part of official dogma, but are a vivid part of popular religion. In the horror genre, magic, ghosts, witch doctors, voodoo, angels and demons, Egyptian curses and so on. are recurrent themes. However, even though the themes are not part of an official religion, the conflicts are often solved in accordance with liturgical conventions: Demons exist. The priest (and only the priest) can exorcize the demon. Faith does move mountains. The crucifix does keep the vampires away. In popular cinema it is characteristic that the (popular-)religious universe is used on a grand scale—and it is taken for granted. This type of film does not end with a negation of the metaphysical universe. As such, official religious scripture, religious institutions, religious dogma and religious experts play a part in this type of film.

Further, the issue of secularization is interesting when seen from the perspective of the study of religion. Whereas the general secularization thesis was dismissed long ago, the way religion is used, formed and created is changing. As Arnfríður Guðmundsdóttir's and Jesper Tang Nielsen's chapters exemplify, Jesus films are still produced, but it is individual directors who decide how the figures should be interpreted, not religious institutions. Furthermore, it is the media industry that decides when and where religious elements should be present—or whether it is necessary to do this correctly. One famous example of the way religious scripture is misquoted occurs in *Pulp Fiction* (Quentin Tarantino 1994), where Jules

(Samuel L. Jackson) throughout the film uses a citation from the Bible that he at one point explains is Ezek. 25.17. However, apart from a few sentences, this citation does not exist. It is just used by the scriptwriter to portray a character. Perhaps it is a sign of secularization that it is representatives of the media who decide how and when religious themes are relevant to show, and not representatives of the Church.

In sum, seen from the perspective of the science of religion, the use of religion in film is more about how religious sources are used than why they are used. In short, how religious elements are used is affected by the relationship, the development and the changing links between religion and society.

The relationship between theology and popular culture has never been simple. When the film was invented in the very last years of the nineteenth century, the first moving pictures were shown at market places and popular gatherings. Quickly the cinema was considered just another fringe of low culture and escapism and thus not worthwhile mentioning in serious studies. In the last decenniums, however, the study of popular cinema has become legitimate in various fields of scholarship.

The seemingly escapist world outlook of Hollywood films is the subject of Chris Deacy's article, which opens up the book. Taking his clue from Gordon Lynch's definition of theology as 'the process of seeking normative answers to questions of truth/meaning, goodness/practice, evil, suffering, redemption, and beauty in specific contexts', Deacy discusses the possibility of going beyond the escapism. The creation of ideal worlds is not just a characteristic of popular cinema—furthermore, in theological thinking, popular films should be seen not as delusions, but as a theological resource. Through examples of a wide selection of popular films, Deacy shows how themes like truth-telling, personal growth, familial perfection, accomplishment of good and the like are exemplified in popular cinema. Thus even escapist films can contribute to the task of human flourishing.

Whereas Deacy's approach to the study of cinema is based on theological reflections, the author of the second chapter of the book applies an approach coming from media studies. Mikkel Eskjær presents an overview based on film sociology of the relation between institution, communication and religion in Danish contemporary cinema. As both cinema and religion are modes of communication, Eskjær seeks to analyze how religious matters are turned into cinematic communication and how cinematic codes and conventions are adjusted to religious communication. He does that by presenting a model that arranges film along a vertical and a horizontal axis. Along the vertical axis, religious matters in films are represented along a continuum, with unofficial or 'banal' religion at one end and the representation of official or explicit religion at the other. On the horizontal axis, films are distinguished along a continuum from genre cinema (the classical Hollywood narration) to art cinema (e.g. films inspired by European modernism). By applying this model to a variety of Danish films of the last decenniums, the author shows the relations between different modes of narration and different types of religious cinema. This leads him to argue that it is not as much the role and function of religion that differs in the two types of cinema as the way it is adapted to the narrative conventions of the two genres. This approach enables Eskjær to show that religion is used in cinema only when it is part of society's cultural fund and contributes to the cultural horizon of experience. However, cinema also gives religion a new and different life through the negotiations of identity and intimacy as seen in genre cinema, or through the more reflexive struggle with modern conditions found in art cinema.

The first two chapters of the book address theoretical and methodological approaches to the study of contemporary cinema, while the next chapters take a deeper look into specific themes of the films. Thus, Árni Svanur Daníelsson concentrates on how the Christian theological concept of salvation is used in contemporary films (especially *In America*, 2002; *Levity*, 2003; and *Tsotsi*, 2005). In his chapter, he analyzes how sin, sacrifice and resurrection are used as frameworks for the films and thus shows how modern characters and a modern setting can make theological themes both touchable and relevant for contemporary society. By focusing on the way the narratives are mediating classical biblical themes, his contribution exemplifies the fruitfulness of a theological 'reading' of these films.

The popular theme of Adam and Eve is the subject of Thorkell August Ottarsson's chapter. By dividing the vast amount of films into two subgroups, *traditional* and *eclectic* interpretations, Ottarsson shows how the Eden myth is an ever-relevant framework for recent releases (as well as earlier films). The way of sin, the plight of Eve, the invasion of evil, the dubious role of Adam and the battle for Eden are all recurrent and persisting themes in the cinema. However, Ottarsson also analyzes examples of the large quantity of films that show how the myth is interpreted in individualistic ways. The plot may be turned around so that man is the creator, the Fall of Man is interpreted as a positive development for humankind or God may simply be executed or even driven to suicide. As such, the various interpretations of the Eden myth show, on the one hand, how biblical references are construed in accordance with individualistic societal development, and, on the other hand, that the biblical myth keeps its relevance.

In his chapter, Gerard Loughlin presents a close reading of a scene from the 1983 film *Nostalghia* by the Russian director Andrei Tarkovsky. The description of the scene is surrounded by the description of another scene from *Nostalghia* and by reflections on Tarkovsky's latest film, *The Sacrifice*. What binds the two films together in Loughlin's analysis is the presence in both films of a painting of the Madonna—the *Madonna del Parto* by Piero della Francesca in *Nostalghia* and the *Adoration of the Magi* by Leonardo in *The Sacrifice*. The one painting is showing the Madonna in waiting, ready to bring forth her child, and the other is showing her after having given birth to the child. Both paintings are about birth, Loughlin points out. In the first painting the Madonna reveals a tear, a sign of the birth as both giving life and causing death as embedded in the Christian drama of the divine incarnation. Loughlin's text is an example of a tight combination of analyses of film and paintings that are made possible by his theological perspective.

A fourth example of biblical themes in films is evident in Caroline Vander Stichele's chapter on the role of Mary Magdalene in motion. Exploring the image of Mary Magdalene in *The Passion of the Christ* (2004), *The Da Vinci Code* (2006) and *Mary* (2005), together with examples from other Jesus films, Vander Stichele shows how the character of Mary Magdalene shifts in the three films. In *The Passion*, she plays the part of the loving but passive woman, who grieves over the death of the suffering hero, and who is completely silenced. In *The Da Vinci Code* she is given a more prominent role as the wife of Jesus, the idea of the sacred feminine and the mother of his child. However, even though this idea of Mary Magdalene opens up an interpretation that is more satisfying to a feminist reading of the scriptures, she is still mainly the wife and 'the sacred vessel'. The third example in Vander Stichele's chapter shows a Mary Magdalene figure who is much more prominent. In *Mary* she is neither a prostitute nor a wife, but the most important of the disciples. Nevertheless, all the films have the view of Mary Magdalene as the 'other' to the male protagonist. She changes her appearance in accordance with the taste of the director, but the male stays the same.

In Arnfriður Guðmundsdóttir's chapter, Mel Gibson's *The Passion of the Christ* is examined from a theological and scholarly point of view, analyzing Gibson's use of extra-biblical sources of inspiration, especially Anne Catherine Emmerich's nineteenth-century work *The Dolorous Passion of our Lord Jesus Christ*, and criticizing his claim of authenticity. She also discusses how classical interpretations of Christ's death, as victorious, as satisfactorious and as exemplary, are present in Gibson's film, but concludes that the spiritual significance of violence is overemphasized in the film and thus legitimizes bloodshed and aggression.

The use of the Bible in film is not restricted to cinematic films, but is also widespread in television serials. This is the subject of Jesper Tang Nielsen's chapter, where he examines the Danish Christmas tradition of broadcasting a TV Christmas Calendar in 24 episodes. Whereas the subject for the TV calendars usually had been traditional Christmas topics, such as the spirit of Christmas, the importance of the family coupled with popular belief (Christmas pixies and Santa Claus), in 2003 the serial had the title *Jesus and Josephine*. For the first time, the subject of Jesus and Christianity was introduced in the TV Christmas calendars. Jesper Tang Nielsen shows how popular beliefs of Christianity permeate the script and thus give an impression of how Christianity is seen in Denmark today. On the surface it appears as an irrational mythology that is only believed by woman and children. However, using the actantiel model of Greimas Nielsen, he also shows how the plot of the serial goes beyond a simple interpretation. It turns out that Christianity and the Bible constitute the very foundation of contemporary Danish culture and that without Christianity, Denmark would be pure Hell. In this way the Christmas calendar supports a very conservative understanding of Christianity as well as Danish culture.

Concluding the book, Britt Istoft shows a different approach to the study of religion in film. Taking her lead from *The Star Trek* universe, she shows how religion permeates the science fiction and fantasy genre. During the decenniums of its existence, the *Star Trek* culture has developed groups of adherents (now in their second generation) with behaviour, dress, moral rules, ethical worldviews, and so on, that are comparable to the development of new religious groups. In her analysis she also points out how religion and religious traits come into existence and develop, and thus how the cinema has been capable of reversing the picture. Recently, religion in the cinema is not just about how religion is treated in film, but also about how these recent releases are influencing religion.

'ESCAPING' FROM THE WORLD THROUGH FILM: THEOLOGICAL PERSPECTIVES ON THE 'REAL' AND THE 'REEL'

Christopher Deacy

The aim of this article is to examine the manner and extent to which popular film is capable of comprising a potential site of theological engagement. From the outset, it is worth bearing in mind that, according to a number of biblical and theological critics, cinema is an infelicitous and ultimately undemanding medium which, a few exceptional instances notwithstanding, is intrinsically incapable of contributing to any serious or constructive theological discourse. For example, David Jasper's contention is that film is only effective insofar as 'it seems to offer the viewer the power to understand without the need seriously to think or change' (Jasper 1997: 243) and is simply 'there to help us through the tedium of inactivity' in what comprises, at root, 'an art of illusion' (1997: 235). Theology, in marked contrast, is, according to Jasper, a much more creative and 'two-edged' (1997: 244) sphere of activity, which 'emerges from more problematic and disturbing material than Hollywood dare show' (Jasper 1997). Insofar as Hollywood is an industry that revolves, as do all successful commercial and business enterprises, around 'money and profit', in which 'stars are paid enormous sums of money' (1997: 235)—it is not uncommon for the likes of Jim Carrey and Tom Hanks to be paid in excess of $25 million per picture[1]—and who 'all too often fall from their dizzy heights as dramatically as they climb to fame' (1997: 235), there is, invariably, a kernel of truth behind Jasper's critique. However, as this article will demonstrate, it would be facile to assume that film is capable of nothing more substantial than rendering audiences passive. Underlying Jasper's argument is the assumption that theology can critique film because it is capable of a level of intellectual rigour which the manufactured, illusory and escapist medium of film by definition cannot, and this leads us to the heart of the matter. Jasper's perception of film is largely one-sided (rather than 'two-edged'), in the respect that he is allowing—indeed, stipulating—that theology can (and

1. See http://www.hollywood.com/news/Hanks_Will_Be_Top_Hollywood_Earner/3681990, accessed 17 April 2007.

must) critique film, but he overlooks the very real sense in which theology is being allowed to say about film what film cannot say in turn about theology. No matter how tempting it may be for the theologian to critique a film, Gerard Loughlin perceptively notes that 'except when discourses on theology and film are reports of actual conversations between film-makers and theologians, such dialogues are nearly always acts of ventriloquism, since film itself is a cultural product about which we may talk, but which is not itself a conversing partner' (Loughlin 2005: 3). In other words, whereas theology is an intellectual and scholarly discipline, practised in university and ecclesiastical institutions, film is an entertainment medium, which is susceptible only to being appropriated *unilaterally* by the theologian.

What is more, Jasper's over-emphasis on the intellectual domain of theology—which he sees as being 'ironic, difficult and ambiguous' (1997: 244)—is not entirely representative of all that goes on in religious communities where emotional (and devotional) commitment often takes precedence over intellectual assent, to the point that it would be misleading to suppose that God favours the academic! As David Ford attests, 'A great deal of theology is done by those who write little or who may not write it down at all' (2005: 14), thus giving sustenance to the possibility that there is more to theology than the composition and dissemination of sophisticated, erudite, written texts. Indeed, Ford continues, 'A lifetime's theological wisdom may be channeled into prayer, politics, family life, coping with suffering, teaching or other activity' (2005: 14), and this raises the question of the extent to which it is viable to draw the kind of distinction that is intrinsic to Jasper's argument between highbrow theology and base, intellectually barren popular culture. If, as Gordon Lynch indicates, theology can be defined as 'the process of seeking normative answers to questions of truth/meaning, goodness/practice, evil, suffering, redemption, and beauty in specific contexts' (Lynch 2005: 94), it is difficult to argue for a strict line of demarcation to be drawn between where 'good' and 'bad' theology may be seen to lie. As Ian Markham puts it, one can have a theology of anything 'as long as the purpose is to explicate the implications of belief in God for that topic' (Markham 2006: 194), and although the specific examples adduced by Markham in this instance are work and sexuality, it is hard to justify the exclusion of the agencies of popular culture from the orbit of theology. On this basis, it could therefore be said that theology is failing to fulfil its academic commitments unless there is a readiness on the part of the theologian to engage fully in areas that have previously been supposed to lie outside its frame of reference. As Ford points out, it has become increasingly difficult in recent years for theologians 'to privatize or cordon off religion and reduce its public significance' (2005: 14). Although the specific remit of his discussion is the social and political issues that have emerged in our post-9/11 world, recent controversies that have emerged within the realm of 'secular' culture—including the alleged blasphemy of *The Jerry Springer Opera* (Peter Orton 2005) and the gross misreading of early Christian sources that underpins the fictional *The Da Vinci Code* (Ron Howard 2006) wherein we are led to believe that Christ was married to Mary Magdalene and had a child, whose last living descendant is alive today—could also be said to go some way towards demonstrating that 'the flourishing of the world' in the present day 'depends to a considerable extent on how various religious and secular forces learn to live together' (Ford 2005: 14).

ILLUSION AND DELUSION

With these considerations in mind, this article will investigate whether film is able to provide rich answers to questions pertaining to theological discourse. Insofar as 'movies are controlled by crass commercial interests' and 'merely provide escape or indulge our prejudices and fantasies, oversimplifying life in the process' (Johnston 2000: 87), Rob Johnston is correct to exercise some element of caution before looking to films to provide theological fruit. As my previous work on escapism has suggested, there is often a tendency among audiences to hope and wish for a real world that follows the same conventions as that of the *reel* world which, as John Lyden puts it, 'offer[s] a vision of the way the world should be', to the point that we have a propensity to 'hope and wish for a world like the movies even though we must return to a very different world at the end of the show' (Lyden 2003: 4). These tendencies notwithstanding, the situation is not as clear cut as Jasper's more one-sided critique initially (and persuasively) suggests. True though it is that romantic comedies, for example, 'may have done more harm than good in society because people tend to rush into relationships, and even marriage, with illusions of perfection culled from the movies' (2003: 187)— to the extent that 'Love is depicted as a matter of magic and moment, not a matter of a relationship that must develop with time' (2003: 190)—it is not entirely inconceivable that works of escapism are able to critique and challenge the very conventions on which escapism rests. Cinema may well comprise, in Jasper's words, a 'house of illusions' (1997: 244), but Clive Marsh is also correct when he affirms that even a 'frothy' film (and the example he has in mind here is *Shirley Valentine* [Lewis Gilbert 1989]), 'should be allowed to do more than its critics, and theologians, often expect' (Marsh 2004: 138). In Loughlin's words, 'before we ask more of film-makers and the systems within which they work, we should ask more of ourselves as viewers, demand more of the films we watch', in order that we might find 'that the films have more to give', and that 'their writers and directors have given us more than we first think' (Loughlin 2005: 2). After all, 'illusion' need not be synonymous with 'delusion', and there is plenty of evidence to support the counter-hypothesis that illusion plays a vital and necessary role even within theology, rather than comprise an anathema to it. Although theology does not purport to be about illusions, the Christian Eucharist, for instance, entails worshippers knowing both that the bread and wine remain bread and wine while also representing, in terms of Luther's doctrine of con-substantiation, the body and blood of Christ. Theologians have for centuries grappled with the manner in which the material bread and spiritual body of Christ are coterminous (see McGrath 1998: 197-98), just as they have understood the nuances of how Christ can be both fully human and fully divine at one and the same time (see Young 1996: 75-79 in relation to the Council of Chalcedon).

Illusion need not, therefore, be seen as something that stands in opposition to realism. Rather, as Marsh puts it, 'The illusions of film are functionally no different from the truthful fiction of a thoughtful novelist. They may merely be fictions in visual form', and which, moreover, we 'need in order playfully to reflect on life' (Marsh 2004: 86). Failure to acknowledge the role of escapism and illusion thus amounts to a failure to understand the rudiments and very edifice of cinema. Jasper is thus wrong to see cinema as incapable of doing anything other than just emulating, or mimicking, theology (see Jasper 1997: 237) and as merely 'offering the viewer a commodity which can be consumed without fear of significant change or disturbance' (1997: 244). Rather, films have the capacity to challenge, change and even transform people—to the point of, in Johnston's words, making us 'aware of both who we are and what our relationship with others could be', and even ushering 'us into the presence of the holy' (2000: 87). Of course, different audience members will glean something different from any one film. But, is there not something potentially educative about a medium that invites this kind of possibility? Despite having been constructed by someone else's imagination, Johnston correctly notes that 'It is on first reflection incredible that we can view a story about someone or something else that takes place in a different place and time and yet say, "This is important to me". Or, "I agree". Or perhaps, "Wonderful"' (2000: 120). For some people, the film that moves them in this way might be a work of *film noir*, such that, as Eric Christianson sees it, the troubled and gritty individuals who comprise the *noir* world become 'deeply embedded nostalgic icons, signs for coping with the uncertainty of dangers long gone and yet strangely familiar' (2005: 151). For others, though, a work of escapism may have just the same effect. Contrary to the discussion generated in Chapter 2 of *Faith in Film*, in which I set up—in a manner not wholly distinct from that of Jasper—a dichotomy between those films which are, and are not, amenable to constructive theological engagement *vis-à-vis* their respective escapist vs. redemptive world-views, I am recommending here that escapism can be justified if and when it does not simply enable audiences to hope and wish for happy endings to come about in their lives, too. Rather, escapist films can be theologically productive if any of the satisfactions and joys that we characteristically associate with escapism—its predilection for happy endings, wish fulfilment and its overall delineation of a fantasy world—can come to be qualified within the context of life *as a whole*. Lyden has produced one of the best contributions to this topic in recent years, in his suggestion that the goal for viewers (and theologians) is not simply to conclude that the real world falls short when compared to the ideal world of a Hollywood fantasy but to 'find ways to bring that ideal into relation with the real, however partially or fragmentarily' (Lyden 2003: 104).

IDEAL WORLDS

While it is undoubtedly the case that some so-called feel-good films 'aim to take us away, for a moment, from 'ordinary life' and immerse ourselves for a while in a different and supposedly 'better' world' (Clarke 2005: 60), it is questionable that this is their sole, or exclusive, function. This is because audiences, rather than passive and docile consumers, are afforded the opportunity, when watching a film, to reflect on the discontinuities and tensions between the real and the reel, the actual and the ideally constructed, and to glean some kind of profit from this interchange or dialectic. As Clarke puts it, 'It may be seen as escapist to make a film full of images of peace in a time of war, but, on the other hand, to live in this other world for a brief moment may help us to reflect on the reality we know' (2005: 60-61). To give an example, the ending of *Meet Me in St. Louis* (Vincente Minnelli 1944)—in which a large, happy family in turn-of-the-twentieth-century Missouri is spared the trauma of having to uproot and re-locate to the unfamiliar urban world of New York through what Coates refers to as the traditional matriarchal values of rootedness and fantasy coming to override the 'patriarchal law of political economy' (1994: 6)—may well turn on 'a transformation so improbable in its context that it has to be read as utopian' (1994: 6). But, in delineating the belief that 'utopia is possible here and now' (1994: 6), the film could also be construed as a means of preventing 'defeatist acceptance' of what Coates identifies as 'the hardships of 1944, the film's year of release' (1994: 6). That *Meet Me in St. Louis* is overtly escapist in nature is not in dispute. Indeed, film author and critic David Thomson recalls that, upon seeing Vincente Minnelli's musical in his youth, it made him wish 'for older sisters, a large fond family, and the precious aura of St. Louis in 1904', to the point that 'long before I heard the word escapism I made the journeys [such] films allowed' (Thomson 1978: 21). At the same time, however, escapist films can constructively shed light on real-life pressures and traumas. The films of Frank Capra—arguably cinema's greatest proponent of escapism—may, similarly, be 'permeated by nostalgia for a vanished America, an idealized pre-urban America, where a purer, better, freer way of life was lived' (Richards 1976: 77), but Capra envisaged some good coming out of what we may be inclined to see as an ostensibly backward-looking and regressive mentality. Capra identified the cause of the malaise at the time of the Depression 'in the disappearance of good neighbourliness', such that if one's 'friends rallied round and people loved and helped one another' (1976: 77) then many of the *present* problems in society may be resolved. These same themes have also arisen in more recent Hollywood works, such as *Field of Dreams* (Phil Alden Robinson 1989), *The Horse Whisperer* (Robert Redford 1998) and *The Legend of Bagger Vance* (Robert Redford 2000), where a deliberate attempt is made to set aside our largely materialistic and media-saturated culture and to pursue instead what Collins refers to as 'an almost forgotten authenticity' and 'purity' in which 'the problems of the present are symbolically resolved' (1993: 257).

Significantly, this is precisely the same sort of dynamic that lies at the kernel of many of the biblical passages that Jasper construes as comprising sound theology. Despite Jasper's contention that 'the fire of religious passion' (1997: 238) that underscores the writings of the Hebrew prophets is ontologically different from the reassuring and secure ambience of a Hollywood blockbuster, both the Old Testament prophets and escapist films are involved in a related enterprise. Both are predilected to juxtapose the inadequacies of present reality with the promise of a more utopian order or realm, which is facilitated by the intervention of (and deliverance by) an external 'other'. The agency may be different: in the case of Hollywood, we require the likes of Spiderman, Superman, the Terminator and the Pale Rider to deliver oppressed and defenceless individuals and communities from various manifestations of evil and suffering, whereas Amos prophesises a future free from oppression and social exploitation in which it is thanks to *God's* judgment and mercy that justice rolls 'down like waters and righteousness, like an everflowing stream' (Amos 5.24). Both the words of the prophets and the screenplays of many escapist movies are redolent in positing a present unsatisfactory human condition (whether physical or psychological) from which deliverance is sought by a trans-human redeemer. Yet, instead of requiring the suspension of our rational faculties, as Jasper's critique would suggest is the inescapable corollary of escapism, something far more nuanced is going on here.

Simply because, in the 'real' world, life does not work out as neatly as it does in the filmic universe where 'happy endings' are normative, Jasper does not seem to allow for the possibility that audiences do not necessarily subscribe to these 'illusions' lock, stock and barrel. When I recently showed my students clips from the romantic comedy *You've Got Mail* (Nora Ephron 1998), whose fantasy denouement typifies the Hollywood 'happy ending'—wherein the protagonists' implausible reconciliation offers, in Paul Fiddes' words, nothing more than 'an escape from life, a happy-ever-after world which fails to connect with the world in which we are living' (2005: 110)—the unanimous response was one of derision. After all, Joe Fox (Tom Hanks) is a corporate shark (though a rather tame one) while Kathleen Kelly (Meg Ryan) runs a small, family corner shop, which puts its customers' welfare above financial greed and business acumen, yet all conflict is miraculously spirited away at the film's end. At the same time, it was clear from questioning my class that almost everybody had previously seen—even, in some cases, purchased the DVD of—the film. How may we account for this paradox? Lyden may not be too wide of the mark in his attestation that 'One escapes to the world of film in order to return better equipped to this world, and so even the "idealist" aspect of film serves a "realist" function' (2003: 50). Theologically, this has a number of ramifications. As Lyden sees it, 'Even if we cannot be *perfect* parents and *perfect* career women/men at the same time, as our filmic counterparts manage to be, the model proposed in [films] can serve as an ideal to which we aspire, however inadequately, and one that helps us partially resolve the conflict in our daily lives' (2003: 76). In much the same way, theological values and ideals are rarely, if ever, attained, but this does not mean to say that the aspiration is compromised or rendered deficient. Writing in 1941, William Temple made a distinction between 'men as they are' and 'men as they ought to be', and advised that part of the task of Christian ethical exploration 'is so to order life as to lead them nearer to what they ought to be; but to assume that they are already this, will involve certain failure and disaster' (quoted in Gill 2006: 165). In other words, due to human imperfection, the Church has to acknowledge the unattainability of a perfect social order, to the point, indeed, that even the attempted *sketch* or *outline* of such a utopian state is fraught with difficulties. As Temple saw it, any attempt to establish 'the order that would work best if we were all perfect' could never come to fruition—indeed, 'we should wreck it in a fortnight' (2006: 165). Similar tensions are evident in Augustine's *City of God*, in which it is noted that there are two divisions in society—'one city of men who choose to live by the standard of the flesh, another of those who choose to live by the standard of the spirit' (Augustine 1984: 547). Nevertheless, the fact that there are competing and irreconcilable conceptions afoot concerning how one should best aim to lead a good and fulfilling life does not annul, for Christians, the pursuit of *agape*. Whatever tensions there may be between the earthly and the heavenly cities, to appropriate Augustine's metaphor, Christians are still required to 'love God and his fellow-Christians' (Kelly 1958: 414), even if it will only be at the end of history that the city of God will exist in perfection. For now, those who belong to the kingdom (or city) of God are merely 'on pilgrimage in this condition of mortality' (Augustine 1984: 877) in what amounts to a mixed body of brethren where the members of the two cities are inextricably 'interwoven and intermixed in this era', before being separated 'at the last judgement' (1984: 46).

Frustrating though it may be for the Christian that this is a fallen and defective world in which we need laws, courts, prisons and other corrective agencies rather than one in which 'all would tell the truth, respect the property…of others, and would be self-less and self-giving' (Gill 2006: 141), it does not follow that Christians feel required to escape from the world because it does not live up to the ideal of the heavenly city. Instead, both in the case of theology and escapist films, a compromise has to be struck. Since Christian businesspeople, for example, are 'not working in a society composed solely of sincere Christians', then they have to be attuned to the reality that 'if they were to follow the injunctions of the Sermon on the Mount literally, their business would probably collapse' (2006: 141). Even among Christians whose *telos* is the heavenly city, it is impossible to completely separate oneself from human culture, as St Paul identified in his dealings with the Corinthian Church, many of whose members had no qualms about eating meat that had been sacrificed to pagan gods (1 Cor. 8.4-13). These questions provide the very benchmark of H. Richard Niebuhr's fourth model of the relationship between Christianity and culture, *Christ and Culture in Paradox*, that is documented at length in his classic 1952 publication *Christ and Culture*. There, Niebuhr notes that 'man is seen as subject to two moralities, and as a citizen of two worlds that are not only discontinuous with each other but largely opposed' (1952: 56). Nevertheless, there is no alternative, for those who subscribe to this model, to being caught up in the affairs of this world. Provided that Christians derive their knowledge about what to do in the secular sphere from their Christian ethics, beliefs and values—so that they live out, as best as possible, a Christian life—then the fundamental tensions between Christ and culture can and must be (albeit paradoxically) held together, with a view to gaining new insight from that dialogue and exchange.

ENRICHING ESCAPISM

With films, similarly, perfection may be as unattainable in real life as it is attainable on the silver screen, but this is not to say that our response to escapism should be as disparaging as Jasper counsels. At the very least, a movie can provide an entry-point to discussions about all manner of theological questions. Films may not be capable of supplying all of the answers, but by the same token it would seem churlish to castigate the Sermon on the Mount because human society today is as self-centred, divisive and has the same propensity to seek war over peace as was the case two thousand years ago. As Lyden puts it, 'there is no reason to automatically assume that films designed to challenge people normally fail in their aim simply because most people do not make radical, life-changing decisions after viewing them' (2003: 30). Not everyone who reads the words of Amos will suddenly be disposed to give all of their money to the poor afterwards, but it is never easy to quantify the effect a film has on an audience. In Lyden's words, 'The people who loved the movie *Gandhi* [Richard Attenborough 1982] may not have become pacifists, but perhaps the film had an effect on their subsequent behavior or political views' (2003: 103). Similarly, *Cape Fear* (Martin Scorsese 1991) can provide a possible entry-point to questions about truth-telling, confessing one's sins or atoning for the transgressions of the past, without necessarily preaching to an audience about precisely how they should behave or conduct their lives (see Deacy 2001: 139-40). The fact that the film tackles issues of alienation and redemption is the key consideration, irrespective of whether it posits a remedy that will be satisfactory or appropriate for everyone (inevitably it will not be). Marsh similarly argues that we may identify or relate to Morgan Freeman's character, the convicted murderer, Red, in *The Shawshank Redemption* (Frank Darabont 1994) not because we are murderers ourselves but because we may be able to tap in to 'the sense of guilt or remorse' that we 'feel about a past action of our own' (Marsh 2004: 92), in a manner that is analogous to what happens in Darabont's film. Even in an ostensibly escapist film, such as *Mrs Doubtfire* (Chris Columbus 1993), in which much humour is served up in the visual spectacle of Robin Williams' character dressing up as a female nanny, any mawkishness on display must be seen within the context of the film's presentation of broken, single parent families and the extremes a father feels he must go to (which are not, perhaps, entirely removed from the antics of the Fathers for Justice campaign in Britain, which has gone to all manner of extreme lengths, including scaling the walls of Buckingham Palace, in order to advocate its cause) in order to be close to his children. Such a film asks, in Marsh's words, 'hard questions about how people grow and develop, both in relation to primary relationships within families, and to other relationships which develop through education, work and life events' (2004: 44).

On this basis, to 'escape' into the world of a movie is not simply bound up with illusion. In Lyden's words, 'We willingly enter another world in the cinema, one that we realize is not the empirical world, but one that has power over us nonetheless' (2003: 52). The effect need not be seen as wholly distinct from a religious ritual, wherein a worshipper enters sacred space with a view to seeking an encounter with another dimension of existence, which he or she knows is not the empirical world but which nevertheless charges the empirical world with meaning and value following the experience of transcendence and an encounter with, to borrow Rudolf Otto's term, the *numinous* (Otto 1959: 21). Both cinema and church thus enable people to achieve a degree of separation, or escape, from the restrictions and limitations of the 'real' world before their 'return' to the everyday, which is, subsequently, imbued with new significance (see Segal 1999: 127-28). As Lyden puts it, 'We desire alternate worlds because we find our own imperfect; but such desires to flee also entail a desire to return, renewed and refreshed, to the everyday' (2003: 53). Similar ideas have been expounded within liberation theology by Leonardo Boff, who has noted that 'Modern studies have shown convincingly that fantasy is not mere fancifulness or a mechanism for escaping from conflict-ridden reality' (2004: 285). Rather, it is 'the key to explaining authentic creativity', not least the ability to 'break away from things that are taken for granted, to abandon accepted presuppositions and begin to think in unorthodox ways' and 'set off on a different road or head in a different direction' (2004: 285). Escapism thus plays a powerful theological role in that, through the encounter with an alternative, fantasy world, the inadequacies of the real world can be stripped away and exposed and, what is more, brought into relationship with, and shed new light upon, the real world, which, at the end of the day, is what Boff calls 'stronger than the structures that serve as its support and framework' (2004: 285). We can thus be enriched, rather than impoverished, by escapism, to the point, even, that Boff sees in fantasy 'the richest source of human creativity', and even as, in theological terms, 'the image of the creator God in human beings', and 'the soil in which humanity's capacity for invention and innovation flourishes' (2004: 285). Fantasy is thus capable of *enriching* our apprehension of the empirical world, with all of its trials, obstacles and impediments, rather than (as Jasper would see it) *distancing* us from them.

   To give an example, Lyden makes the point that the Steven Spielberg fantasy *Hook* (1991) 'holds out an ideal of familial perfection…not because [Spielberg] believes this is literally attainable, but because the fantasy invokes an image of the world as we would like it to be' (Lyden 2003: 201). In other words, without seeing the world of fantasy and escapism as anything other than a realm of wish-fulfilment, hope and idealism, there is always the possibility that such a vision will 'rub off on reality' (2003: 201) and engender in audiences the hope that this world, for all its imperfections, has the capacity to improve.[2] In contrast to the world of *film noir* which, arguably, presents the world as it presently is, the advantage with escapist films is that they have the capacity to inject into this present world a measure of hope

---

2.   The thinking of Walter Rauschenbusch, a leading figure in the Social Gospel movement in the United States, comes particularly to mind here. See Livingston 1971: 263-66.

and aspiration as to how life could, and even should, be. This links with the premise of Bernard Brandon Scott's 1994 publication, *Hollywood Dreams and Biblical Stories*, in which the thesis is advanced that cinema comprises a rich repository of modern mythology, through which 'we work out who we are and negotiate the problems of modern life' (Scott 1994: 4). In offering resolutions to conflicts in life that are unresolved, or remain irresolvable, Scott sees a children's film such as *Home Alone* (Chris Columbus 1990) as significant because it is able implicitly to confront the anxieties of its adult audience regarding the safety of children in a dangerous world, and could only do so, moreover, in terms of a happy ending since an ending that was pessimistic and downbeat (indeed, realistic) would fail to convey to an audience that it is possible for good to triumph over evil. While acknowledging that many people may deride 'popular films as not worthy of serious attention'—and Jasper's critique comes particularly to mind—Scott is right in his attestation that 'their very popularity demands explanation', and that it is not adequate simply to attribute their appeal 'to the audience's lowbrow taste' (1994: 4). Rather, there is something far richer (and more subtle) taking place.

A film with a wish-fulfilment sensibility can therefore play an integral role in theological discourse, since it can offer constructive models of human negotiation and interaction. As Peter Francis says of Clint Eastwood's Westerns, for example, the likes of *High Plains Drifter* (1973), *The Outlaw Josey Wales* (1976), *Pale Rider* (1985) and *Unforgiven* (1992) 'capture something of our persistent need to have utopias of freedom that give us some hope in the present', even to the point of enabling us 'to understand how to build an inclusive community and leave behind old hatreds' (Francis 2005: 197). We may not choose literally to emulate the characters on screen—indeed, it would be worrying if we all turned into vigilantes as a consequence of watching Eastwood's Preacher in *Pale Rider* taking the law into his own hands because, like him, we want to start saving oppressed communities from being driven from their land by marauding bands of gold prospectors, or their modern day counterparts. Rather, it is sufficient that, as Lyden puts it in the context of a discussion of gangster films, 'the ideal world of the myth is set up in contrast to the real world we live in, not as a literal model to follow in every respect but as a challenge to our ordinary ways of seeing and doing things' (Lyden 2003: 156). Quite how audiences actually appropriate films is a different matter, but it is sufficient that, in an imperfect world (as Augustine and Temple saw it), films are able to supply visions of how love, mercy, goodness and justice can be accomplished and realized, albeit incompletely. The visions may be more reel than real, but, in Lyden's words, the 'imaginary constructions within them' can nonetheless 'serve to convey real truths about the nature of reality and how it is believed to be' (2003: 54), and, perhaps, provide a template as to how we would like the 'real' world to function.

SLOPPY THINKING AND FUTILE IDEALISM?

Of course, in a fundamental sense this is easier said than done. One of the great joys of *film noir*, for example, is that its delineation of an ambiguous, fallen and capricious world also contains much in the way of theological potential. This may be a body of film in which, as Christianson puts it, 'audiences are generally morally disempowered', and 'not offered a secure vantage point from which to pass judgement' (2005: 154) on what is unfolding on the screen, but this is not to say that audiences cannot 'do' theology with films that portray a world devoid of hope and wish-fulfilment. Speaking about the downbeat—even hope-less—ending of *Chinatown* (1974), which portrays a world in which good demonstrably does not triumph over evil, the director, Roman Polanski, argued in a BBC interview that,

> If it all ended with happy endings, we wouldn't be sitting here talking about this film today. If you...feel...there's a lot of injustice in our world, and you want to have people leaving [the] cinema with a feeling that they should do something about it in their lives, [then] if it's all dealt for them by the filmmakers they just forget about it over dinner, and that's it (quoted in Deacy 2005: 37).

Similarly, in the words of Donald Levine, 'ambiguity can be productive if it is taken not as a warrant for sloppy thinking but as an invitation to deal responsibly with issues of great complexity' (quoted in Christianson 2005: 163). Roy Anker is a theologian who even goes so far as to suggest that the greater the darkness on display, the more incandescent the light. In his words, 'it is by arriving at a clear purchase on what afflicts the human creature that people have some hope of understanding the Light or 'good' that might dispel evil's distortion and malice' (Anker 2004: 20). Despite the Manichean—even Gnostic—perspective that appears to inform his vision, Anker makes the judicious theological point that since it is darkness, rather than light, which constitutes 'the natural human condition', and that 'people are beset by evil inside and out, and cannot find their way to any slight portion of Light, whether as rescue, safety or love' (2004: 19), then even though we may look for a better, more idealistic world our quest will be futile. For, according to Anker, 'Even though people may want a better world, they not only lack sufficient sense or virtue to find or forge a path to that destination, but their best efforts to get there will more than likely only aggravate their already grievous fix' (2004: 19). On this basis, there is no profit to be found in using escapist films as a tool for gaining theological insight, to the point, perhaps, that Jasper may not be entirely wide of the mark after all in his attestation that theology 'emerges from more problematic and disturbing material than Hollywood dare show' (Jasper 1997: 244). Indeed, only those films that are, like theology, 'two-edged, ironic, difficult and ambiguous' (1997: 244)—and *noir* perfectly fits this bill—would qualify as even remotely able to contribute to serious theological discourse.

Towards a Re-Drawing of the Boundaries

However, this is somewhat tautological, since Jasper appears to have already pre-determined that Hollywood film and the discipline of theology make for very incompatible bedfellows. Underlying his critique is the supposition that only limited dialogue can accrue between theology and film on the grounds that theology is invariably, and consistently, more stable, meaningful and fecund than Hollywood escapism could ever be. Yet, for there to be any serious dialogue or interaction between any two entities, it is a basic pre-requisite that both 'sides' in the debate need to be at least amenable to the possibility of change. The way Jasper sees it, theology is always going to be too serious and intellectually superior for any meaningful dialogue with Hollywood film to result. Is this always the case, though? As Marsh sees it, 'to imply that religious meanings are somehow always inevitably more transparent and morally truthful than what one sees on screen seems overly optimistic' (2004: 86), although I have to confess that this is a line I have previously adopted in *Faith in Film* where I indicate that theology's dealing with redemption is more serious and efficacious than anything Hollywood can do in the context of escapism (Deacy 2005: 26). However, for dialogue to be serious, theology must be prepared to gain something from—and even be challenged by—film rather than simply amount to a static discipline whose message is timeless and beyond growth. As Christian history has shown, there is no such thing as an immovable or fixed theology. In the early Church, for example, the challenge of Gnosticism in the second century precipitated the drawing up, by the likes of Irenaeus and Tertullian, of the so-called rule of faith, which endeavoured to combat those influential contemporary currents of thought that sustained the view that the physical world was an evil that must be escaped in order that one may become more spiritually enlightened (see Young 1996: 22-29). Likewise, at the turn of the fifth century, Augustine came to the view that, in light of the challenge to the Church presented by the Donatist controversy, there were situations in which it was legitimate to invoke the secular arm, and to employ coercion by the state, in order to bring a schismatic church body—the metaphorical lost sheep, as it were—back into the Catholic fold (1996: 61).[3] In both cases,

---

3.   To cite another example, the Council of Chalcedon in 451 CE was an attempt to offer a compromise between two competing tendencies—one, the Alexandrian approach, which held that, through the Incarnation, God had become united with human nature in order that human nature can share in the life of God (such that there was only one divine nature), while the other, Antiochene position vigorously defended

theological thinking was at the mercy of all manner of social, cultural, intellectual and political currents of thought, which radically transformed the way in which theology was thenceforth able to operate. Indeed, the 'rule of faith' constituted a radical break from previously unregulated and spontaneous theological wisdom, which, as brought to a head in the Montanist movement of the second century, witnessed a progressive shift away from spontaneity and improvization (in the form of apostles, preachers and teachers) towards institutionalization and orthodoxy (in the form of bishops, presbyters and deacons), while the use of coercion was subsequently taken to justify the use of state power to suppress various heresies and to impose penalties (including death) on heretics throughout the medieval and early modern periods.

On the grounds that theology is thus inescapably dependant on historical and cultural circumstances, the challenge for theologians today is to ensure that theology does not comprise a self-important and immobile—even retroactive—discipline, but one that is capable of taking stock of changes in cultural paradigms and is able to cope with what Ford calls 'the novelty and disruption of modernity' (2005: 2). Jasper is by no means unaware of this, as demonstrated by his acknowledgment that in the cinema of Scorsese, for instance, 'life and film are more complex than simple religious readings would allow' (Jasper 1997: 242). However, when Jasper then illustrates his argument by pointing to the fact that *The Last Temptation of Christ* (Martin Scorsese 1988) is capable of transgressing 'the demands of its audience' (Jasper 1997: 243) in a way that Hollywood escapism is characteristically unable to achieve, it is apparent that, for Jasper, although not all films are theologically barren, a dichotomy exists between mainstream theology and mainstream cinema which will (and should) never be reconciled. So long as there is a tendency among theologians to scorn the output of Hollywood, then theologians are susceptible to the charge of misreading what does, and does not, constitute a legitimate repository of theological activity. Jasper may consider escapism as too shallow and superficial to be of any durable theological value, but the idea that we therefore ignore or denigrate something that we do not believe in has a number of unfortunate ramifications. Taken to the extreme, it is not fundamentally different from the way in which the early Church fathers decided that the best way of defeating the challenge of Gnosticism was to suppress it, and to destroy its texts (although Jasper in no way goes this far with respect to filmic texts!), or that the best way of defeating the rival claims of the Donatists was to employ against them a systematic programme of force, administered by the state, in order that they

the independence of the two natures and understood Christ as both fully human and fully divine. For Antiochenes, the two natures were held together by the grace of God in the form of the hypostatic union (see Deacy 2001: 87).

may come to see the error of their ways. A far better, and more intellectually viable, approach is to employ a greater sense of reciprocity and to allow for the possibility that, through whatever means—whether erudite written texts or crude escapist films—the key thing is that individuals and communities are enabled to harness their own resources and gifts and strive to attain their potential, and thereby be in a position to move towards what Bedborough refers to as 'the unique design for which God intends us' (2005: 128) and what, for Jürgen Moltmann, amounts to the 'movement of history toward the fulfillment of human destiny in the kingdom of God' (2005: 157).

CONCLUDING REMARKS

Often, of course, Hollywood films richly deserve to be critiqued by theologians. As Peter Francis comments, in the context of a discussion of discerning Christ-figure motifs in *Pale Rider*, a film in which a mysterious, even supernatural, agent comes down from above in order to dispense justice 'to those who need empowerment' (Francis 2005: 191), raises a number of theological problems. Francis is concerned about the way in which Eastwood's Preacher conforms to all the 'stereotypes of flawed masculinity' and comprises a detached figure 'who only descends to dole out judgement or to flex his miraculous muscles' (2005: 191). Using theistic parallels, Francis is perturbed by the fact that 'This is a God who remains aloof, unknown and unnamed' (2005: 191) and whose 'supernatural help' is actually disempowering, rather than empowering, for the community concerned as 'The Preacher does it all for them, they are not participants in the struggle for freedom' (2005: 191). In such a context, a theological critique is not wide of the mark.[4] However, as the above discussion on escapism has demonstrated, the fact that a film presents a wish-fulfilment and fantasy world in no way means that all audiences are incapable of responding in a spirit of anything other than passivity, docility and submission. As liberation theology has demonstrated, the fact that one third of the population of Latin America live in a state of abject poverty does not ensure, on the part of all Church activists, that the only response is one of acceptance of the status quo and the tendency (as critiqued by Marx) to direct one's *telos* to an afterlife where the trials and tribulations of this present age will be overcome and restitution guaranteed. Likewise, Augustine's contention that the Church on earth is

---

4.   For more on this, see Deacy 2001: 146, where I argue that since the filmic action hero 'is single-handedly capable of saving the world from catastrophe, by taking risks and executing stunts which are beyond the competence and means of the average human being, there is a fundamental sense in which the film viewer is being forced to abdicate responsibility in favour of a quasi-messianic, fantasy redeemer-figure who will shoulder our burdens'.

qualitatively distinct from the heavenly city to which we are called in no
way precipitated, on Augustine's part, a spirit of resignation or complacency.
Rather, the onus was to ensure, in the present, that the person of faith
should not 'hesitate to obey the laws of the earthly city by which those
things which are designed for the support of this mortal life are regulated'
(quoted in Gill 2006: 120), even if this meant—as his dealings with the
Donatists best exemplified—that a necessary evil (coercion) can sometimes
be justified in order to bring about a greater good (Church unity and catho-
licity). As Moltmann's theology of the Cross has shown, furthermore, one
does not transform the world by rejecting the manner in which people are
presently engaging with it. Rather, if there is to be any radical change in
society, this must take the form of 'a political praxis of solidarity with the
victims', wherein 'desire for radical change must result from real solidarity
with the victims of society and be rooted in their actual interests' (Bauckham 2005: 157). In other words, only by relating to what actual individuals
and groups are doing on their own territory in a spirit of empathy and
openness, rather than assuming a position in which the answers have already
been pre-determined by outside channels and dogmas, can constructive
theological activity take place. Escapist films may therefore have their shortcomings, but unless films, from whatever genre, are allowed to participate in
the task of human flourishing and fulfilment, and are grounded in 'the
created dignity and eschatological destiny of humanity as the image of God'
(2005: 157), then we have a very long way to go before film and theology
can be brought together as discerning, and reciprocal, dialogue-partners.

BIBLIOGRAPHY

Anker, Roy M.
    2004   *Catching Light: Looking for God in the Movies* (Grand Rapids: Eerdmans).
Augustine, St
    1984   *The City of God* (trans. Henry Bettensen; London: Penguin).
Bauckham, Richard
    2005   'Jürgen Moltmann', in Ford with Muers 2005: 147-62.
Bedborough, Sally
    2005   'Taking the Waves by "Surprise": Master and Commander', in Clarke and
            Fiddes 2005: 23-135.
Boff, Leonardo
    2004   'Liberating Grace', in G.E. Thiessen (ed.), *Theological Aesthetics: A Reader*
            (London: SCM Press): 284-85.
Christianson, Eric
    2005   'An Ethic You Can't Refuse?: Assessing The Godfather Trilogy', in
            Christianson, Francis and Telford 2005: 110-23.

Christianson, E.S., P. Francis and W.R. Telford (eds.)
    2005   *Cinéma Divinité: Readings in Film and Theology* (London: SCM Press).
Clarke, Anthony
    2005   'Gaining Fresh Insights: Film and Theological Reflection in a Pastoral Setting', in Clarke and Fiddes 2005: 59-79.
Clarke, A.J., and P.S. Fiddes (eds.)
    2005   *Flickering Images: Theology and Film in Dialogue* (Oxford: Regent's Park College).
Coates, Paul
    1994   *Film at the Intersection of High and Mass Culture* (Cambridge: Cambridge University Press).
Collins, Jim
    1993   'Genericity in the 90s: Eclectic Irony and the New Sincerity', in J. Collins, H. Radner and A. Preacher Collins (eds.), *Film Theory Goes to the Movies* (London: Routledge): 242-63.
Deacy, Christopher
    2001   *Screen Christologies: Redemption and the Medium of Film* (Cardiff: University of Wales Press).
    2005   *Faith in Film: Religious Themes in Contemporary Cinema* (Aldershot: Ashgate).
Fiddes, Paul
    2005   'When Text Becomes Voice: You've Got Mail', in Clarke and Fiddes 2005: 97-111.
Ford, David
    2005   'Introduction to Modern Christian Theology', in Ford with Muers 2005: 1-15.
Ford, D.F., with R. Muers (eds.)
    2005   *The Modern Theologians: An Introduction to Christian Theology Since 1918* (Oxford: Blackwell).
Francis, Peter
    2005   'Clint Eastwood Westerns: Promised Land and Real Men', in Christianson, Francis and Telford 2005: 182-98.
Gill, Robin
    2006   *A Textbook of Christian Ethics* (London: T.&T. Clark International, 3rd edn).
Jasper, David
    1997   'On Systematizing the Unsystematic: A Response', in Clive Marsh and Gaye Ortiz (eds.), *Explorations in Theology and Film: Movies and Meaning* (Oxford: Blackwell): 235-44.
Johnston, Robert
    2000   *Reel Spirituality: Theology and Film in Dialogue* (Grand Rapids: Baker Academic).
Kelly, J.N.D.
    1958   *Early Christian Doctrines* (London: A. & C. Black).
Livingston, James C.
    1971   *Modern Christian Thought: From the Enlightenment to Vatican II* (London: Collier Macmillan).

Loughlin, Gerard
    2005   'Cinéma Divinité: A Theological Introduction', in Christianson, Francis and Telford 2005: 1-12.
Lyden, John C.
    2003   *Film as Religion: Myths, Morals and Rituals* (New York: New York University Press).
Lynch, Gordon
    2005   *Understanding Theology and Popular Culture* (Oxford: Blackwell).
Markham, Ian
    2006   'Theology', in R.A. Segal (ed.), *The Blackwell Companion to the Study of Religion* (Oxford: Blackwell): 193-210.
Marsh, Clive
    2004   *Cinema and Sentiment: Film's Challenge to Theology* (Carlisle: Paternoster Press).
McGrath, Alister E.
    1998   *Historical Theology: An Introduction to the History of Christian Thought* (Oxford: Blackwell).
Niebuhr, H. Richard
    1952   *Christ and Culture* (London: Faber & Faber).
Otto, Rudolf
    1959   *The Idea of the Holy* (Harmondsworth: Penguin Books).
Richards, Jeffrey
    1976   'Frank Capra and the Cinema of Populism', in B. Nichols (ed.), *Movies and Methods* (2 vols.; London: University of California Press, 1976): I, 65-77.
Scott, Bernard Brandon
    1994   *Hollywood Dreams and Biblical Stories* (Minneapolis: Fortress Press).
Segal, Robert A.
    1999   *Theorizing about Myth* (Amherst: University of Massachusetts Press).
Thomson, David
    1978   *America in the Dark: Hollywood and the Gift of Unreality* (London: Hutchinson).
Young, Frances
    1996   *The Making of the Creeds* (London: SCM Press).

Religion in New Danish Cinema

Mikkel Fugl Eskjær

This chapter offers a sociological overview of religion in new Danish feature films. The aim is to highlight some institutional constraints that define Danish cinema and thereby the representation of religion in cinema. Danish cinema is supported through a mixture of private and public funding, resulting in a film form halfway between art cinema and genre cinema. This has important consequences for the presence and the treatment of religion in new Danish cinema.

This chapter focuses on the relations between institution, communication and religion in Danish cinema by presenting a model that accounts for the link between religion and different types of cinema (sections 1-2). This is followed by a description of how religion is treated in new Danish art films and genre films (sections 3-5). Finally, the chapter discusses how and why religion features in new Danish cinema by referring to dramaturgical and social conventions surrounding film and religion (sections 6-8).[1]

Methodologically, this chapter is concerned with the communicative aspects of film and religion. Cinema and religion constitute different areas of human communication. Cinema is a medium of communication oriented towards art and entertainment (Eskjær 2006). Religion is communication that, according to Geertz, formulates 'conceptions of a general order of existence' (2000: 90). When combined, these forms of communication lead to a particular representation and observation of religion by adopting the communicative strategies of art and entertainment.

However, such a coupling of different types of communication far from guarantees success. Today we are offered an enormous amount of media content from a handful of different media platforms. In what has been called the global 'mediascape' (Appadurai 1996) or the 'new media system' (Castells 2000), old and new forms of media technology and media platforms are constantly competing for our attention. In such a media-saturated environment, the question becomes why anybody would be interested in religious

---

1. The expression 'new Danish cinema' mainly refers to feature films and is restricted to the last two decades. Documentary films are not included in the current analyses.

films, or any other type of mediated communication for that matter. Contrary to face-to-face communication, where the sheer presence of *alter* guarantees that the communication of *ego* is somehow received, no such guarantees exist in the area of mass communication. Thus, as a heuristic device, mass communication in general, and the coupling of cinema and religion in particular, can be considered an improbable type of communication (Luhmann 1981, 2000).

The advantage of such an approach is that it focuses our attention on the communicative means and devices employed in order to solve or reduce the improbability of communication. We thereby have to consider how religion is enclosed in the formal systems of cinema and how religion fulfils important dramaturgical functions in popular narratives. For instance, if religion is represented within familiar narrative patterns of conflict, heroic deed, sacrifice and forgiveness, it is more likely to meet audience expectations and thereby facilitate communicative acceptance than would a film representing religion in an abstract or hyper-spiritual visual language.

The relation between cinema and religion is therefore a question of how religious matters are turned into cinematic communication and how cinematic codes and conventions are adjusted to religious communication.

1. FILM AND RELIGION

Religious cinema far from represents a homogenous group of films. One way of analyzing the variety of religious filmmaking is to differentiate religious films along an axis, or continuum, ranging from overtly explicit religious content to implicit, sometimes even hardly discernible, religious elements. At one end of the continuum are films that deal with theological questions and issues, often associated with official religion. The simplest form is perhaps used to illustrate or adapt religious texts like the Bible or Mahabharata, a tradition as old as cinema itself (Holloway 1977: 37; Abel 1994: 95, 163-66). Another form constructs narratives with conflicts of a religious character, which are then solved in accordance with liturgical conventions (Fraser 1998).

The other end of the continuum consists of films portraying religious matters that belong to either non-official religions (McGuire 1994) or what have been termed 'banal' religions (Hjarvard 2005), a term that draws on an analogy of Michael Billig's (1995) study of banal nationalism. This type of religious cinema is not so much concerned with official religion and liturgical conventions, but instead integrates religious elements and representations in a rather simple and often implicit manner. This can either be done through references to non-official religions, like superstitious beliefs, or through references to figures like witches, fairies and goblins, or it uses religious symbols in depicting the fight between, for instance, good and evil, well known from popular genres such as horror or action films. Belonging to this category also are the hardly noticeable appearances of religious representations, as when the camera makes an apparently innocent pan and by doing so reveals the presence of a traditional church in a Danish village, a gothic cathedral in a European city, or perhaps a mosque in an 'exotic' location. In all these instances, the presence (or 'flagging') of religious representations serves a specific function, whether it is to offer geographical clues, mark ethnic differences or indicate historical and cultural traditions.

Another method of differentiating cinema is to distinguish between genre cinema and art cinema, where genre cinema is synonymous with classical Hollywood narration (Bordwell, Staiger and Thompson 1985; Bordwell 1995) and art cinema refers to a mode of narration inspired by European modernism (Bordwell 1985, 2002; Neal 2002). Combining this distinction with the differentiation of religious cinema, we get a picture of the relations between different modes of narration and different types of religious cinema. Illustrated as two independent axes standing at right angles to each other, the model is depicted in Figure 1.[2]

The model illustrates how theological films can be found in both genre cinema and art cinema, even though they employ different communicative strategies and different modes of production. This is best exemplified by the difference between, for instance, *La Passion de Jeanne d'Arc* (Carl T. Dreyer 1928) and *Joan of Arc* (Victor Flemming 1948), or between *La procés de Jean d'Arc* (Robert Bresson 1962) and *The Messenger* (Luc Besson 1999).

The model also indicates that art cinema is more inclined towards explicit religious matters, whereas genre cinema operates in both areas, perhaps with a preponderance of implicit religion, taking the popularity of genres like fantasy, horror and science fiction into consideration.

2. RELIGION AND DANISH CINEMA

If the model is applied to a Danish context, it becomes clear that the structural conditions of Danish film production are influencing both the extent and the character of religious representations. Despite certain tendencies towards mainstream cinema, the majority of Danish films are located in the area between (commercial) genre cinema and (author-based) art cinema. One looks in vain for spectacular religious narratives in the tradition of *Ben*

2.   The purpose of the model is to offer a framework by which to differentiate between different types of religious filmmaking. In its present form, the model should be regarded as a heuristic device rather than an absolute claim about the nature of the films included in the model. Thus, the exact location of each individual film can probably be debated, but is still within the overall pattern of the model.

Hur or *The Ten Commandments*. Similarly, there exist relatively few Danish films that typically include elements of banal religion, such as horror films, fantasy and science fiction.

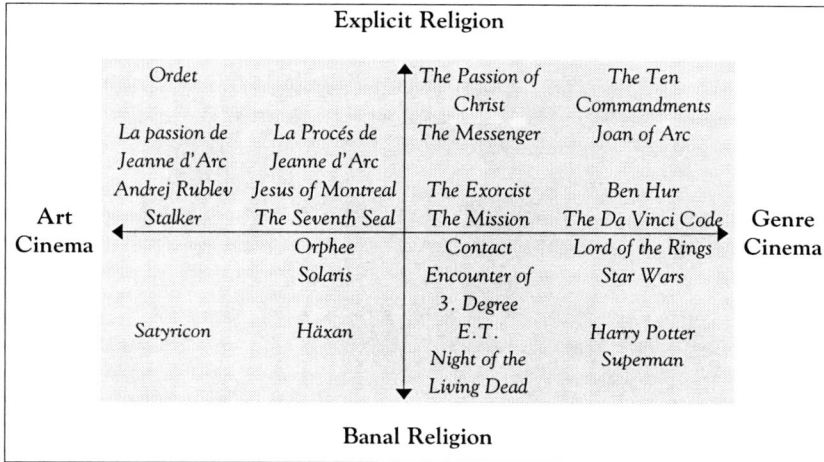

			Explicit Religion		
	Ordet		*The Passion of Christ*	*The Ten Commandments*	
	La passion de Jeanne d'Arc	*La Procés de Jeanne d'Arc*	*The Messenger*	*Joan of Arc*	
Art Cinema	*Andrej Rublev* *Stalker*	*Jesus of Montreal* *The Seventh Seal* *Orphee* *Solaris*	*The Exorcist* *The Mission* *Contact* *Encounter of 3. Degree*	*Ben Hur* *The Da Vinci Code* *Lord of the Rings* *Star Wars*	Genre Cinema
	Satyricon	*Häxan*	*E.T.* *Night of the Living Dead*	*Harry Potter* *Superman*	
			Banal Religion		

Figure 1.

Expressed in more theoretical terms, Danish cinema has traditionally avoided the type of action-orientated genres (westerns, gangster, detective, war, science-fiction) that according to Thomas Schatz are concerned with aspects of *social order*; it has mainly been dominated by genres (comedy, social melodrama) that celebrate values of *social integration* (Schatz 1981; Bondebjerg 2005).

This situation is partly due to the nature of Danish film production. Danish cinema is a public matter in more than one sense. The majority of Danish films receive public funding in one form or another, either for script development, production, or distribution support, or a combination of all three. The historical background can be found in the 1960s, when changes in the media landscape (primarily the popularity of television) made film production a financially untenable business. In order to secure a national film production, the first Danish film act was passed in 1964 with the purpose of 'promoting film art in Denmark'. Eight years later, the Danish Film Institute (DFI) was created in order to administrate public film funding (1972). Since then, different types of financial support have been created.

Today, support is given to films based on artistic criteria and commercial qualities (DFI 1998). This double line of support reflects the intention of creating a pluralistic support system. In reality, however, the actual output does not differ much. The DFI has been very concerned with public and political reception of their use of taxpayers' money. The result has been a high demand for audience attendance figures, on the one hand, and cultural quality, on the other hand, which has pulled art cinema in the direction of popular cinema and commercial films in the direction of more ambitious filmmaking. As a consequence, the majority of Danish film production has been located in the grey area between (commercial) genre cinema and (ambitious) art cinema (Grodal 2006)

It is, however, a picture that is undergoing important transformations. Recent years have witnessed a movement towards a more genre-conscious cinema and an increased interest in genres concerned with questions of *social order*; genres that traditionally have been absent from Danish cinema. This has also influenced the relation between film and religion. The serious and everyday realistic treatment of religion, so typical of former Danish cinema, has been followed by a more spectacular use of religion, seen in, for example, *The Kingdom* by Lars von Trier and a handful of productions with Anders Thomas Jensen as either scriptwriter (e.g. *Mifune* 1999) or director (e.g. *Adam's Apples*).

In the following, I will distinguish between what could be termed *popular art cinema*, which has constituted the backbone of Danish cinema over the last three or four decades, and a more commercial and *genre-conscious cinema*, which has gained terrain in recent years.

3. IRONY AND REALISM: RELIGION IN NEW DANISH ART FILM

When analyzing new Danish art cinema, one person stands out as a key figure in its revitalization. The importance of Lars von Trier can hardly be underestimated, both as a filmmaker and the driving force behind the *Dogme Movement*. Nor can the milieu surrounding the production company Zentropa (Hjort and Bondebjerg 2000: 209-11). As part of that endeavour, von Trier has also been instrumental in creating a small, but important group of films with religious motifs.

Religious and metaphysical references can be traced to von Trier's early works, like the Tarkovskij inspired *The Element of Crime* (1984), but come centre stage in later films like *Breaking the Waves* (1996) and *Dancer in the Dark* (2000). Both films are (along with *The Idiots*) part of what Danish film scholar Peter Schepelern (2000) calls von Trier's *Golden Heart Trilogy*, with reference to the female protagonist who sacrifices herself in order to save either her husband or her son. However, both films are also part of von Trier's turn towards popular genres such as melodrama and musical. Von Trier has explained that '*Breaking the Waves* clearly belongs in the sentimental department. That film's synopsis outlines a story that...is really far out, almost in the ladies magazine genre' (Hjort and Bondebjerg 2000: 214). The quote indicates that the turn towards popular genres contains an element of cultural defiance; a counter reaction turned against the cultural contempt for popular fiction typical of elitist modernism. Von Trier has explained how his family was characterized by 'modern thoughts and very clear ideas about what was noble and what wasn't. The sentimental was deemed hollow and false' (quoted in Schepelern 2000). Some of von Trier's later films are evidently a reaction against such prejudices.

There are a number of religious layers and elements in von Trier's films, like references to the 'holy fool', the juxtaposition of body and soul, guilt, sacrifice, and so on. Meanwhile, all these religious elements go hand in hand with melodrama and sentimentality, making it hard to decide whether the religious themes are part of von Trier's revolt against 'good taste' or expressions of genuine religious preoccupation. The latter would place von Trier within the tradition of modern religious art cinema, along with Robert Bresson, Ingmar Bergman or Tarkovskij. The former would be an example of how religion is one element of the director's toolbox, a means to enhance melodramatic effects or to explore new cinematic territory.

Regarding the Dogme phenomenon, it is hardly an exaggeration to claim that the Dogme movement has enhanced a characteristic feature of Danish cinema in general, namely a widespread preoccupation with everyday realism. This is a direct consequence of Danish cinema's long association with art cinema, which has always defined itself as the opposite of Hollywood and the escapism associated with commercial genre cinema (Bordwell 2002). The everyday realism affects the handling of religious matters, as pointed out by the film scholar Anne Jerslev (2006). Both *Italian for Beginners* (Lone Scherfig 2000) and *Forbrydelser* (*In Your Hands*) (Annette K. Olesen 2004) illustrate this.

The latter is probably the one film that most explicitly deals with the questions of faith in a modern world. The film is set in a women's prison and portrays a young priest whose sudden miraculous pregnancy forces her to confront her faith, or rather lack of faith. This is evident most clearly in one of the last scenes, when a medical test predicts the probability of her giving birth to a multi-handicapped child, forcing the priest to choose between her faith in life/God or in modern science. Both the setting and the film's socially concerned content illustrate the tendency to depict religion within a realistic framework.

Italian for Beginners is more typical in its treatment of religious authorities as ordinary people struggling with mundane problems. The film follows a young priest arriving at his new parish in a lower middle-class suburb. The main story, however, is a typical modern multi-character narrative (Tröhler 2000), dealing with several 'main' characters (all members of a municipal language course) and their personal problems of isolation, identity and sexuality. Each person in this group represents what Tröhler calls a narrative 'vector'—including the priest. The film ends by suggesting that the priest, who has lost his wife, has overcome his own personal tragedy through participation in the community surrounding the Italian lessons, rather than through religious self-examination.

In this respect, the priest in *Italian for Beginners* is reminiscent of another priest in a more recent Danish film, *Menneskedyret* (*Truly Human*) (Carsten Rudolf 1995). *Truly Human* is about a boy's identity problems in relation to the loss of his father and his mother's search for a new husband. Complications arise because of the local priest, who had an affair with the mother when they were young, and may be the boy's biological father. Furthermore, the priest is still in love with the mother, as well as being the employer of the boy, who works as his church assistant. The main conflict concerns questions about love and father identification. The compassionate and anti-authoritarian priest functions as a contrast to the blunted and authoritarian school master who has becomes the mother's new partner. The conflict between the two father figures concerns the boy, who is clearly revolting against the school master as his new father, as well as the mother, who seems constantly to repress a longing for her former relation with the priest. In both cases, the role and function of the priest can be read either in terms of secular conflicts about identity and love, or as a Christian analogy.

The film demonstrates a rather typical ambiguity towards religion in new Danish art cinema. On the one hand, 'God is not as he used to be', as the priest explains to the boy, illustrating his point by making the boy look into a surveying binocular that turns everything, in this case the church, upside down. On the other hand, the film is conveying, despite this poetic but heavy-handed symbolism, a clear religious message, through the central position of the priest. As a constant background figure, he is the possible father of the boy, the only person who understands the confused boy, and the repressed love of the mother.

The TV serial *Strisser på Samsø* (Eddie Thomas Petersen 1997) adds to the picture of priests as everyday people preoccupied with problems of intimacy. The serial is about a policeman who is transferred to a small island after the death of his wife. To stress the sense of provinciality on the island, the local priest is a prominent figure. However, in order to make this constellation interesting—at least for the male protagonist—the priest is a young, beautiful, alcohol-consuming woman and the fiction suggests (but only suggests) that she is seeking an erotic adventure as a result of an unhappy marriage. We are first introduced to the priest as she curses a car driver, but the most emblematic picture of how the priest is portrayed in everyday settings is a scene where she is playing billiards with the local drunkards.

All this indicates how representatives of official religion in Danish art film are stripped of their lofty and authoritative character, and placed at eye

level with the rest of society. Priests and religion seem less to fulfil metaphysical functions than to be figures of crystallization regarding conflicts of
contingency and existential uncertainty. At times, Danish cinema appears to
be more interested in young (female) priests as intriguing representatives of
problems of identity and intimacy regarding love, sexuality and pregnancy,
rather than incarnations of religious doctrines; so much, in fact, that a
female Danish priest complained about the tendency to depict her profession
as consisting of young, uncertain females more concerned with their private
lives than preaching the gospel (Plum 2004).

4. GOOD, EVIL AND SPECTACULAR:
RELIGION IN DANISH GENRE FILM

Although the institutional background of Danish cinema seems to encourage
a kind of popular art cinema, regular genre films have become more widespread in recent years, both within television and feature film production.

Riget (*The Kingdom* 1994) represents von Trier's experiment with television as a narrative medium. Although the serial would probably qualify as so-
called art television, due to its satirical and self-conscious style, as well as its
curious blend of avant-garde and TV serial (Thompson 2003), it was still a
highly successful and popular product. The serial illustrates a typical feature
in religious genre films, where the topic often centres on the inexplicable or
the inadequacy of science, symbolized by reference to irrationality and the
occult (in *The Kingdom*, by having Lars von Trier himself making the sign
of the cross and the devil at the end of each episode). *The Kingdom* is a
deconstruction of the entire fundament of rationality that medical science is
symbolizing, by sympathizing with the clairvoyant Ms Drusse, while mocking
the medical staff—who themselves are performing secret obscure rituals,
giving birth to a monstrous baby or trying to poison each other with voodoo
medicine. As we are told in the introduction to each episode, the hospital
where the action takes place was built on the location of a former bleaching
pond:

> The bleachers gave way to doctors and researchers, the best brains in the
> nation and the most perfect technology. Now life was to be charted, and
> ignorance and superstition never to shake the bastions of science again.
> Perhaps their arrogance became too pronounced [as did] their persistent
> denial of the spiritual. For it is as if the cold and damp have returned.

However, as in von Trier's religious films, it is hard to know whether he is
actually presenting us with a positive alternative. Does the irrational and
supernatural represent a positive force or is it just an advanced MacGuffin, a
narrative device to create suspense and humour? In the second part of *The*

Kingdom, alternative medicine appears just as incompetent and inhuman as its rational counterpart, offering no positive alternative to the harsh attack on conventional medical science.

One of the most productive figures in new Danish cinema, and one of the people responsible for turning Danish cinema in a more genre-conscious direction, is Anders Thomas Jensen. He is the scriptwriter behind some of the most successful films in recent years, both in terms of box office figures and critical acclaim. Meanwhile, he has developed his own career as a film director, starting with three Oscar-nominated short films, and later moving into feature film direction based on his own manuscripts.

Adam's Apples completes a tendency that goes back to his early films and manuscripts, where religious themes become a vehicle for spectacular narratives. Already, the short film *Ernst and the Light* (1996) uses the Second Coming of Jesus to make a humorous description of our time, which leaves little room for religious ideals and demands. 'There is no use for you here', Ernst tries to explain to the son of God: 'The market is gone. Pull yourself together. Invest your know-how in something new and find out where you are to any use'. When the son of God asks whether 'none of you have kept faith and want to be saved?', Ernst, a small-time businessman, replies: 'God no. People want sex and violence, and sex and sex and then cleaning articles'. However, the son of God insists upon being the salvation of humankind, to which Ernst replies: 'You are going to save nobody here. You just mind yourself'.

The film *I Kina spiser de hunde* (*In China They Eat Dogs* 1999) tells the story of a bank clerk who prevents an attempt to rob his local bank. When hearing that the money was meant for an operation (which turns out to be a lie), he regrets his actions and decides to help the accomplice by stealing the money himself. The plan includes his criminal and violent brother as well as his two foolish assistants. The story ends by having a representative from both heaven and hell dividing the casualties from the film's final shoot-out. This is both an ingenious and convenient way of ending a story that otherwise is devoid of religious references and without a clear narrative closure. The religious ending appears as a narrative *deus ex machina* as well as an effort to add a certain (shady) morality to the narrative's black humour and fascination with small-time crooks and criminals.

Although the religious elements in the films of Anders Thomas Jensen such as *Adam's Apples* can be interpreted theologically (see Tudvad 2006), they also have a clear dramaturgical function. A paraphrasing of the book of Job, the film plays on the contrast between an evil, brutal and violent neo-Nazi and a good, forgiving and reality-denying priest to create a popular comedy about how the good in man eventually prevails over evil and ignorance. In a highly secular society, such as the Danish one, religion is an easy victim for the type of black (and disrespectful) humour that has become the trademark of Anders Thomas Jensen. Poking fun at religion is effective communication, since one can play on the audience's horizon of expectations as well as activate a relatively low (but also unproblematic) threshold of indignation.

This use of official religion as a means to create disrespectful humour and gentle indignation was anticipated by *Nattevagten (The Nightwatch)* (Ole Bornedal 1994). The film is about two law students who decide to have a final taste of carefree youthfulness before the conformity of their future profession will govern their lives. In order to do so, they challenge each other to perform socially transgressing actions, such as dining with a prostitute, getting into a fight and behaving in an uncivilized way in a church. The latter is done by refusing absolution and vomiting in the baptismal font. This storyline is attached to another story about a psychopathic serial killer. But it is telling that the film's description of the calculated evil of the killer is without any references to religion or religious symbolism. Religious elements only appear as a setting for the final proof of the two young men's transgressions of social norms and behaviour as a kind of *rite de passage*.

Nattevagten anticipated another important tendency in new Danish cinema by employing traditional horror aesthetics, which in a Danish context is rather unusual. The film thus indicated a change of guard in Danish cinema by obtaining a relatively high success within a genre that traditionally has been marketed towards a much smaller audience segment than the usual Danish family drama.

5. TENDENCIES IN NEW DANISH RELIGIOUS FILMMAKING

A general view on religion in new Danish cinema reveals two tendencies linked to the distinction between art film and genre film. First, religion often appears in films that touch upon fundamental questions in life. Basic human conditions get linked to religious terms like faith, sacrifice, guilt, forgiveness, evil and so on. For that purpose, religion can be used both dramatically (von Trier) or humorously (Anders Thomas Jensen). Second, official religion is often staged in an everyday realistic setting associated with art cinema, whereas the supernatural and the mythological are staged in the more spectacular fashions associated with genre cinema.

The first tendency reveals that religious matters closest to official religion and liturgical conventions tend to appear more often in art cinema than in genre cinema. This also suggests why questions concerning existential problems are more widespread in art cinema, in contrast with genre cinema, where supernatural conflicts are more common.

The second tendency indicates that within the everyday-realistic frame-work, religion appears as something partial. Religion is portrayed as a social function among others and priests are performing a profession like any other profession. In these films, religion is not necessarily all-embracing, but rather one aspect of a complex reality. The main conflicts need not be of a particularly religious nature, even though they unfold around a religious person or setting.

In contrast, mythological and supernatural themes often permeate the entire narrative universe in genre films. The film *Dykkerne* (*Beyond*) (Åke Sandgren 2000) provides a good example. The film is about two brothers who discover a German submarine from WWII containing secret information about life-preserving experiments developed by the Nazis. These experiments were performed on children and based on a diabolic technology that keeps the children encapsulated in water tanks. The younger brother has an accident while diving inside the submarine and his soul is retained by the confused souls of the Nazi guinea-pigs. Thus, the film contains a number of religious references, most of them in relation to elements of unofficial religion such as superstition (the younger brother forgot his amulet in the boat before the fatal accident), mysticism (voices from the dead), exorcism (performed by a clairvoyant woman), growing up (the two brothers are allowed to dive without an instructor when they discover the submarine), descending to the land of the dead (the older brother returns to the site of the accident to free his brother's soul), resurrection (invocation of Christian, the name of the older brother, during the rescue operation) and the salvation of the lost souls (as they dramatically ascend into heaven in the final scene).

Thus, *Dykkerne* is a good example of how genre cinema creates a religiously saturated universe, by combining aspects of both official and non-official religion. The film illustrates how 'The official model is often overlaid with nonofficial religious themes, perhaps drawn from folk religion, mythology, popular culture, or…[a] "misinformed" view of the official model' (McGuire 1994: 102).

6. DRAMATURGICAL FUNCTIONS

Despite their very different nature, it can be argued that film and religion possess related mythological and ritual functions (Lyden 2003). On the one hand, cinema is performing important social rituals like celebrating 'sacred' times such as birthdays, weekends and holydays. On the other hand, cinema is re-enacting fundamental mythological conflicts and narratives. In order for that to succeed, a handful of operative preconditions have to be in place.

Film and religion need to be combined on both a narrative and dramatur-gical level. This implies an internal power struggle between religious and narrative intentions. Either the film has to adjust to the demands of religious communication, or the religious demands have to adjust to the dictates of the narrative. Only in rare cases does the combination of film and religion seem to form a synthesis on a formal level, where the communicative expres-sions of the film by itself possess a religious or spiritual dimension. These rare instances have been called different names such as *sacramental film* (Fraser 1998) or *transcendental style* (Schrader 1972) and include films by, for example, Bresson, Tarkovskij and Dreyer.

In new Danish cinema there would be few, if any, examples of such a style. Rather, the synthesis between film and religion is to be found within the framework of an aesthetic of everyday realism, or through the play with genre conventions. In the case of Lars von Trier, these two options seem to merge.

Lars von Trier: Between Transcendence and Sentimentality
Despite obvious references to Dreyer and Tarkovskij, one can hardly speak of *transcendental style* in relation to von Trier's films. To be sure, a number of components contained in Schrader's definition of transcendental style are found in the work of von Trier. This includes (1) a formalized everyday realism (the handheld camera in *Breaking the Waves* and *Dancer in the Dark*) confronted with (2) emotional outbursts, or what Schrader calls 'over-whelming compassion', leading to a 'decisive action' (Bess's sexual humilia-tion in *Breaking the Waves*, Selma's fatal fight for her money in *Dancer in the Dark*), followed by (3) a final *stasis*, the culminating moment, when the disparity between the everyday and emotional compassion freezes into a form that points to 'something deeper than itself, the inner unity of all things' (Schrader 1972: 51).

The endings of von Trier's films can be read as a kind of genre parodying *stasis*: the bells in heaven that end *Breaking the Waves* or the absolute silence (in a musical) that follows the execution of Selma in *Dancer in the Dark*. However, as these examples illustrate, von Trier seems more concerned with exploring (and challenging) genre conventions than creating transcendental allusions. Von Trier unfolds his religious elements in relation to the norms and conventions of classical genres such as melodrama and musical.

Thus, the presence of religious elements can be explained partly by reference to dramaturgical needs and narrative conventions. A look at the development of the films by Lars von Trier demonstrates the point. In *Dancer in the Dark*, the tragedy revolves around Selma's hereditary, and rapidly increasing, blindness, which will also become the destiny of her son, unless Selma can pay for an expensive eye operation that will save his vision. However, in an early draft, the hereditary disease was not blindness but the inability to walk (Schepelern 2000). By changing the story to an issue of blindness, the film obtains two things. First, it refers to other historical melodramas about blind women, like *City Lights* (Chaplin 1931) or *Magnificent Obsession* (Sirk 1954). Second, and more importantly, it relates to a religious antinomy between body and soul symbolized by the traditional association of blindness with wisdom. Thus, the melodramatic content is intensified by turning Selma's disease into a problem of blindness. In accordance with the melodrama's stressing of destiny, Selma's blindness is a symbol of her fate as a victim of invisible forces (losing her job, money, freedom and eventually her life). Furthermore, the figure becomes more religiously pure, since blindness is traditionally associated with innocence, piety and devotion.

The transformations of the manuscript of *Breaking the Waves* are even more extensive. The main character, Bess, was originally called Caroline, mother to a child and married to a language professor. The action was placed in a European capital in 1962 and the characters were described as 'not particularly religious' (Schepelern 2000). In a later draft, Caroline (Bess) is married to Yan, captain on a tanker and living in Ostende. The final version is about Bess from a small Scottish village and her marriage to Jan who works on an offshore oil rig. However, the early versions and the final version share the same main conflict about the husband, who becomes disabled; in an early draft as a result of sickness, in the final version because of an accident. As a result of his disablement, the husband demands that his wife have sex with strangers, which eventually leads to *his* miraculous cure, but *her* ruin and death.

Thus, Caroline from a European capital has become Bess from a Scottish village. The 'not particularly religious' Caroline has become the devout Bess who has dialogues with God. The secular environment has been substituted by first a Catholic setting (Ostende) and later a devoted Protestant community, since, as Schepelern explains, 'the miracle will be more effective in a miracle-hostile puritan universe such as the Scottish' (Schepelern 2000: 195). Small but important changes also take place in the main story about the promiscuous behaviour of the sacrificing wife. From being first conceived of as having a rather perverted sexuality, in the tradition from Marquis de Sade's *Juliette*, Bess ends up performing her sexual encounters, as demanded by her disabled husband, with evident dislike and aversion, turning Bess into 'a sacrificing, suffering and "pure" heroine'. According to Schepelern: 'the moderation of the sexual element is a result of the realization that the pious and sentimental, which he [Trier] wanted to express through the character of Bess, hardly could be combined with sexual desire' (2000: 210-11).

These changes of manuscripts indicate that religious elements are to a certain degree functions of dramaturgical needs. Religious or existential conflicts about suffering, sacrifice, devotion and so on. often call for an explicit religious setting in order to be handed down to the audience in a clear and meaningful manner. The story about the sexually sacrificing Bess from a Protestant community could *mutatis mutandis* also be presented as the story about Caroline from an urbane university environment. However, the explicit religious framework functions as communicative assistant, by constituting a horizon of expectations and understanding regarding the line of action and the range of possible interpretations.

Enlargement, Proxies and Contrast: Narrative Functions of Religion
As indicated by the examples mentioned above, one of the dramaturgical functions of religion is to enlarge themes and conflicts. Religious symbols and practises serve as means to sharpen characters and conflicts, as when the miracle following Bess' sacrifice in *Breaking the Waves* is taking place in a Protestant community. A similar mechanism governs the earlier mentioned *Forbrydelse*, where the choice between faith in God or in modern science is forced upon a priest. In *The Kingdom*, the references to occultism and the supernatural serve to underline the overall theme, namely, the gradual undermining and erosion of the kingdom of rationality. Thus, references to religious themes offer the viewer adequate schemas and scripts to deal with themes like sacrifice, faith and irrationality, which otherwise may appear too abstract.

In modern Danish cinema, religion often functions as a proxy. Religion creates the frame in which questions of community, love, death, forgiveness and so on, can be approached. Modern Danish cinema is populated by marriages and funerals. It has seldom much to do with salvation or metaphysical blessing, but is a convenient and effective frame to deal with problems and conflicts concerning love and intimacy, grief and despair. Religion delivers the scene and the setting, rather than the answers. It is a means to diagnose, rather than to cure, contemporary problems.

Priests and churches also function as dramaturgical centres of rotation in modern multi-protagonist narratives like *Italian for Beginners* or *Strisser på Samsø*. They symbolize community and unity and are thus natural rallying points. As such, they become a kind of narrative incarnation of hotel lobbies and railway stations in classical cinema; that is, locations and situations that force people into joint projects.

Finally, religious symbols and characters create highly dramatic contrasts. *Ernst og Lyset* tells the story about the Second Coming and Jesus' difficulties in persuading modern man to believe in his mission. One can hardly imagine a more unlikely disciple than Ernst, a petit bourgeois travelling salesman who sells cleaning products. His total denial of unearthly concerns eventually frustrates Jesus to the point that he disappointedly returns to heaven without having accomplished his mission. *Adam's Apples* contrasts a brutal neo-nazi and a good, but reality-denying priest. The action is based on the meeting and confrontation of brutality and forgiveness, glorification and denial of violence, the political and the spiritual, evil and goodness. As a paraphrasing of the book of Job, the film did not need a priest as the main character. From a dramaturgical perspective, however, in a secular society, a priest is the most clearly defined representative of belief and the most obvious contrast to evil, represented by a violent neo-nazi.

Forbrydelse also plays on the contrast between a priest and a women's prison. The director, Kirsten Olesen, explains how 'Everything is so full of contrast within a prison. The edges are very sharp, and the contours very clear. In a way the roles are given in advance' (Nysten 2004). Here the contrasts work in order to thematize religious terms like guilt and forgiveness. The contrasting and well-defined roles and relations between priest and prisoners make it possible to investigate how guilt and crime exist on several levels; juridical, human and moral.

7. THE STATUS OF RELIGION IN NEW DANISH CINEMA

The role and function of religion in modern Danish cinema point in several directions. First of all, they show that religion is not about to disappear from Danish cinema. On the contrary, religion appears to be thriving in popular narratives, offering a codified communicative frame in which to address existential problems—even in a highly secular society.

On the other hand, 'God is not what he used to be', as the priest explains in the film *Menneskedyret* (*Truly Human*). Or as we are told at the very beginning of *Italian for Beginners*, 'Things haven't been easy of late. We feel perhaps that we haven't felt Gods presence very much'. Something has changed. The everyday realism that characterizes new Danish cinema's depictions of religion indicates that religion is no longer a lofty and grave matter, as it was in the modern art cinema of Dreyer, Bergman or Tarkovksij. The religious figures in new Danish cinema are not desperately demanding proof of God's existence (as does the crusader in *The Seventh Seal*) or searching metaphysical zones (as in *Stalker*). Religion seems to have lost its metaphysical attraction and has rather become a social framework for negotiating problems of identity and intimacy.

Furthermore, there is a certain suspiciousness surrounding characters who are true believers in Danish cinema. In *Italian for Beginners*, the wife of the young priest possibly died of a combination of religious devotion and schizophrenia, while the old priest, for whom he is substituting, has renounced his faith all together following the death of his wife. In the film *Sekten* (*Credo*) (Susanne Bier 1997), we get a demonizing portrait of new-age religion as sectarian, brutal and brainwashing, while the second episode of *Strisser på Samsø* portrays a devout Protestant community as a collection of darkened, incestuous, fanatics ready to sacrifice their own children in the name of salvation and true belief. In *Adam's Apples*, faith stands between the priest and raving madness. And in *Ernst og Lyset*, the Son of God is simply told that he is selling a bad product.

Thus, in new Danish cinema we find an almost total demystification of official religion combined with a social stigmatization of excessive belief. The only place where religion is really allowed to unfold is within the self-contained and self-regulated universe of genre film. Here, metaphysical connections between the earthly and the beyond are established, giving form and identity to evil, the unknown and the irrational.

In Denmark, this area of popular cinema has traditionally been the domain of American films (Bondebjerg 2005). But now, when Danish cinema is becoming more orientated towards mainstream cinema, it is symptomatic that there is greater interest in the supernatural, the mystical and the mythological. Viewed from a normative perspective, it will be interesting to follow this development and see whether this orientation towards mythology and 'banal' religion will result in a more national/Danish representation of religion or whether Danish cinema will comply with the genre conventions of Hollywood in dealing with religious matters.

8. RELIGION AND THE INVERTED FUNCTION OF ART AND POPULAR CULTURE

All this leaves us with a surprisingly familiar picture. In new Danish cinema, official religion is mainly the subject of the more 'serious' art films, while alternative, unofficial and spectacular religion is relegated to the area of popular culture and spectacular narratives. More surprisingly, the representation of religion one encounters in serious art films is in accordance with classical sociological descriptions of religion as a subfield in a complex and differentiated society. In Danish cinema, priests and religious elements are fulfilling important functions, but they are given no privileged status. Meanwhile, excessive belief is portrayed as a kind of social anomaly.

If we allow a few generalizations this familiar picture nevertheless contains some surprising consequences. First of all, with a few exceptions (*Breaking the Waves*, *Adam's Apples*), there is little room for 'biblical variations' in Danish cinema. The everyday realistic manner in which official religion is portrayed often stresses the human and professional aspects of Protestantism rather than liturgical questions according to the scriptures.

Second, and more interestingly, when it comes to religion, the role and function of art cinema and popular cinema is almost inverted. Traditionally, the self-conscious art film is where one would expect official descriptions and values to be challenged. *The Idiots* by Lars von Trier would be a typical example, challenging the lifestyle and values of bourgeois family structure and self-realization. On the other hand, popular culture, especially genre cinema, normally reproduces hegemonic structures and values (such as celebrating national symbols, gender relations, the nuclear family and so on). All this is inverted when it comes to religion. Here, serious art cinema is almost reproducing official definitions of religion as an entirely private matter. By contrast, popular genre films seem to recognize religion as an all-pervasive aspect of life and as a challenge to the technical-rational hegemony. These films offer descriptions of, for instance, evil as something more and different than a purely political or social-psychological outcome, as well as allowing the supernatural to intervene in earthly matters. Thus, it is popular cinema rather than art-house cinema that seems open to new aspects of religious communication in modern society, introducing elements of non-official religion to the religious discourse of popular culture.

Perhaps the treatment of religion in Danish art cinema indicates that official religion has become demystified to the point that religion is just another component in the overall social fabric, neither representing any exceptional authority nor being a source of exceptional existential unrest. On the other hand, the persistent interest in religious matters within genre cinema indicates that religion still offers a framework for handling cultural and social antinomies between the ordinary and the exceptional, belief and reason, science and intuition, good and evil.

This last point can be read as religion's contribution to the re-enchantment of popular culture (Murdock 1997), but it can also be regarded as religion's incessant ability to negotiate cultural and social antinomies. *Dykkerne* depicts a supernatural world of spirits, rites of initiations and a symbolic descent to the kingdom of death. However, the spiritual and physical contact with this non-rational side of reality is mediated by modern technology and instruments of rationality like radars, computers and diving technology, offering the viewer a narrative solution, rather than a logical solution, to the antinomy of rationality and irrationality.

This ability to negotiate and partly overcome cultural and social antinomies, however, is not restricted to religious films. It has always been an inherent part of genre cinema (Schatz 1981), suggesting an altogether different question of whether religion and popular narratives share the same functions.

This brief examination of the role and function of religion in new Danish cinema confirms the picture drawn by theories of de-secularization (Casanova

1994; Martín-Barbero 1997), which suggest that despite a ceaseless development of the technological-rational hegemony, or modernization in the direction of a 'second' or 'reflexive' modernity (Giddens 1994; Beck and Williams 2000), religion is not about to disappear from modern society. Within cultural expressions such as cinema, religion, on the contrary, has proven to be an effective means to negotiate, for instance, the arrogance of science and rationality (*Riget*), the scientific risk connected with pregnancy (*Forbrydelse*) and the confrontation with death and the beyond in a modern tale of coming of age (*Dykkerne*).

Thus, religion functions on two different levels and should be regarded from a double perspective. From an internal perspective, religion is part of the dramaturgical repertoire of narrative cinema. The role and function of religion have been adjusted to the narrative conventions and demands of art cinema and genre cinema to such a degree that we can talk about more or less autonomous systemic operations. On the other hand, it is obvious that in order to function as dramaturgical means and solutions, religious references must evoke a cultural response. Religion contributes to relevant and modern narratives only as long as religion constitutes a part of society's cultural fund and contributes to the cultural horizon of experience. In that respect, cinema makes use of the communicative functions and cultural capital of religion, while also giving religion a new and different life (that is, new and different cultural functions), through the negotiations of identity and intimacy as seen in genre cinema, or through the more reflexive struggle with modern conditions found in art cinema.

BIBLIOGRAPHY

[n.a.]
  1964   Lov om film og biografer [Law on Movies and Cinemas] ([n.c.], [n.p.], Law
          no. 155 from 26 May).
[n.a.]
  1972   Lov om film og biografer [Law on Movies and Cinemas] ([n.c.], [n.p.], Law
          no. 104 from 2 February).
Abel, Richard
  1994   The Ciné Goes to Town: French Cinema 1896–1914 (Berkeley: University
          of California Press).
Appadurai, Arjun
  1996   'Disjuncture and Difference in the Global Cultural Economy', in Arjun
          Appadurai (ed.), Modernity at Large (Minneapolis: University of Minne-
          sota Press): 27-47.
Beck, Ulrich, and Johannes Williams
  2000   Samtaler med Ulrich Beck. Frihed eller kapitalisme (Copenhagen: Hans
          Reitzels Forlag).

Billig, Michael
    1995   *Banal Nationalism* (London: Sage).
Bondebjerg, Ib
    2005   *Filmen og det moderne. Filmgenrer og filmkultur i Danmark 1940–1972*
            (Copenhagen: Gyldendal).
Bordwell, David
    1985   *Narration in the Fiction Film* (London: Routledge).
    1995   'Den klassiske Hollywoodfilm. Fortællemæssige principper og procedure',
            Tryllelygten 2.2: 57-78.
    2002   'The Art Cinema as a Mode of Film Practice', in Fowler 2002: 94-103.
Bordwell, David, Janet Staiger and Kristin Thompson
    1985   *The Classical Hollywood Cinema: Film Style and Mode of Production to 1960*
            (New York: Columbia University Press).
Casanova, José
    1994   *Public Religions in the Modern World* (Chicago: University of Chicago
            Press).
Castells, Manuel
    2000   'Materials for an Exploratory Theory of Network Society', *British Journal of
            Sociology* 51: 5-24.
DFI
    1998   *Det danske filminstitut. En institution og et hus for levende billede. Det danske
            filminstituts 4-årige handlingsplan* (Copenhagen: DFI).
Eskjær, Mikkel
    2006   *Film som kommunikationsmedie. En systemteoretisk analyse* (Copenhagen:
            Institut for Medier, Erkendelse og Formidling, Københavns Universitet).
Fowler, C. (ed.)
    2002   *The European Cinema Reader* (London: Routledge).
Fraser, Peter
    1998   *Images of the Passion: The Sacramental Mode in Film* (Trowbridge: Flicks
            Books).
Geertz, Clifford
    2000   'Religion as a Cultural System', in C. Geertz, *The Interpretation of Culture*
            (New York: Basic Books, 1973): 87-125.
Giddens, Anthony
    1994   *Modernitetens konsekvenser* (Copenhagen: Hans Reitzels Forlag).
Grodal, Torben
    2006   'Film for enhver smag?', *Ekko* 35: 27-29.
Hjarvard, Stig
    2005   'Medialisering af religiøse forestillinger', in H.R. Iversen and M.T. Højs-
            gaard (eds.), *Gudstro i Danmark* (Copenhagen: Anis): 167-86.
Hjort, Mette, and Ib Bondebjerg
    2000   *The Danish Directors: Dialogues on a Contemporary National Cinema*
            (Bristol: Intellect).
Holloway, Ronald
    1977   *Beyond the Image: Approaches to the Religious Dimension in the Cinema*
            (Geneva: World Council of Churches).

Hoover, S.M., and K. Lundby (eds.)
    1997   *Rethinking Media, Religion, and Culture* (Thousand Oaks, CA: Sage Publications).

Jerslev, Anne
    2006   *Præsten som filmisk figur i nye danske film* (Copenhagen: Department of Media, Cognition and Communication).

Luhmann, Nicklas
    1981   'Die Unwahrscheinlichkeit der Kommunikation', in N. Luhmann, *Soziologische Aufklärung*, III (Opladen: Westdeutscher Verlag): 25-35.
    2000   *Sociale Systemer. Grundrids til en almen teori* (Copenhagen: Hans Reitzels Forlag).

Lyden, John C.
    2003   *Film as Religion: Myths, Morals, and Rituals* (New York: New York University Press, 2003).

Martín-Barbero, Jean
    1997   'Mass Media as a Site of Resacralization of Contemporary Cultures', in Hoover and Lundby 1997: 102-16.

McGuire, Meredith B.
    1994   *Religion: The Social Context* (Belmont, CA: Wadsworth Publishing).

Murdock, Graham
    1997   'The Re-Enchantment of the World: Religion and the Transformation of Modernity', in Hoover and Lundby 1997: 85-101.

Neal, Steve
    2002   'Art Cinema as Institution', in Fowler 2002: 103-20.

Nysten, Jes
    2004   'Interview med Annette K. Olesen om "Forbrydelse"' (http://menighedsraad.dk/fileadmin/userupload/Gabrielprisen/2004_interview_Annette_K._Olesen.pdf, accessed 21 December 2006).

Plum, Karen F.
    2004   'Nye præsteroller på film og tv', *Politiken* (1 May): 5.

Schatz, Thomas
    1981   *Hollywood Genres: Formulas, Filmmaking, and the Studio System* (New York: Random House).

Schepelern, Peter
    2000   *Lars von Triers film: Tvang og befrielse* (Copenhagen: Rosinante).

Schrader, Paul
    1972   *Transcendental Style in Film: Ozu, Bresson, Dreyer* (Berkeley: University of California Press).

Thompson, Karen
    2003   *Storytelling in Film and Television* (Cambridge, MA: Harvard University Press).

Tröhler, M.
    2000   'Les films à protagnistes multiples et la logique des possibles', *Iris* 29: 85-101.

Tudvad, Peter
    2006   'Jobs bog ifølge Jensen', *Ekko* 33: 50-53.

IMAGES OF SALVATION IN *TSOTSI*, *IN AMERICA* AND *LEVITY*

Árni Svanur Daníelsson

[W]hy should we assume that only preachers and theologians can bring out the significance of Christ's redemption? (Sherry 2003: 10).

INTRODUCTION

The goal of the current chapter is to examine images of salvation in the films *Levity* (Ed Solomon 2003), *In America* (Jim Sheridan 2002) and *Tsotsi* (Gavin Hood 2005). In the process, a basic framework for the analysis of images of salvation is introduced. The purpose of this is twofold: on the one hand, to examine how Christian theology can be useful in the analysis of specific themes in films; on the other hand, to examine how films can be used to give insight into and reflect upon central theological issues.

The three films discussed in this chapter were chosen because they are good examples of different ways in which salvation is portrayed in films. Two of them, *Levity* and *Tsotsi*, explicitly deal with these themes, whereas the theme is more implicit in *In America*.[1] The films provide diverse accounts of the human condition, problems and solutions, as is discussed below. They raise questions regarding the nature of sin and sacrifice and the connection between life and death. Last, but not least, the films echo three approaches to salvation: liberation from evil (*Tsotsi*, *Levity*), cleansing from guilt (*Levity*) and the transforming power of love (*In America*, *Tsotsi*).[2]

Tsotsi is an Academy award winning film by South African director Gavin Hood. It tells the story of a young gang member, named Tsotsi, whose life is transformed when he finds a child in the backseat of a car he has stolen. This becomes a life-changing event that turns him away from a life of crime and violence. Tsotsi is a powerful analysis of alienation, individualism and

---

1. A tagline for *Tsotsi* reads 'In this world...redemption just comes once'. The director of *Levity* writes that the film is about a man seeking 'the redemption that he doesn't believe possible for himself' (Solomon 2003).

2. This terminology stems from Gerald O'Collins, who discusses these approaches in detail in *Jesus our Redeemer* (2007: vii and Chapters 6–9).

violence in society. It deals with sin on an individual and societal level. The film examines the need for forgiveness and dealing with the past; for making right what was done wrong. It is also a witness to the redemptive power of love, exemplified in the child that Tsotsi/David kidnaps, who reminds him of his mother's love. This in turn leads to a radical re-evaluation of his own life.

In America is a recent film from the Irish director Jim Sheridan, who based the film partly on his own life. He is well known for films like *My Left Foot* and *In the Name of the Father*. *In America* tells the story of an Irish family that moves to New York to start a new life. They have suffered the loss of a family member and are still dealing with their grief. The film shows the family struggling in a new land; underneath this are themes of grief and salvation. The story intertwines the mystery of life and death in a memorable scene and leaves the audience with questions about the connection between death and life and resurrection and what it means for one person to die for someone else.

Levity was written and directed by Ed Solomon. It tells the story of Manual Jordan, a murderer who is released from prison. He is still dealing with feelings of guilt over a murder he committed as a young man, a long time ago. In an attempt to make up with the past, he seeks out and befriends Adele Easely, the sister of the murder victim. In the end, he gets a second chance to do what is right. The film stars Billy Bob Thornton as Manual, Holly Hunter as Adele, with Morgan Freeman and Kirsten Dunst in supporting roles. *Levity* centres on release from guilt and shows that sometimes drastic steps need to be taken to work through it. It also illustrates that what oppresses can come from within. The scene discussed in this chapter is an interesting meditation on the nature of sacrifice and on the way one man's sacrifice can be of value for another. It also illustrates how a person can both give and receive salvation at the same time.

SALVATION IN FILM: A FRAMEWORK

In theology, the word salvation refers to 'God's activities in bringing humans into a right relationship with God and with one another through Jesus Christ' (McKim 1996: 247). David Ford has pointed out that '[t]he root meaning of salvation is health', which 'can be physical, social, political, economical, environmental, mental, spiritual and moral' (Ford 1999: 111). Salvation is one of a number of terms used in soteriology; others include redemption, atonement and sacrifice. Of these, salvation has the widest connotations and could be said to encompass the other terms. It is used in this chapter for this reason.

Most images of salvation in the Bible were 'drawn either from everyday life in the ancient world or from the cultic and legal language of ancient Israel' (Daley 2004: 152). Thus, already in the Bible itself, we can see a dialogue between contemporary culture and religion. We also find a variety of images of salvation in contemporary art, including film. Individual films in some cases make use of these images from the Bible and reflect upon them (through parallels or direct references). They may also take one further step and 'attempt to show how the process of redemption, which is described in the Bible in general terms...is worked out in individual lives here and now' (Sherry 2003: 168).[3]

It has been noted previously that 'often the seemingly most straightforward versions of a redemption story contain complications and ambiguities of definition' (Kiely 2004: 278). For this reason, it may be helpful to have a framework to organize the various themes. Such a framework might entail looking at: (1) various film characters in need of salvation; (2) their situations; (3) the process they go through; (4) the agents of salvation; and finally (5) the nature of their salvation.[4]

1. Character(s)
The first task is to look at the character that is the subject or focus of salvation in the film. Which character is this? In some cases more than one character in a film can be in need of salvation and/or may experience it (e.g. *Levity* and *Magnolia*, Paul Thomas Anderson 1999). It is also possible to look at sin and salvation as structural or institutional and thus affecting society or even the environment (e.g. *Tsotsi*; cf. O'Collins 2004: 4).

2. Situation
We next examine the character's situation in the film and ask questions like: What is the nature of his/her troubles or why is there a need for change and salvation? One can also examine how the self-knowledge of a character is presented in the movie (e.g. is he aware of his need for salvation?). This can entail looking at what Kenneth Surin has called *a phenomenology of moral evil*, in other words, '[making] explicit the moral evil which permeates the very depths of our lives' (Surin 1989: 144; referred to in Sherry 2003: 58). When analyzing the salvation themes from a Christian theological perspective, it can be useful to keep in mind the various images of sin in the Bible and the history of theology. These images include: being enslaved by

---

3. Some scholars have even wondered whether we 'find the richest witness to redemption in liturgy, art, music, literature, and the best films?' (O'Collins 2004: 22).

4. The basis for this framework is from my own research, along with Sherry, O'Collins and Kiely (Cf. Sherry 2003: 49; O'Collins 2004; Kiely 2004: 278).

hostile powers (Eph. 2.1-2), being unclean or defiled (Ps. 51.2, 7), alienation (Gen. 3.16), lack of compassion (Lk. 16.19-31; O'Collins 2006: 2-3), a need for forgiveness (Ps. 51) and a need for release from guilt (Ps. 38).

3. and 4. *Process and Agent*

Next, we look at how salvation takes place in the film. At what cost? What is the 'method' of salvation or process that takes place in the film (Kiely 2004: 278)? Closely connected to this is an examination of the agent of salvation. Who is the redeemer and in what way is he or she an important character? Does he confront? Provoke? What is his function? Can the characters perhaps redeem themselves or do they need the intervention of someone else (2006: 278)?

5. *Nature of Salvation*

The final step involves determining the nature of salvation in the film. What is the result of the process? In what way is the character redeemed? We can look to the New Testament for a variety of images in this regard. Salvation is described as: a cure (Lk. 6.9), exorcism (Lk. 8.36), liberation from the dominion of sin or from being slaves to sin (Rom. 6.18; 8.2; 1 Jn 3.8), forgiveness of sins (Mk 2.5, 10; Eph. 1.7), reconciliation (Rom. 5.10-11; Daley 2004: 152-53), resurrection, life and immortality (Jn 5.24; 1 Cor. 15.22-23, 2 Tim. 1.10), having a renewed relationship with God or new access (Mt. 27.51; Hart 1997: 194-95) and having a new perspective on death (O'Collins 2004: 5).

In this respect, Robert Kiely points to an important distinction between material and spiritual salvation, when he asks: 'Is the nature of the release exclusively material? Are the wounds to be healed, debts to be paid, chains to be broken literal or are there moral and spiritual components of the release which may or may not coincide with the physical evidence?' (Kiely 2004: 278). The *Shawshank Redemption* (Frank Darabont 1994) and *Levity* are good examples of films that show salvation both in a literal and a spiritual form. In both films, the protagonists get out of prison; these are literal chains that are broken or the *secularized salvation*, as Clive Marsh calls it in his discussion of *The Shawshank Redemption*. There is also the issue of overcoming guilt in *Levity* (see below) and receiving forgiveness for past wrongdoings in *The Shawshank Redemption* (Marsh 2004: 48-51).[5]

---

5. Clive Marsh discusses salvation in *The Shawshank Redemption* in detail in *Cinema and Sentiment*, and suggests that there are four images of salvation in that film: secularized salvation, salvation as the receipt of forgiveness, salvation as transcendent utopia and salvation as freedom from structure(s) (Marsh 2004: 48-59).

NARRATIVES OF SALVATION

What constitutes a salvation narrative and what characterizes salvation in film? Clive Marsh describes redemption motifs in film as follows:

> Films which contain redemption as a key motif often have a simple purpose: to tell the story of someone who undergoes a massive change from a destructive form of life to one which is more hopeful (Marsh 2007: 98).

In an article on redemption in literature, Robert Kiely offers the following definition:

> Some person is in an undesirable situation (of pain, bondage, debt) from which he or she hopes, against all odds, to be released. Against the hope of the victim is the hatred and mockery of an enemy who does not believe release is possible and, in any case, does not want it to take place (Kiely 2004: 278).

On the surface, this may look like a typical definition of a narrative, but let us take a closer look at the description of the undesirable situation. Marsh uses the terminology 'destructive form of life' and Kiely speaks of 'pain, bondage, debt'. Salvation narratives need not, by definition, differ from other narratives in structure but they do differ in content, that is, in the way they define the problematic situation and how they describe the solution.[6] An example from *The Incredibles* (Brad Bird 2004) might help to clarify this. There are a number of subplots in the film, which show Mr Incredible or some of the other superheroes saving people and pets from various kinds of troubles. One such subplot has Mr Incredible helping out an old woman whose cat is stuck in a tree. Using his super-strength he is able to rip up the tree and save the cat. This narrative may share the same structure as narratives of salvation and it could even be fit within the scheme presented in this chapter, but it falls short of being a narrative of salvation on two counts: the nature of both problem and solution is such that the narrative does not lend itself to a religious interpretation.

We now move on to examples from the three films introduced above, from which we will get a better idea of the kind of problems and solutions found in salvation narratives.

Tsotsi: *Returning*

Tsotsi (Gavin Hood 2005) is a South African film that takes place in Johannesburg. It tells the story of a young and ruthless gang leader who

---

6. Cf. also Trevor Hart's article 'Redemption and Fall', where he writes: 'Humans, Christians contend, need to be rescued from a plight which currently distorts and ultimately threatens to destroy their creaturely well-being under God, but which lies utterly beyond their control or influence. But just what sort of threat is this? And by what means are we to think of it as having been met' (Hart 1997: 189).

experiences a profound change in his life when he takes responsibility for an infant he finds in a car he stole. Before this happened, he shot the infant's mother. In the first part of the film, he is depicted as a particularly ruthless character who never shows any feelings or remorse (e.g. when a member of the gang challenges him on this, the man is beaten up quite severely).

The audience gets glimpses of Tsotsi's former life from a few flashbacks he experiences. We learn that his real name is David (Tsotsi, which means 'thug', is a nickname) and he had a family and a home, but was 'orphaned' when his mother, who suffered from AIDS, died. He seems to have had an abusive step-father (or father) and he ran away from home.

The abducted infant along with Miriam, a young woman he forces to breastfeed the infant, are the agents of Tsotsi's salvation. The infant can be seen as a mirror image of Tsotsi's younger self. It reminds him of what he once had and awakens new (or perhaps old) feelings in him. Miriam, on the other hand, confronts him, appeals to his conscience and pleads for him to return the infant.

Through his relationships with Miriam and the infant, in terms of a theological understanding, he could be said to 'come to himself' (cf. Lk. 15.17) and perhaps in the process, he becomes David again, rather than continuing to be Tsotsi. He seems to care for others, he acknowledges his wrongdoing and tries to do what is right. He asks for forgiveness from people he has treated badly (his colleague Boston and a beggar he had harassed). The most dramatic change is perhaps that he tries to stop the cycle of violence in himself and others (he kills the gang member Butcher and then dismantles the gang).

In the final scene of the film, he returns the baby. Here we witness two things. The first is a shaken young boy who has let his defences down. Earlier in the scene, we see him bring the infant to the gate, in a bag. He puts the bag down and intends to leave, but finds that he cannot. A bond has developed that cannot easily be broken. So he returns and the scene unfolds. This is a dramatically different Tsotsi from the one seen at the beginning of the film; barriers and defences have been removed, literally and symbolically. As was stated before: Tsotsi has become David again.

Second, there is a visual style and *mise-en-scene* that serves to underline the main themes of the film. People are behind bars, isolated, and the bars finally are set aside so that the infant and its parents can be reunited.

This scene highlights a different layer of the film. While the main narrative deals with Tsotsi or David's story and salvation, the film is also a reflection of a society characterized by distance between people and by violence. The people portrayed in the film are literally walled in; the rich have put themselves behind bars. There is a disquieting distance and emptiness between people, excellently portrayed in the *mise-en-scene* and illustrated in the final scene discussed above. In the background of this narrative is the question of social justice in a society plagued by an AIDS epidemic and poverty, and thus of structural sin and a society's need for salvation.

In America: *Overcoming*
In America (Jim Sheridan 2002) portrays a different theme. The main focus is on grief. The film tells of a family of Irish immigrants in New York: Johnny and Sarah and their two daughters Christy and Ariel. The family is dealing with the after-effects of the death of Frankie, Johnny and Sarah's only son. We learn that he died from an inoperable brain tumour. This in many ways has shaped the family, especially Johnny, who seems to have gotten stuck along the way. He finds himself unable to cry and unable to grieve. This has put a serious strain on his relationships with his wife and daughters. This is well illustrated in a scene where the family sits at a restaurant. The younger daughter, Ariel, is reminiscing about the past and complaining that she has no one to play with. The following exchange takes place:

> Ariel: And you don't play with us anymore.
> Johnny: I do play with youse.
> Ariel: Not like you used to.

Another scene takes place in the girls' bedroom. Sarah, who is pregnant, has been reminiscing about when she was pregnant with the girls. Johnny is sitting behind her. The baby is kicking and the girls are excited but Johnny seems distant. When Sarah asks Johnny if he can feel the baby kicking he replies: 'I can't feel anything'. This short reply seems to sum up not only the scene but his situation. A bit later Sarah gives her take on this when she says to Johnny: 'If you can't touch somebody you created, how can you create somebody that'll touch anybody'. Johnny is out of place, distant, cold, perhaps not unable to feel but unable to express his feelings.

In a confrontation between Mateo, one of their neighbours, and Johnny, the former says that Johnny does not believe. Johnny replies: 'In what? God? You know, I asked him a favour. I asked him to take me instead of him. And he took the both of us. And look what he put in my place. I'm a fucking ghost. I don't exist. I can't think. I can't laugh. I can't cry. I can't...feel!'[7]

---

7.   It is worth noting that after this twofold confrontation with Sarah and then Mateo, we cut to a scene in the girls' school where Christy is singing a solo. The song fits well with Johnny's situation and perhaps hints at where the possibility for salvation lies: 'Desperado, why don't you come to your senses...come down from your fences, open the gate... You better let somebody love you before it's too late'. Perhaps these three scenes constitute a turning point in the movie.

In America shows how sorrow can become a burden that overshadows life. It also gives an example of how this can be worked out. Mateo is a key figure in that respect. He is an artist who lives a few floors down. The girls first meet him on Halloween as they go trick-or-treating in the apartment building where they live. Following that, Mateo becomes a friend of the family. He also becomes a voice of truth and optimism for them. At the same time he is a powerful reminder of the reality of death because he has AIDS and is dying.

As the film progresses, there is an interesting dynamic between *fear* and *hope*. Sarah becomes pregnant. The pregnancy is not without problems, which becomes a source of distress for all of them, especially the parents, who fear they could not live with the loss of another child. Thus the unborn child is at the same time a representative of fear and hope. Mateo encourages them and reassures them that everything will be all right. He also becomes an important figure in the life of the girls, perhaps substituting for a depressed father, who is unable to touch his daughters.

The birth of the child and Mateo's death form the climax of the film. Death and life meet in a superbly edited scene where cross-cutting is used in an innovative way to bring together an end of one life and a beginning of another. Christy introduces the scene with the words 'We were waiting for the baby to show some signs of life'. Then the camera cuts between shots of Mateo dying and the newborn child struggling for its life in an incubator after it has received a blood transfusion. By graphically matching the shots and using sound bridges, the film connects life and death. A time of sorrow becomes a time of hope and new life.

It may be possible to see in this an analogy of death and resurrection. Not in the sense that Mateo dies for the newborn girl, but rather that his death seems in some way to be interconnected with the infant's life and with her being alive, as is emphasized in the editing of the scene. Furthermore, this marks the beginning of Johnny feeling alive again. The writer/director, Jim Sheridan, says about this scene: 'I wanted to suggest that...[he] dies and through the child the spirit of the paternal is reintegrated in the father...' (Sheridan 2004, min. 1.26). Salvation is thus described by the director as Johnny becoming whole again. This is made tangible in touch, first when he touches his newborn child and then as the relationship with his older daughters is restored.

Mateo is also the family's savior in a material sense, because he pays the hospital bills for the birth and treatment of mother and daughter (this recalls interpretations that see Jesus' death on the cross as a payment for the sins of humankind).

There are several elements in the narrative that follows that point to a dramatic change for the family: their apartment is full of life, which is best seen in a party held after the infant comes home. Their neighbours from the building come together in joy. Some of them have sobered up and/or gotten rid of their addictions. Johnny gets an audition for a play and last but not least he is able to say goodbye to Frankie and can finally express his feelings and weep over the family's loss. They are whole again.

Levity: Sacrificing
In *Levity* (Ed Solomon 2003), the main focus is on forgiveness and release from guilt. On the cover of the DVD, the film is described as a 'parable on forgiveness and redemption'. The film tells the story of Manual Jordan, a murderer released on parole after serving 23 years of a life sentence. He has a clear image of his crime and takes full responsibility for what he did.

Even though Manual is released from prison, he is still in bondage. He is held captive by guilt and sees no way out, and has no hope of forgiveness or salvation. Manual isn't the only character in the film in need of salvation. All the protagonists of the film and some of the supporting characters are also in need of salvation. One of these is Abner Easely, nephew and name-sake of the man Manual murdered all those years ago. He is a troublemaker and gang-member who seems to be headed in the same direction as Manual was.

Twice in the film, Manual refers to an eleventh-century text (by the Jewish rabbi and philosopher Moses Maimonides) about how one can make up for past sins and be redeemed. One needs to:
1. acknowledge one's sin
2. show remorse
3. make right with one's neighbour
4. make right with God
5. do the right thing in the same situation

Manuel's lack of belief in the usefulness of this is evident. In the beginning of the film, after outlining the five steps, he says:

> Only I can't bring Abner Easely back like he was some stolen chicken. Certainly made sure of that 23 years ago. And I don't believe in some God that's gonna open his arms to me…even if I did. So there goes steps three and four. And as for step five…time makes sure we're never in the same place twice…no matter how much we wish it. Which is why, for me, I know I'll never be redeemed.

Again, in a scene at the end of the film, Manual discusses these steps. He writes a letter to Adele, the sister of the man he murdered. She is also the mother of the young Abner mentioned earlier. While she is reading the letter, her son is in an alley next to their house. He is there to kill a member of a rival gang. Were he to succeed in this, he would be embarking on a road similar to that taken by Manual 23 years earlier. Adele and Manual are both aware of this danger, and earlier in the film, at Adele's request, Manual spoke to the boy, but this had no effect on him.

In the scene that follows, we see Manual stepping into a potentially dangerous situation in order to defuse it. We can also be fairly sure that even if he were to interrupt the boy at this time and prevent the murder, this might only be delaying the inevitable. Even though nothing is said about this, we can assume that Manual would be aware of it, but he doesn't stay away and puts himself in danger in order to do good (this actually recalls the fifth step mentioned above).

In the struggle Manual is shot, probably by accident. Thus the intervention becomes a sacrifice of some sort. Judging from young Abner's response, the sacrifice is not in vain. Shooting a man has shaken him to the core. Thus Manual becomes the agent of young Abner's salvation (and vice versa) by saving him from the life that Manual had led until then.

Manual survives and having gone through the five steps, he is able to move on, which is expressed in the film by him leaving town. Clearly he is no representative of God and he is anything but sinless. The film emphasizes this. He is, however, a good example of someone who sacrifices himself (unwillingly or not) so that another may be saved. In doing this, he may also have had a chance to redeem himself.

CONCLUSION

These three films illustrate different perspectives on sin and salvation. All of them indicate that in order to move on, one needs to make up with the past. Children or youths play an important role in the films. Baby Sarah becomes a beacon of hope, young David functions as a mirror for the older David, young Abner is both on the receiving end of salvation and is the agent of Manual's salvation. Perhaps the children are so important because they are seen as a representation of innocence and purity or the possibility of this.

As we have seen, these three films touch on a variety of issues, but they also touch upon three important topics for theology: sin, sacrifice and resurrection. They approach this effectively by showing us that 'the process of redemption or salvation is worked out in individual human lives here and now' (Sherry 2003: 168). Perhaps that is precisely where we find the power of film as a medium: it makes the abstract concrete, touchable—it shows what theology analyzes.

BIBLIOGRAPHY

Corrigan, Timothy, and Patricia White
    2004   *The Film Experience: An Introduction* (Boston: Bedford/St Martins).
Daley, Brian
    2004   'He Himself is our Peace', in Davis, Kendall and O'Collins 2004: 149-76.
Davis, Steven T., Daniel Kendall and Gerald O'Collins (eds.)
    2004   *The Redemption: An Interdisciplinary Symposium on Christ as Redeemer* (Oxford: Oxford University Press).
Deacy, Christopher
    2001   *Screen Christologies: Redemption and the Medium of Film* (Cardiff: University of Wales Press).
Fiddes, Paul S.
    1989   *Past Event and Present Salvation: The Christian Idea of Atonement* (London: Darton, Longman & Todd).
Ford, David
    1999   *Theology: A Very Short Introduction* (Oxford: Oxford University Press).
Hart, Trevor
    1997   'Redemption and Fall', in Colin E. Gunton (ed.), *The Cambridge Companion to Christian Theology* (Cambridge: Cambridge University Press): 189-206.
Kelsey, David H.
    2005   *Imagining Redemption* (Louisville, KY: Westminster/John Knox Press).
Kiely, Robert
    2004   'Graven with an Iron Pen', in Davis, Kendall and O'Collins 2004: 277-94.
Marsh, Clive
    2004   *Cinema and Sentiment: Film's Challenge to Theology* (Studies in Cinema and Culture; Carlisle: Paternoster Press).
    2007   *Theology Goes to the Movies: An Introduction to Critical Christian Thinking* (London: Routledge).
McKim, Donald K.
    1996   *Westminster Dictionary of Theological Terms* (Louisville, KY: Westminster/John Knox Press).
O'Collins, Gerald
    2004   'Redemption: Some Crucial Issues', in Davis, Kendall and O'Collins 2004: 1-22.
    2007   *Jesus Our Redeemer: A Christian Approach to Salvation* (Oxford: Oxford University Press).
Sheridan, Jim
    2004   Commentary on In America (*Jim Sheridan: 2002*) 20th Century Fox (DVD published by 20th Century Fox).
Sherry, Patrick
    2003   *Images of Redemption: Art, Literature and Salvation* (Edinburgh: T. & T. Clark).
Solomon, Ed
    2003   'Director's statement, Levity', www.sonyclassics.com/levity/index-withflash.html, accessed 9 September 2007.

Surin, Kenneth
    1989   *The Turnings of Darkness and Light: Essays in Philosophical and Systematic Theology* (Cambridge: Cambridge University Press).
Voytilla, Stuart
    1999   *Myth and the Movies: Discovering the Mythic Structure of 50 Unforgettable Films* (Studio City: Michael Wiese Productions).

EDEN REVISITED:
CATEGORIZING EDEN THEMES IN FILM*

Thorkell Ágúst Óttarsson

The story of Adam and Eve is probably the second most used biblical theme in film (the first being Christ references). Of the 487 films reviewed on the Icelandic *Deus ex cinema* website (www.dec.is/is), 69 make a *direct reference* to the story of Eden or can be considered a *parallel* to the story. Direct references range from the story being mentioned or hinted about to its use as the basis of the plot. Films that are classified as parallel have a plot similar to the story of Adam and Eve, without any direct references to it or any obvious indication that the film-makers had the biblical story in mind.[1]

After categorizing the films in terms of direct references and parallels to the story of Adam and Eve, these films can be divided into a variety of different groups, which can be assigned to one of two main categories:

1. Traditional Interpretations.
2. Eclectic Interpretations.

Although my emphasis will be on the second category, Eclectic Interpretations, I will describe Traditional Interpretations first.

TRADITIONAL INTERPRETATIONS[2]

These sub-groups follow a traditional Christian understanding of the story. Some differ in terms of where the blame is laid (i.e. on the snake, on Adam

* I would like to thank Gunnlaugur A. Jónsson, Árni Svanur Daníelsson, Annika Hvithamar and Geert Hallbäck for their valuable criticism and cooperation, and Arzanne De Vitre Vesthaug for proofreading the article.

1. This is not to say that I believe that the intentions of the film-makers matter at all when discussing films. It is the film itself that should always speak for itself. We often do not know the intention of the film-makers and the film-maker is not always capable of expressing his/her intentions. The film therefore may say the opposite of what the film-maker intended. D.W. Griffith, for example, denied that the infamous *The Birth of a Nation* (1915) was racist. Few would agree with him on this point.

2. I call this category Traditional interpretations (instead of Literary interpretations or something in that vein) to underscore that traditional interpretations are not necessarily closer to the original meaning of the story or the intent of the author(s) than are 'untraditional' interpretations.

and/or on Eve), while others play with the symbolism of the original story, putting it in a new context without interpreting it anew.

1. *The Way of Sin*

In this group of films, the responsibility for the Fall lies with the characters in the movie who represent Adam and/or Eve. The initiative is theirs and their sin leads to perdition. As such, the plot is certainly *film noir*. *A Simple Plan* (Sam Raimi 1998) is a good example. It is about a married couple who steal a bag filled with drug money (together with two other men) to make their life a little easier, but end up destroying everything they had. They find the money in a forest, and it is surrounded by crows, a symbol of misfortune, disease, war and death (Biedermann 1992: 280-81). There are no direct references to the story of the Garden of Eden in the film, but the plot is in essence the same as the traditional interpretation of the story.

U *Turn* (Oliver Stone 1997) is also about a character that tries to take a shortcut in life, this time through involvement with crime, and ends up destroying his life. The likeness to the story of Adam and Eve is mainly in the structure (as with *A Simple Plan*), but there are also some direct references, especially to the snake.

Evas Øye (Berit Nesheim 1999) is also a good example. Eve is a poor, single mother who dreams of a better life. She steals a fortune from her deceased girlfriend, but one sin follows another and soon her life is in worse shape than it was before the crime. Eve keeps the money in her father's cellar, close to a box full of apples.

2. *Invasion of Evil*

The snake character bears all or most of the responsibility for the Fall in this sub-group. He or she causes it and it is his/her fault. The main characters are mostly innocent victims. Most films about *Snow White* are good examples of this category. *Snow White and the Seven Dwarfs* (Walt Disney and David Hand 1937) is maybe the best example. Snow White plays the role of Adam/ Eve and the stepmother is the Devil/snake, who, out of jealousy (just like Lucifer), tries to kill Snow White with an apple. Snow White (just like Adam and Eve) breaks the only rule she was required to follow (not to speak to strangers) and pays with her life. She is, however, saved by the prince (who perhaps can be regarded as a Christ-figure) after he kills the evil stepmother. In the end, they ride to a heavenly castle in the clouds, just like the heavenly Jerusalem in the book of Revelations.

Alien III (David Fincher 1992) is an example of a film with a parallel plot, where Ripley can be seen in the role of Adam/Eve and the Alien is a snake figure. Ripley lands on a prison colony. The inmates are all men who have formed their own religion, which they practice in isolation from the rest of the universe. Their peace is disturbed when Ripley crashes on their planet, followed by an alien who could wipe out the whole colony and subsequently all life on Earth if it got there. It is only through sacrifice that Ripley saves humankind, when she jumps to her death, in a crucifix position.

Lost Paradise is also an important theme in *Ivan's Childhood* (Andrei Tarkovsky 1962).[3] The movie begins in a veritable Eden, where Ivan, like a newly created Adam, discovers nature and plays with the animals. We are quickly made aware that WWII has robbed him of his Eden, and throughout the film, especially in the dream scenes (apples are quite significant in the third dream), we are reminded of this fact. The film ends with a dead tree; the Tree of Knowledge of Good and Evil is often associated with death, because its fruit is believed to have made humankind mortal.[4]

3. The Story of Eden, Backwards

Here the Christian interpretation of the story is starting backwards, with the disharmony of Adam and Eve, and ending in their union, often in some kind of Eden. *Blast from the Past* (Hugh Wilson 1999) is an excellent example of the story of Eden, backwards. The film is about an eccentric father in the 1960s who locks his wife and soon-to-be-born son in a fallout shelter for 35 years, because he believes that the Soviet Union dropped a nuclear bomb on America. The son's name is Adam, because they believe he is the first child of a new beginning. Adam is 35 years old when he first sees the outside world; he is sent up to the surface to obtain supplies when his father falls ill. He soon finds out that he needs help with his errand in this new and strange society, and hires Eve for the job. Adam and Eve are quite different. Adam is naive, good-hearted and innocent, whereas Eve is independent, intelligent and world weary. Adam scares Eve at first, but later she believes he is just a simpleton and is embarrassed by him. Nevertheless, she stays with him because he needs help and she needs the money. Adam falls in love with Eve the moment he sees her, but it is not until the end of the film that Eve realizes that she has also fallen for him. The film ends with them building a house in the countryside, with paradise-like surroundings. The constructor even remarks that it is like the Garden of Eden.

3. I have written a paper on religious themes in *Ivan's Childhood*, which was published in the volume *Through the Mirror: Reflections on the Films of Andrei Tarkovsky.* (2006: 168-87). There I discuss the Eden theme in much more detail. Paradise lost is also an underlying theme in Tarkovsky's *Nostalghia* (1983). See a paper by Gunnlaugur A. Jónsson in the same book (2006: 219-37).

4. In baroque art, the skeleton of death is often shown holding an apple, symbolizing that the price of the original sin is death (Biedermann 1996: 17). The cross of Christ is also believed to have been made out of the Tree of Knowledge, and the tree is even sometime shown as a skeleton (1996: 351).

The Garden of Eden (Lewis Milestone 1928) is another example from this group. It is about a poor young woman, Toni le Braun, who is invited to a hotel called Eden. There she meets a rich young man, Richard Dupont. They fall in love in the garden of the hotel, called The Garden of Eden, where they discuss the original Eden and the love between Adam and Eve. But there is trouble in Paradise because of their difference in social status and Richard's family is not too keen on their plan to marry. All goes well in the end, however, when they finally unite in the hotel Eden.[5]

The *Twilight Zone*, episode Two (Montgomery Pittman 1961) is a good example of a parallel. There are only two survivors after an apocalyptic battle, a man and a woman. Unfortunately they are from opposing sides, sworn to kill each other. They start out as enemies but unite in the end, take off their military uniforms and declare peace.

4. *The Plight of Eve*
In general, Eve seems to be a much more interesting film character than is Adam, if the number of films in which an Eve-character plays a decisive role is any indication. Films in this group are all about the plight of an Eve figure, who is a wild, sexually active and independent woman, with no interest in children or domestic work. It is almost as if she has no choice in the matter, she was simply created like that. She is the sinful Eve.

Et Dieu...créa la femme (*...And God Created Woman*) is a famous French film with an Eve character, directed by Roger Vadim in 1956.[6] It starts with Juliete sunbathing in her back garden, as naked as Eve in Eden. Eric, a powerful elderly businessman, walks in on her and says he has an apple for her. When she asks which apple he is referring to, he answers 'The forbidden fruit'. It turns out that the forbidden fruit is a red toy car he has in his pocket, but the indication is that she can have a real one only if she becomes his lover. Juliete is the tramp in her hometown. She is shameless, impolite, careless and lazy. She is not too keen on getting married, not because she is against the institution, but because she is afraid of herself. Juliete gets married to avoid being sent to a monastery and she tries to play the wife part, but is in fact like an alcoholic who tries to stay sober, a day at a time. She caves in, at the end, and sleeps with her brother-in-law under a dead tree, in paradise-like surroundings.

5.   The producers of the film did everything they could to point out the connection to the story of Eden. Posters had the words Adam, Eve and Eden on them and pictures of a tree and a big apple. Lobby cards were called leafs from Eve's Diary (even though no one is called Eve in the film) and the first sentence in the original 1928 Press book for the film is as follows: 'Apples, serpents, fig leaves and Paradise are only symbolically present in this "Garden of Eden"—for it is a modern clothes version of the oldest story in the world'. See extra material on the DVD from Flicker Alley.
6.   Roger Vadim remade the film in America in 1988.

The Lady Eve (Preston Sturges 1941) is another good example from this group. It is about Jean, a con-artist, who on returning from a year in the Amazon studying snakes, decides to clean out a rich man (Charles). The wild and independent Jean is eating an apple the first time she lays eyes on Charles, which she then drops on his head to get his attention.

Choose Me (Alan Rudolph 1984) is maybe the best example of a film with an Eve character. The references to the Eden story are many and quite explicit. The film starts with the name 'Eve' written on a neon sign above a bar. The owner of the bar is named Eve, as was the owner before her. Both the Eves were promiscuous and had 'man troubles'. The present owner was a prostitute (who used to work at Adams Street) before she bought the bar. She walks around in a red dress and smiles to almost any man who shows any interest in her and usually ends up in bed with him. She has no hope of ever marrying because she has 'ruined too many marriages to have one of [her] own' and because she knows herself too well: 'There'd always be another moment', she says, 'with another man. I don't think I can make marriage last with anyone.' She is, according to herself, 'the prisoner' and the 'victim' of sex. In one scene, she even blames her name for her troublesome life: 'I'm never going to forgive my father for calling me that'. It is almost as if the name itself is cursed.

A red apple is the symbol of the TV series *Desperate Housewives* and the main title design at the beginning of the show is all about the story of Adam and Eve. It starts in the Garden of Eden and then follows the lives of Eves though the history of humankind, ending with the main characters under an apple tree, with apples in their hands. The women in the show are as manipulative as Eve (according to tradition). Men may think that they run the show, but women will always have the last word. The heroines of the show are, however, much more complex and diverse than the Eves in the films previously mentioned.

5. Adam (?)

It is questionable whether films about Adam deserve their own sub-group. Adam is sometimes included in the films about Eve, but he is usually in a supporting role and rather dull and unadventurous. There are very few films where Adam is without the wild and dominant Eve, and they can be classified as belonging to other subgroups. It is therefore difficult to generalize about 'Adam' films. *Young Adam* (David Mackenzie 2003) and *Adams æbler* (Anders Thomas Jensen 2005) are perhaps the best examples of films with Adam characters (without Eve).[7]

---

7.   *Young Adam* also fits perfectly in 'The Way of Sin' sub-group and *Adams æbler* fits in the 'The Eden Story, Backwards' sub-group.

Young Adam describes humankind's sinful condition after the Fall. It is about Joe (a totally self-centred man), whose only goal in life is to fulfil his own needs and desires. Joe gets a job on a barge, from Ella, the barge owner, and her husband Leslie. Leslie and Joe become friends, but Joe has an affair with Ella. One day Joe and Leslie find a drowned woman's body in the harbour and we soon find out that Joe knows more about the matter than he wants to admit.

There has been a lot of speculations about the title, since no one in the book or in the film is called Adam. Adam from the Bible is often called the 'Old Adam', because we are all in a sense Adam. He was just the first one. The New Adam refers to Christ, who comes to mend what was broken. I am not aware of any theological use of the title Young Adam and strongly believe it is something the author (Alexander Trocchi) made up. I suggest that Young Adam refers to all of us: i.e. sinful humanity.

There are not many direct references to the story of Adam and Eve in the film, aside from the name of the film. The barge is the most obvious reference, but it is called 'Atlantic Eve'. The most interesting scene is the infamous frontal nudity scene of Ewan McGregor (which was cut out of the film by the US censors, very much against McGregor's will). There is no direct reference to the story of Adam and Eve in the scene, but it strongly echoes the third chapter of Genesis. Joe and Ella fall asleep in the barge after lovemaking. Ella's husband comes back to the barge and finds them in bed together. They wake up when they hear him tramping above them. Ella says: 'He's tramping around like the day of judgment' and then asks Joe if he is not getting out of bed and pulls the sheet off of him, revealing his nakedness. This very much resembles what happened to Adam and Eve after they ate of the fruit and realized that they were naked. The frontal nudity scene therefore can be seen as a reminder of the sin of Adam and Eve. It is also interesting that Ella compares her husbands tramping to 'judgment day', something Adam and Eve both felt strongly in the Bible when they heard the 'sound of the LORD God as he was walking' and therefore hid from him.

Adams æbler is about Adam, a self-centred Neo-Nazi who is given a chance to serve part of his prison sentence in community service at a church. There Adam learns to love God and his fellow man while taking care of an apple tree.

Adam, in the film *All About Adam* (Gerard Stembridge 2000), is, however, an interesting exception. In this film he is more like Eve (he helps people with their problems by sleeping with them), but then again the film can be seen as a parody of Eve films; even the title refers to the famous film *All About Eve* (Joseph L. Mankiewicz 1950).

6. *The Battle for Eden*
Films in this subgroup concern someone who has found or created Eden and
two or more parties battling for control or possession of it. This is a popular
theme in science fiction films, as in *The Star Trek* movies II and III (Nicholas
Meyer 1982; Leonard Nimoy 1984), which in a way are really one film in
two parts. In the films, scientists are working on a device called Project
Genesis, the goal of which is to create life out of nothingness. They choose a
lifeless planet and turn it into paradise, so powerful that it can resurrect the
dead. The planet is, however, quite unstable and ages rapidly, and it is this
instability of Project Genesis that makes it dangerous. It could be used as a
weapon if it falls into the wrong hands. The crew of the Enterprise has to
stop Kahn, its main nemesis, from getting Genesis, something he greatly
desires, and the battle for Paradise begins.

   Pi (Darren Aronofsky 1998) is another interesting example. The film is
about a mathematical genius who has found the number behind everything
that happens in the world. The number is the same as the name of the Lord
and he who has it has the key to Eden and can unlock its gate. The problem
is that two other parties (a Jewish sect and some stockbrokers) want the
number to gain power, and they will do anything to get their hands on it.

7. *Apocalyptic Films*
References to the Eden story are quite prominent in apocalyptic films, such
as when the devil appears as a snake, with snakes or with snake-like qualities, and the apple or the tree of knowledge is used to symbolize man's sin
and the fallen world. Films in this sub-group do not interpret the story in a
new way, but rather use the traditional symbolic language of the story of
Adam and Eve to underline the terror of Judgment Day.

   There is an interesting use of an apple in *End of Days* (Peter Hyams
1999). The Devil has chosen a bride, Christine York, who is to carry his
child, the Anti-Christ. She does not know it yet, even though she has been
raised for the task by Devil worshipers. At one point in the film, she cuts an
apple in two. Suddenly the apple is full of worms, which turn into tortured
human beings. The scene obviously refers to the traditional belief that the
fruit of the Tree of Knowledge of Good and Evil brought nothing but
suffering and sin into the world and this suffering is going to increase with
the birth of the Anti-Christ. There is also an interesting reference to the
snake in the film. Christine York is marked with the last letter of the Greek
alphabet, Omega, but the letter also looks like a snake. Omega stands for the
End (of Days) which starts with the union of Christine York and the Devil.

   The Prophecy films (Gregory Widen 1995; Greg Spence 1998; Patrick
Lussier 2000; Joel Soisson 2005) are about a heavenly war waged on Earth by
renegade angels. A key scene in the second film takes place in Eden, now an

industrial dump, devoid of all greenery, except for a tree that stands by the gate of Eden. There is one apple on the tree, which Izzy, a young helpmate of the archangel Gabriel, intends to eat. Gabriel warns her before she plucks the apple: 'Don't eat that! Trust me!' Again, the apple stands for the evil in the world, and nothing but bad is to be gained from it.

ECLECTIC INTERPRETATIONS

We now turn to Eclectic interpretations, which will be analyzed in greater detail. The reason for making them the primary focus is twofold: (1) I think they shed interesting light on the story of Adam and Eve, because their interpretations are in many ways untraditional; but more importantly, (2) they might shed interesting light on our society.

1. *Man as Creator*

Most films in this group are science-fiction films. They are quite critical of man's unrestrained search for knowledge. All the films are about what happens when man seats himself on the throne of God and tries to create in his own image or when humankind creates something that threatens its existence.

Blade Runner is a good example of a film in this category. Humankind has managed to create a perfect replication of itself. These creatures are called replicants; they have been created as slaves and are only given four years to live, so that humankind can control them better. The film was made at the end of the cold war and is very much the product of that era. The future is bleak. Almost all animals are extinct due to pollution and food is scarce. Humankind has been forced to leave earth, but only the strong are permitted to go. Anyone who does not pass a physical test has to stay behind on the dying and starving planet. You could say that humankind has lost its humanity. Even the replicants show more compassion and emotions than does humankind itself.

Tyrell, the creator of the replicants, is the most powerful man on earth. He lives in a pyramid, like the pharaohs of old, and is as mighty as any man can be. He is the most intelligent person on earth and he controls the life-span of the replicants. He has, in a way, both the tree of life and the tree of knowledge in his hands. It is therefore quite fitting that he has two trees on his desk in the pyramid. Tyrell is a poor substitute for God. He has no love for his creation, but creates only out of greed and self-glorification and then sells his creatures into slavery and prostitution.

Replicants are not allowed to enter Earth, most likely to protect Tyrell and his company. Deckard—the protagonist of the film—is an ex-member of the squad that specializes in killing replicants. He thinks he is human, but finds out later in the film that he is, in fact, a replicant, used by man to kill his own kind.[8] Deckard is sent to kill four replicants that came back to Earth to try to get an extension on their lives. They have in a way re-entered Eden to eat from the tree of life and Deckard could therefore be said to be in the role of the cherubs, preventing humankind from entering.

The fifth replicant, Rachel, is later added to his execution list, but the problem is that Deckard falls in love with her. Deckard and Rachel are both unaware of the fact that they are replicants. They are in many ways like Adam and Eve. They are expelled from Eden/Earth the moment they find out that they are replicants, or in other words, when they gain self-knowledge. But there is an important difference here from the Bible version. Deckard and Rachel are not thrown out of Eden, they escape from it.[9]

Everything is turned upside down when a man plays the role of God. Eden is a lifeless place, kindness is turned into oppression and salvation is found in turning away from the Creator.

The message of *Blade Runner* is the same as in almost all the *Frankenstein* films. In a way, there are two sets of Adam and Eve in *Mary Shelley's Frankenstein* (Kenneth Branagh 1994). The first set includes Victor Frankenstein and Elisabeth, his sister by adoption, whom he falls in love with and plans to marry. Frankenstein has been hungry for knowledge since he was a young boy and becomes obsessed with overcoming death when his mother dies.

Frankenstein goes about playing God when he decides to create a human being, a fact emphasized in an electricity experiment. He asks Elisabeth how she is feeling and almost touches her finger when she answers 'Alive!', thereby recreating 'The Creation of Adam' motif, painted by Michelangelo, on the ceiling of the Sistine Chapel.

The motto of the school Frankenstein enters is 'Knowledge is power only through God' and he is warned repeatedly that his pursuit is illegal and immoral and against God's will.

Frankenstein thought his creature would be perfect from Day One, but he tries to kill it when he realizes that he has to father it and teach it the ways of life. The Creature does not know how to use its emotions. It accuses Frankenstein of neglect later in the film when it says: 'You gave me these emotions. But you didn't tell me how to use them. And now two people are dead because of us. Why?' And later: 'Did you ever consider the consequences of your actions? You gave me life, and then you left me to die.'

The creature, just like Adam, desires a friend, a companion, someone like himself, and forces Frankenstein to create a woman for him. 'I do know that for sympathy of one living being I would make peace with all. I have love in

---

8.   For an overview of the debate on whether Deckard is a replicant or not, see Chapman 2005.

9.   See Kerman 1991 for an in-depth discussion on *Blade Runner*.

me the likes of which you can scarcely imagine. And rage, the likes of which
you would not believe. If I cannot satisfy the one I will indulge the other.'
Here we have the second set of Adam and Eve.

Frankenstein promises to create an Eve for his Adam, but fails to keep his
promise and, instead, the creature kills Elisabeth on her wedding night with
Frankenstein. His quest for knowledge and eternal life (the two trees in the
Garden of Eden) destroys everything that is dear to him, and costs him his
life in the end. This fact is underscored at Frankenstein's funeral when
Eccles. 1.17-18 and 12.14 are read:

> And I gave my heart to know wisdom, and to know madness and folly: I per-
> ceived that this also is vexation of spirit. For in much wisdom is much grief:
> and he that increaseth knowledge increaseth sorrow. For God shall bring
> every work into judgment, with every secret thing, whether it be good, or
> whether it be evil.

The moral conclusion of the films in this sub-group seems to be that
humankind should leave creation up to God; otherwise it might threaten its
own existence. God was, in a way, right when he warned Adam and Eve
against eating the fruit of the Tree of Knowledge of Good and Evil. Man's
knowledge threatens his own existence. This has never been more true as in
the last 100 years, when all life on earth can be wiped out with the push of a
button (as in the Cold War Era when *Blade Runner* was made) and more
recently the impending threat of climate change, which *Mary Shelley's
Frankenstein* might reflect.[10]

2. The Beautiful Fall

The so-called Fall is glorified in this second sub-group. The interpretations
may vary in detail, but they all reject the idea that Adam and Eve 'fell'.
Instead they were freed. It may very well be that humankind lost its innocence and life became harder, but instead it gained knowledge, sex and free
will, everything that gives life meaning and makes it worth living—according to these films.

The main questions posed by these films are: Could humankind mature in
a perfect world? Is there any goal in life if humankind can never make
mistakes? Is a perfect world really perfect? Is a perfect world against our
nature, since a perfect world excludes free will, the basic factor that distinguishes us from the animals? Those who interpret the story in this way are of
the opinion that humankind did not have 'everything' before the so-called
Fall, but lacked many things. It is even questioned if Adam and Eve were
human before they ate of the fruit.

---

10. Frankenstein has been interpreted in various ways in films (see Svehla and
Svehla 1997). The emphasis in this film is on science gone bad (Lundquist 1997).

I will use the film *Pleasantville* (Gary Ross, 1998) as an example of this sub-group. The film is about siblings, David and Jennifer, who are sent by a TV repairman into a black and white television show called Pleasantville. Pleasantville is a very nice place, a world before the Fall, the perfect Eden, free of all strife and difficulties. Nothing can burn there, it never rains, everything is possible, people get what they want, no one is homeless and nothing is unhealthy. Sexual or impure desires do not exist. No one makes love and there are no toilets, simply because there is no need for them. Pleasantville is not just pleasant—it is simple, and therefore it is very fitting that it is filmed in black and white. Nothing changes; the town, the people and daily life are always the same. The reason for this is simple—free will does not exist.

David is the main character of the film. His dream is that the modern world could be as simple and innocent as Pleasantville, but later on he realizes that a seemingly perfect world is not that perfect. What is important is not that everything goes our way, but quite the opposite: that we experience mistakes, despair and suffering. For example, what is the fun in playing basketball if one always scores? Basketball is not very interesting until the possibility of losing enters the game. And is life worth living if we cannot make independent decisions? If we cannot decide what to learn, where to work and with whom to fall in love? David and Jennifer start willingly to 'corrupt' this seemingly perfect world, which turns everything that has anything to do with the 'fall' into colour.

There is a scene in the film that is reminiscent of the chastisements Adam and Eve got in the Garden of Eden, with some differences. The TV repairman who sent David and Jennifer into the TV show has had enough of all the changes that have been taking place since he introduced them into his Paradise. He addresses David through a TV and the following exchange takes place:

> TV Repairman: 'What the hell do you think you're doing? Get in here. Now! [David enters.] You think this is a toy? You think it is your own little goddamn coloring book?'

> David: 'Look, it just sort of happened.'

> TV Repairman: 'A deluge doesn't just happen. Bolts of lightning don't just happen.'

> David: 'I didn't do anything wrong.'

> TV Repairman: 'Oh, no? Let me show you something.' [Shows David on the TV screen where a young girl says: 'Go on, try it' and offers him a big red apple. Then we get a close up of David biting the apple. The film freezes and the TV repairman draws an arrow which points at the apple and makes circles

around it.] 'Boom! Right there! What do you call that? Huh? You know, you don't deserve this place. You don't deserve to live in this paradise. Where is the remote control I gave you?'

David: 'Why?'

TV Repairman: 'Because you're coming home you little twerp and I'm going to put this place back the way it was.'

David: 'I can't let you do that.'

TV Repairman: 'What?'

David: 'I'm sorry. I'm not gonna let you do that.'

TV Repairman: 'Just give me that damn remote!'

David: 'I'm gonna go now.'

TV Repairman: 'You're not going anywhere. You are going to get that remote and come home and we're gonna make everybody happy again.' [David exits]

There are some interesting issues in this scene that I would like to elaborate on. The first thing one notices is that the Adam figure shows no remorse. He does not even try to pass the blame onto someone else. Gone is the remorseful sinner; instead we have someone who is proud of his own frailties. David argues later in the film that a world without difficulties is against our nature. We learn nothing from it. There is no real happiness there. People could just as well not have been born into that world, because their existence changes nothing and their lives have no meaning.

Another thing that strikes us in this scene is how powerless God is. God in the Bible is almighty. God in Pleasantville cannot even cast Adam and Eve out of his Paradise, let alone destroy his creation. Man can go against God's will, without God having anything to say about it. This image of God is fitting for today's world, where humankind chooses or rejects God and religion, just as easily as picking groceries in the supermarket. It is therefore appropriate that God should appear in a TV, where one can turn him off whenever one wants to.

But the film does not reject God, even though it criticizes the Edenic-state. In fact, God accepts this fallen world. We see him smile at the end of the film, as he drives away, pleased with the changes Adam and Eve have brought about.

Humankind moulds the world according to its own moral values. Or, as said at the end of the film, 'Life is not supposed to be anything specific'. This interpretation of the story of Adam and Eve is therefore quite postmodern-istic.[11]

11. For further discussion of *Pleasantville*, see Deacy 2003; Holmwood 2005; and Reinhartz 2005: 144-65.

Der Himmel über Berlin (Wim Wenders, 1987), or *Wings of Desire* as it is called in English, is also a fine example of this sub-group. The film is about two archangels, Damiel and Cassiel, who watch over Berlin in the late '80s, just before the fall of the wall. Most of the people we encounter are worried, depressed, lonely or lost. Wim Wenders does not try to throw cheap punches in the film. He does not try to hide the fact that life is difficult and sometimes even unbearable. Berlin is bleeding, just like its people. It has scars from the Second World War, the Holocaust and the Cold War and is wounded by the huge wall that runs through it and around its west part.

Most of the first 90 minutes are spent in meditation on life's difficulties and paradise lost. It begins with the opening words of a poem called 'Song of Childhood' by Peter Handke (which was written especially for the film), 'Als das Kind Kind war' or 'When a Child was a Child'. And then the poem describes all the beauty of childhood when 'Everything was full of life and all life was one'. And we 'had a precise picture of Paradise'. It is also noteworthy that the children are the only ones who can see the angels in the film. Most of the grown-ups no longer see the wonders around them. They no longer feel connected to each other. They are like Berlin, an island with walls around it, or as a driver says in the film: 'Everyone carries his own state with him, and demands a toll when another wants to enter'.

This separation is beautifully shown in the beginning of the film, when the camera wanders from one person to the next, all of them alone, occupied by worries and sad thoughts and all separated by thin walls, like small isolated islands.

The archangels have a hard time understanding human beings and they even envy them, just like the angels of old according to various traditions. They resemble in a way Adam and Eve before the Fall. They live a simple carefree life. They are eternal and never have to worry about the future. They exist in a vacuum and have never been part of the world. Damiel admits that it is 'great to live by the spirit, to testify day by day for eternity, only what's spiritual in people's minds'. But he also admits that he's sometimes 'fed up' with his 'spiritual existence' and would be willing to trade it in just to know how it feels to take off one's shoes under a table and 'wriggle the toes barefoot' or 'to guess, instead of always knowing. To be able to say "ah" and "oh" and "hey" instead of "yea" and "amen".' This separation from human experience is emphasized in the movie by filming everything the angels see in black and white and everything humans see in colour.

Damiel falls in love with a circus trapeze artist named Marion, but her thoughts describe quite well the feelings stirring within him: 'Longing. Longing for a wave of love that would stir in me. That's what makes me clumsy, the absence of pleasure. Desire for love, desire to love.' Damiel feels like he has been on the outside of the world long enough and wants to enter it, if only to hold an 'apple' in his hand, an obvious reference to the story of Adam and Eve. But he does not dare to cross over to the human world before he meets Peter Falk, an ex-archangel, played by the actor Peter Falk himself. Peter has been human for 30 years. He could be likened to the snake who talked Adam and Eve into eating the fruit. He uses every opportunity to get angels to forsake their heavenly sphere and try the wonders of human life.

Damiel decides to cross over. His sight turns into colour and he leaves footprints behind him in no-man's-land, between the walls. Cassiel realizes that he might get stuck in the minefield and carries him over to West Berlin. This scene is in many ways symbolic for the whole film. Damiel is not simply crossing the border between East and West or the border between the human and the spiritual realm. He is also crossing the borders confining the Berliners. He is breaking out of the isolation from the world. He is not one of the islands, like everyone around him, but reaches out and enjoys the pleasures life has to offer, and appreciates everything that makes life worth living: the sun, hopping and jumping around, the colour of stones, the horizon, the beautiful stranger, pain, the taste of a fruit, gravity, the sand under his feet. The film ends when Damiel finds the greatest gift of them all: Marion, dressed in red, like a ripe apple. For the greatest thing in life is to love and be loved, whether it be between strangers or lovers. Damiel's life might be more difficult now, but he has no regrets, because now he knows what no angel knows and most people have forgotten—that the Fall is beautiful. Here again, we can spot a postmodernistic view, where absolute truth does not exist and even angels can choose to leave God's service and benefit from it.[12]

3. The Triumph of Reason
The final sub-group is, in many ways, similar to the Gnostic interpretation of the Adam and Eve story. The snake is the saviour, and God is a tyrant. There is, however, no place for divine beings here or even for spirituality. God had a place in 'the Beautiful Fall' sub-group, but humankind can only attain freedom here by executing God or driving him to suicide.

The name of the *Star Trek* episode 'The Apple' (Joseph Pevney 1967) refers to the fruit commonly believed to have grown on the Tree of Knowledge of Good and Evil.[13] The Enterprise is sent to investigate an Eden-like planet where no one has died or gotten sick in over 10,000 years, due to the care and protection of their god, Vaal, represented as a huge snakehead. Vaal

---

12. *Blade Runner* has often been considered postmodernistic (Boozer 1991: 212-28). Some might therefore question why I have not placed it in a sub-group associated with postmodernism. The reason is because its interpretation of the Eden story is not postmodernistic, even though other aspects of it might be considered so.

13. Kraemer (2001) discusses this episode in some detail.

is, in fact, a super-computer that controls everything on the planet, creating the perfect condition for its inhabitants to live forever. In return, the people of the planet have to serve Vaal by obeying his commands (which forbid love and sex) and by collecting energy stones for him, which he needs in order to function.

It is obvious from the beginning that Vaal regards the Enterprise crew as a threat, and rightly so, since the leaders of the crew are very sceptical towards the society Vaal has created. This can be seen in the arguments between McCoy (the ship's doctor), Kirk (the captain) and Spock (a half-Vulcan, half-human science officer) on whether to intervene or not. McCoy and Captain Kirk believe that the natives do not live, they just exist, because they have no free will. They believe, therefore, that they are forced to intervene, even though it means that they are going against the will of the natives and destroying everything that is dear to them.

Humankind does not need God. Rational thought is sufficient. Vaal may be a super-computer, but he is obviously a symbol of God here. And the fact is that it would not have stopped the Enterprise crew if Vaal was a divine being, as can be seen in the episode 'Who Mourns for Adonais?', where they execute the god Apollo. It is in keeping with the negative attitude toward religion that Vaal is represented as a snake, a Christian symbol for the Devil. It is also interesting that his name is Vaal, which sounds very much like Baal, one of the most hated gods in the Bible (see, for example, Num. 25.1-5 and Judg. 2.11-15; 3.7-8; 6.25-32).[14] The followers of Vaal are shown in just as negative a light. They look and act in a primitive way, like uneducated children.

Gene Roddenberry was the creator of *Star Trek*. He was an active humanist and very sceptical towards any form of religion, except maybe Buddhism, which he showed some sympathy towards (see Kraemer, Cassidy and Schwartz 2001: 1-13). His point of view can be seen in many of the shows from the original series, where the Enterprise crew executes God again and again. True freedom is only possible when humankind leaves God behind and learns to rely on rational thought alone. The end of the episode is a good example of this. Vaal has been killed and Captain Kirk tries to calm the worried natives who point out that Vaal has taken care of them till now by putting fruit on the trees and causing the rain to fall. His speech to the natives is almost biblical in its repeated emphasis that they will like it/enjoy it, which can be seen as an echo of the repeated emphasis in Genesis 1 that 'God saw that it was good'.

> Captain Kirk: 'You'll learn to care for yourselves with our help. And there's no trick to putting fruit on trees. You might even enjoy it. You'll learn to

---

14.   Baal in the Bible can also stand for false gods.

build for yourselves, think for yourselves, work for yourselves, and what you create is yours. That's what we call freedom. You'll like it a lot. And you'll learn something about men and women, the way they're supposed to be— caring for each other, being happy with each other, being good to each other. That's what we call love. You'll like that, too, a lot, you and your children.'

The crew is, in a way, in the role of the snake here, a fact that the script-writer emphasizes at the end of the show, where this biblical framework is underscored, with the following lines:

Spock: 'Captain, you are aware of the biblical story of Genesis.'

Captain Kirk: 'Yes, of course I'm aware of that. Adam and Eve tasted the apple and as a result were driven out of paradise.'

Spock: 'Precisely, captain. And in a manner of speaking we have given the people of Vaal the apple, the knowledge of good and evil if you will, as a result of which they too have been driven out of paradise.'

The snake is the good guy here, which came to save humankind from God the tyrant. The humanistic interpretation of the Eden story is that Adam and Eve were freed from the oppression of religion. Salvation is not found in obeying God, but in executing him.

The *Star Trek* shows are far from the only examples of a humanistic interpretation. *Ten Days' Wonder* (Claude Chabrol 1971) is another good example. The film is about Charles and Helene who were both adopted and brought up together by Theo Van Horn, a rich and eccentric man who has decided to live in the same year, 1925, all his life. Everything within his garden has to look like that golden year, from the clothes Charles and Helene have to wear (much against their own taste) down to the car they drive. Charles and Helene fall in love, but their love affair is cut short when Theo decides to marry Helene. Trouble begins in Paradise when Charles sleeps with his stepmother in paradise-like surroundings. Theo finds out about the affair when he watches Helene eat an apple and look passionately at Charles, who responds in the same way. Theo sets out to punish them by playing on their guilt.

Charles invites his friend, Paul Regis, to the estate to help him, because he has been experiencing memory loss (caused by poison Theo has been feeding him) and an anonymous blackmailer (again, Theo is behind this) has been asking for great deal of money for some love letters he had sent to Helene, which have now gone missing. Paul is a man of reason and intelli-gence. We learn early on that he is an old university teacher of Charles, a famous writer, most likely a philosopher, and not religious. He is often com-plimented for his extraordinary analytical brain and intelligence. Theo, as his name suggests, is, however, repeatedly compared to God. Helene says that he was her God and that she worships him. Charles also worships Theo as a God, as is pointed out by Paul in the beginning and the end of the film, and can be clearly seen in the statue he is making of Zeus; it bears the face of his father. Paul and Ludvik, Theo's brother, also accuse him a couple of times of playing God. The film language also underscores the god-like status of Theo. He is usually at the centre of the frame and the one who controls the movements of the frame.

The film is set up as a battle between these two opposite poles: the man of reason and man the God, or reason vs. religion.

Charles and Helene are like Adam and Eve. They are brought up together in an isolated garden, which exists outside of time (beautifully shown at the beginning of the film when the camera pans past a wall, a clock and then further down the wall and out of focus, ending in focus again on Helene, in her 1920s clothes and the antique car in the background). Helene even says once that she grew up in paradise with Charles. Theo has offered them anything they want, anything except love towards each other. The punishment for eating that fruit is death (even though they are never told so). Theo drives Charles mad, makes him break nine of the Ten Commandments, then kills Helene and makes Charles think that he did that too, thereby breaking the only commandment he had not broken. Charles has a mental breakdown, rejects his God, destroys his statue of Zeus, with the face of his father, and commits suicide, in a crucifix position.

Paul is a little slow and does not realize Theo's plot before it is too late. He storms back and accuses Theo of the crime. This is the first time in the film Theo does not dominate the frame. Now Paul hovers over him like a hawk and says: 'You do take yourself for God Theo. Puffed up with pride and sitting in judgment of your puppets below.' [Here is a cut to Helene eating the apple looking passionately at Charles, and Theo looking at both of them.] 'When you discovered the love of Charles and Helene you chose their punishment. Poor Charles. He thought he was guilty. You saw to that. You gave him his sense of sin.' This is another obvious reference to the Eden story. Paul threatens to take his findings to the police and leaves Theo only one way out, suicide.

The God of this paradise thinks first and foremost of himself. The paradise is created according to his needs and pleasure. A good example of this is Theo's reply when Helene says that the clothes she is made to wear are not really her, 'They are you'. He answers, 'As you know darling'. It is also obvious that Helene accepts the incestuous marriage to Theo because she worships him like a god and feels like she owes him her life, not because she loves him as a man. And this God is not only selfish, he is also unjust and even dangerous, as can be seen in the false sense of sin he indoctrinates into Charles and the harsh punishment he hands out. Paul therefore saves humankind from God the tyrant. Again, the humanistic interpretation of the Eden story is that humankind has to be freed from the oppression of religion. Salvation is to be found in executing God. Paul's last words to Theo are therefore quite fitting: 'There is no place among man for gods like you'.

Ten Days' Wonder is very French in its approach. Reason has been more important than faith in France ever since the French Revolution. One could even say that rational thought has become a state religion, as can be seen in recent laws that forbid religious practice and symbols in schools and public workplaces and in the EU constitution, where God is nowhere to be found. *Ten Days' Wonder* is therefore a good example of the secularization in the modern world, where there is no longer a place for God.

CONCLUSION

These different Eclectic interpretations have many things in common. Eden is not as great as one might expect, and its creator is either wrong or plain evil. Their message is, however, quite diverse. The first sub-group criticizes humankind and is open to or even positive toward religion. The second sub-group criticizes any form of dogma about life. God may very well exist, but everyone has to choose his or her own way, with or without God. Life is what each and every one of us wants it to be. This is a very postmodern worldview. There is no place for God in the third sub-group. Rational thought is the only thing humankind can and should rely on. People have to be saved from the evils of religion, even by the use of force, if necessary. This is humanism in its most extreme and dogmatic form.

These groups do not simply reflect different ways of interpreting and using the story of Adam and Eve. They also reflect trends in our own society. Throughout the history of Judaism and Christianity, humankind has used the stories of the Bible to reflect on its own life and to express new ideas. This happened when the texts of the Bible were still an oral tradition, before they were edited in chapters and then finally formed into the Old and New Testaments. That is how it has been through the ages, down to our century. In a way, one could say that the Bible is still being 'written'. And if that is so, then most of its authors are not yet born.

BIBLIOGRAPHY

Biedermann, Hans
    1992   *Dictionary of Symbolism: Cultural Icons and the Meanings behind Them* (trans. James Hulbert; New York: Penguin Books).
Boozer, Jack
    2001   'Crashing the Gates of Insight: Blade Runner', in Kerman 1991: 212-28.

Chapman, Murray
    2005   'FAQ for Blade Runner', *IMDB*, http://www.imdb.com/title/tt0083658/
                faq#.2.1.35, accessed 25 June 2007.

Deacy, Christopher
    2003   'Paradise Lost or Paradise Learned? Sin and Salvation in Pleasantville', in
                Jolyon Mitchell and Sophia Marriage (eds.), *Mediating Religion: Conversations in Media, Religion and Culture* (London: T.&T. Clark International): 201-12.

Holmwood, Christ
    2005   'The Trouble with Paradise: Pleasantville', in Anthony J. Clarke and Paul
                S. Fiddes (eds.), *Flickering Images: Theology and Film in Dialogue* (Macon, GA: Smyth & Helwys): 207-16.

Jónsson, Gunnlaugur A.
    2006   'Alienation, Exile and Paradise Lost: Nostalgia Scrutinized from a Biblical
                Perspective', in Jónsson and Óttarsson 2006: 219-37.

Jónsson, Gunnlaugur A., and Thorkell Á. Óttarsson (eds.)
    2006   *Through the Mirror: Reflections on the Films of Andrei Tarkovsky* (Newcastle:
                Cambridge Scholars Press).

Kerman, Judith B. (ed.)
    1991   *Retrofitting Blade Runner: Issues in Ridley Scott's* Blade Runner *and Philip K.
                Dick's* Do Androids Dream of Electric Sheep? (Ohio: Bowling Green State University Popular Press).

Kraemer, Ross S.
    2001   'Is There God in the Universe?', in Kraemer, Cassidy and Schwartz 2001:
                15-56.

Kraemer, Ross S., William Cassidy and Susan L. Schwartz (eds.)
    2001   *Religions of Star Trek* (Boulder, CO: Westview Press).

Lundquist, Arthur Joseph
    1997   'Mary Shelley's Frankenstein', in Svehla and Svehla 1997: 285-99.

Óttarsson, Thorkell Á.
    2006   'Childhood Lost and the Horsemen of the Apocalypse: Religious Themes
                in Ivan's Childhood', in Jónsson and Óttarsson 2006: 168-87.

Reinhartz, Adele
    2005   *Scripture on the Silver Screen* (Louisville, KY: Westminster/John Knox
                Press).

Svehla, Gary J., and Susan Svehla (eds.)
    1997   *We Belong Dead: Frankenstein on Film* (Baltimore, MD: Midnight Marquee
                Press).

THE MADONNA'S TEAR: BIBLICAL IMAGES IN THE FILMS OF ANDREI TARKOVSKY

Gerard Loughlin

Andrei Tarkovsky (1932–86) is not often presented as a filmmaker who worked with biblical stories, motifs and images. And yet his second major film, *Andrei Rublev* (1966) is about the eponymous icon painter whose most famous image pictures the story of the strangers who came to Abraham as he sat by the door of his tent in the heat of the day: the very arrival of the divine into his home (Gen. 18). And it is this famous icon that reappears in the background of subsequent films, *Solaris* (1972) and *Mirror* (1974), both of which evoke Christian thematics and symbols. *Solaris* ends with an enactment of Rembrandt's picture of *The Return of the Prodigal Son* (1662). But it is in Tarkovsky's last two films, *Nostalghia* (1983) and *The Sacrifice* (1986) that we see most clearly Tarkovsky working with biblical imagery. Indeed, these are more properly biblical films than most, because they are set within two powerful images of the Virgin Mary: the mother who seeks to make a home for God in the world.

Early in the film *Nostalghia*, the Russian poet Gorchakov (Oleg Yankovsky) comes upon a copy of the Bible, *La Sacra Bibbia*, on the dresser in his hotel room. He and his translator, Eugenia (Domiziano Giordano), have just arrived at the hotel. She has gone to her room on the floor above his, and he has been inspecting his room, throwing open the window and finding the light switch for the bathroom.

> Still wearing his overcoat he wanders around his room, looking into the chest of drawers and the wardrobe, then forgetting about them and leaving them open. In one drawer he stumbles across a Bible, its cover torn, and with pencilled notes on the first page. Other pages are stuck together with chewing gum. He takes the book in his hand. Out falls a comb with broken teeth and some dyed hairs caught in it (Guerra and Tarkovsky 1999: 477).

The comb in the film remains in the book, visible when Gorchakov leaves it on the chest of drawers in order to investigate a noise that he has just heard. In the screenplay this noise is '[s]ome movement in the corridor', but in the film it is more unnerving, for it is the sound of something like a coin or button falling in the room that we know to be empty. It indicates an unseen presence in a room that the comb reminds us was once occupied by another. It is, perhaps, the audible ghost of a life now departed. 'Ears cocked, [Gorchakov] carefully approaches the door and opens it. Outside stands Eugenia' (Guerra and Tarkovsky 1999: 477). In the film this movement and disclosure is given an altogether different resonance, a disturbing sense of the uncanny, of Gorchakov's distracted state of mind.

On hearing the dropped coin or button Gorchakov turns toward the camera, listens to the reverberating silence and then exits screen left while the camera moves forward to show us the comb resting on the Bible. We then cut to a close-up of the door as it slowly creaks opens, a sound that we might expect in a horror film. We have not seen Gorchakov walk to the door nor do we see him as he opens it. We just see the door opening. In this way, Tarkovsky ever so slightly unsettles the space he has otherwise established with an almost schematic clarity. The use of the close-up—the comb in the Bible or the opening door—has the effect of dilating the space of the room, of 'deterritorializing' its parts, so that they slip in and out of what Gilles Deleuze calls 'any space whatever'. The object is detached from its setting, and becomes an 'affection-image', though the affect that its isolating effects is not always easily discerned (Deleuze 1986: 97) (Picture 1).

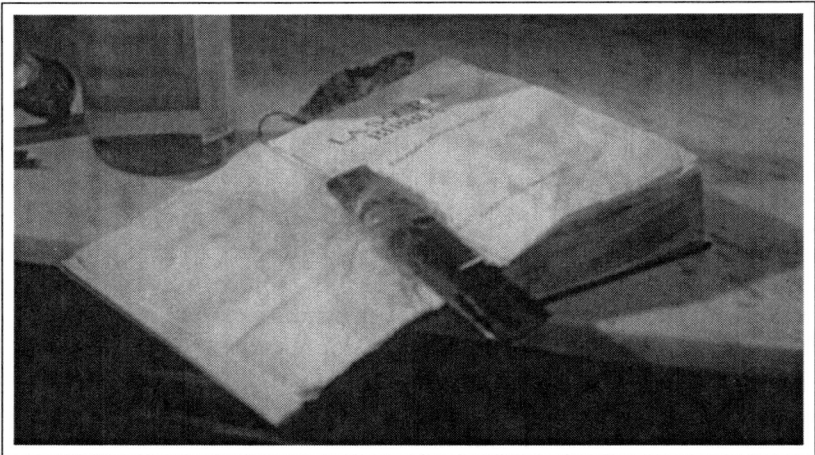

Picture 1. *The comb in the Bible*

The space of Gorchakov's room is later established with a long shot that positions the bed between window and bathroom, with wardrobes and the chest of drawers on the right of the screen. And yet, as Gorchakov moves around the room, its space is made indeterminate through what we are not shown. Even the bathroom into which we can look has an uncertain extent. We never have a shot from within or out of it, and we never see the source of its light. There are several dreamscapes in the film, and these are equally firmly established and yet rendered unstable through having characters appear in different places within the same shot as it slowly tracks across the space. This playing with time and spatial location seeps into the 'real' spaces of the film, so that though they are plain to view, we can never be quite certain where a character is standing, just as Gorchakov is never quite certain as to the time of day.

The door of Gorchakov's room creaks open and we see Eugenia standing in the corridor. She is still wearing her coat and still holding the book of poetry that she was reading in an earlier scene. She is first of all in darkness, but as the door opens further, the light falls full on her face and luxuriant hair (Picture 2). Among Tarkovsky's many beautiful women she is one of the most beautiful. Framed by the doorway, she appears with a haunting stillness and just the shadow of a smile, as in a Madonna by Leonardo da Vinci. And yet, of course, she is neither a virgin nor a mother, and not about to be a mother, and she has come to Gorchakov's room because she wants to incite a response to her own desire for him. She is the Magdalene rather than the Virgin, and longing for a different kind of birth.

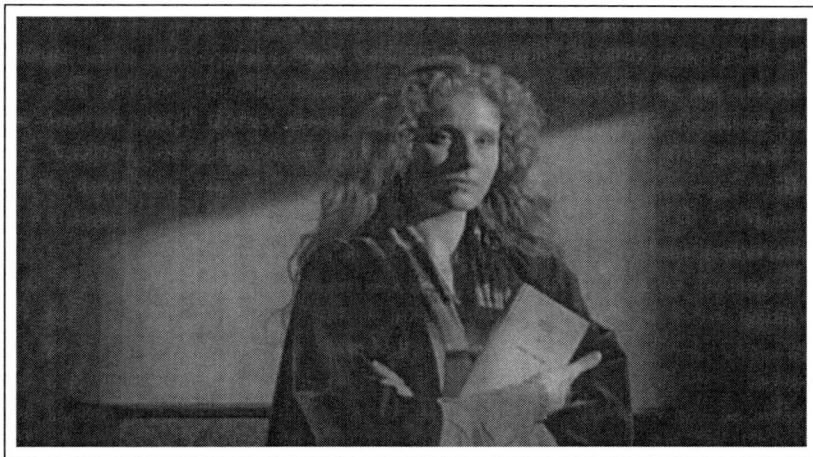

Picture 2. *Eugenia in the corridor*

REFRACTIONS

Nostalghia is as much about birth and what is to come as it is about the past and what has been lost. Openness to the future is often remarked of *The Sacrifice*, which is dedicated to Tarkovsky's son, Andrei, rather than with *Nostalghia*, which is dedicated to Tarkovsky's mother. But birth or the difficulty of bringing to birth is established at the beginning of the film as one of its central concerns. After the credits, the film opens with the arrival of Gorchakov and Eugenia at the church where Eugenia wants Gorchakov to see the fifteenth-century *Madonna del Parto* by Piero della Francesca. Piero's Madonna was originally painted for the Capella di Cimitero of the Santa Maria della Momentana in Monterchi near Arezzo, on the border between Tuscany and Umbria. But Tarkovsky filmed a reproduction, set in the crypt of a Romanesque church in San Pietro. The fresco itself is now in a museum. It is a most unusual Madonna, being a picture of the pregnant Virgin, and so a picture of the Madonna in waiting. It is not an Annunciation, a foreboding of future arrival, but the coming of the future in the becoming of the mother, growing in her maternity as the child has grown within her, the emerging secret of the future.

Piero's *Madonna* is a painting of anticipation rather than arrival, of hope rather than fulfilment. It is the Madonna herself who arrives in the painting, revealed to the viewer by two angels who have drawn back the curtains of a tent to reveal the woman within, who in turn will shortly reveal her interior secret. The angel's parting of the curtains anticipates the Virgin's own partition in bringing forth her child, an opening already anticipated by her indicating, even parting, of her unbuttoned, opened dress. We are told in the screenplay that the Virgin's hand rests upon her dress as upon a wound. 'This unconscious pose protects the still unborn. Who has yet to be born'. And what is anticipated is also feared. 'She has been condemned to stand for thirty-three years, vainly trying to ward off the inescapable horror of the impending and irreversible catastrophe'. For Tarkovsky, or for Eugenia in Tarkovsky's screenplay, the Madonna of the parturition is filled with quiet dread. 'Her look expresses despair and unwavering tenderness' (Guerra and Tarkovsky 1999: 472).

Eugenia's entry into the chapel of the Madonna is caught with a slow tracking shot, as she and the camera move between the pillars of the crypt, until she is standing in the central aisle looking directly toward the camera. The next shot shows us the Madonna in her alcove with the candles of the devout burning before her (Picture 3). The grammar of film naturally leads us to believe that Eugenia is looking at the Madonna. But when in the next shot we come back to Eugenia, she is standing at a different place in the crypt, with an apse on her left (screen right) that must be where the Madonna resides, for when Eugenia attempts to kneel it is in this direction that she turns (Picture 4). She does so because of her conversation with the sacristan, who addresses her from off camera, asking if she has come to pray for a baby or to be spared one. She replies that she is just looking, and the camera tracks left to reveal the sacristan standing in the foreground. Looking away from Eugenia, he explains that nothing happens if there are any onlookers present who are not also supplicants. Eugenia enquires as to what happens and he tells her anything might happen, whatever one most needs. Then he tells her that she should at least kneel down. He walks across the screen and exits on the right. Eugenia becomes self-conscious as she attempts to kneel, finding herself hampered by her long dress and high-heeled shoes, and so, flustered, she stands up again. When the sacristan, again from off screen, points out the praying, kneeling women in the background of the shot, Eugenia responds that they are used to it. He replies that they have faith.

Picture 3. *The ensconced Madonna*

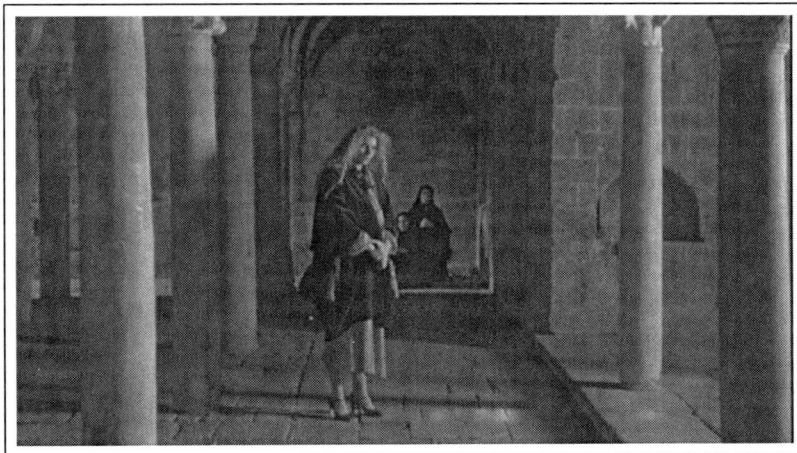

Picture 4. *Before the Madonna (without candles)*

Picture 5. *Entry of the women*

   The film now cuts to the same view and tracking shot as when Eugenia
entered the chapel, but now it is a procession of women who enter. They
are carrying candles, some of them tiered like wedding cakes, and a large
devotional statue of the Virgin, adorned with flowers and jewels (Picture
5). The women enter in silence except for the gentle tinkling of a bell.
The life-sized figure of the Virgin is placed in front of Piero's Madonna. It
is shot from the same point of view as when we thought Eugenia first
looked upon the Virgin. But if so, it must be from where Eugenia is now
standing, with both invisible to the other. A young woman with a white
veil kneels in front of the effigy of the Virgin, her hands held together in
prayer. We cut back to Eugenia, standing in front of the alcove where it is
natural to suppose the Madonna resides. Eugenia walks towards the camera, perhaps, we might think, to get a better view of the ritual that we
think is taking place in the chapel. But in fact she comes forward to speak
to the sacristan, who must be standing just to the right of the camera. She
asks why he thinks that it is only women who pray so much. He replies
that he is only the sacristan, and walks across the screen, from right to left
with the camera following him. The women who are praying before the
figure of the Virgin are nowhere to be seen. Eugenia presses her question
as to why women are more devout than men. The sacristan stops and looks
towards the camera and says that she should know the answer better than
he, but she replies that she has never understood these things. Insisting
that he is but a simple man he replies that he thinks a woman is meant to
have children, to raise them with patience and self-sacrifice. And when
Eugenia asks if that is what woman is for, he replies that he does not
know. Eugenia says she understands and thanks him and now walks across
the screen from right to left. Sensing her frustration with his reply, he

follows her as she now re-enters the picture frame and walks away from the camera. 'You want to be happy, but there are more important things', he calls after her. As he follows her, he reaches the spot where she first stood and looked towards the camera, and he looks towards where Eugenia attempted to kneel, towards the *Madonna del Parto*, towards where, in the next shot, we see the young woman kneeling in front of the statue of the Virgin. And now the camera moves forward as we hear the women praying, closing in on the kneeling woman, who then reaches out to the figure of Mary, and, parting her dress, releases a flock of small birds, their chirping and beating wings drowning out the prayers of the women (Picture 6).

Picture 6. *The release of the birds*

Picture 7. *The Madonna's Tear*

We cut back to Eugenia, who moves as if to get a closer look at what is happening. But in fact it is a repeat of the first shot when she came to a standstill looking towards what we thought must be the Madonna. We then cut back to different shots of the escaping birds, and then to one of the candles in front of Piero's fresco, followed by a close-up of Eugenia, whose face now seems to be warmed with the golden light from the massed candles. Then, for the first time, we are shown a close-up of the Madonna's face, where we see the tear falling from her left eye (Picture 7).

My account of the scene in the chapel has been necessarily laborious, and not least because the scene contains a greater number of cuts than in most of Tarkovsky's scenes, which are usually contained within a few shots, and sometimes within a single one. But what it serves to show is that what we think we see is not quite what we have been shown. As James MacGillivray (2002) notes, most people think that they have seen a ritual of the Virgin performed by the women of the town while Eugenia is in the chapel talking to the sacristan.

Thus, for example, Mark Le Fanu tells us that as Eugenia 'makes her way round the church a sacred ceremony is unfolding' (1987: 116). For Vida Johnson and Graham Petrie (1994: 284) the 'life-sized statue of the Virgin' is brought into the church while Eugenia is talking to the sacristan. This is what anyone would think on first watching the film. But in fact we have seen two scenes cut together. They happen in the same place but at different times, their simultaneity an effect of montage. Moreover, Tarkovsky relocates the apse with its fresco in the scene between Eugenia and the sacristan. This 'exploding of architectural space', as MacGillivray calls it, is not so evident without some knowledge of the building in which Tarkovsky filmed, and it is not so unusual in cinema where different places are often stitched into the same space, most often the outside and inside of different buildings, with characters who can walk through a door from one to the other. But in Tarkovsky's film it is the same place that is stitched together with itself.

The development of the scene might be due to the fact that Tarkovsky decided to film the cult of the *Madonna del Parto* after having filmed the meeting between the sacristan and Eugenia. It does not appear in the published screenplay, where Eugenia encounters a group of women ascending the steps of the cathedral on their knees (Guerra and Tarkovsky 1999: 472-74). However, the effect of Tarkovsky's rendering is to suggest that Eugenia's encounter with the sacristan and the ritual of the birds have both happened in subtly different places or at different times and yet also in the same space and at the same time, suggesting that Eugenia has both seen and not seen what is to view; just as we viewers have seen something that is less linear than we first imagined. We see two different responses to the portrait of the Madonna superimposed upon one another: the traditional supplications of the women and the fearful but fascinated look of the uncomprehending Eugenia who does not find herself at home in the chapel.

But for what do the women pray, and what does the holy mother offer them? In the screenplay, we are told that she 'comforts and gives hope to everyone, who tenderly and feelingly asks that they be blessed with conception' (Guerra and Tarkovsky 1999: 472). Thus, the women ask to bring forth children as will the Madonna, and as symbolized in the film by the release of the birds from her womb: a sympathetic magic. But their prayers are more ambiguous than this. In the film, the sacristan asks Eugenia if she has come to pray for a child or to be spared one, and in the screenplay the women on the steps of the cathedral are in distress at the death of their motherhood through the death of their children. And this is why there is a tear on the face of the Madonna, for she knows that the child she is about to bear will die on the cross. This is why she waits for her son with a heavy heart (1999: 473). To pray for a birth is also to pray for a death.

The last shot of the scene is the close-up of the Madonna's face, and the effect of this, as already noted, is to produce an 'affection-image', abstracted from 'all spatio-temporal co-ordinates' (Deleuze 1986: 96). Indeed, it provides the co-ordinates for the scene we have just watched, as if some event had been refracted through the crystal of the Madonna's tear into different elements. For the structure of the scene is 'crystalline' in the Deleuzian sense that it sets up an indiscernible distinction between the real and the virtual (Deleuze 1989: 69). One becomes the other and there can be no decision as to which has priority. In the chapel of the Madonna we see both faith and its absence, and the conjunction of these opposites—the manner in which Tarkovsky makes them appear together —becomes an analogue for the film's concern with the desire to believe while doubting, with hoping while disbelieving. The scene in the chapel is caught in the Madonna's tear, as is indeed the entire film, for the cause of her joy is also the cause of her sorrow, and both are refractions of a single event: a birth and life and death.

OBJECTIVE AMBIVALENCE

The manner in which Piero's painting gives rise to contrary responses is repeated with regard to several other paintings. Of Leonardo's *Ginevra de'Benci* (c. 1474), Tarkovsky remarked that she is 'at once attractive and repellent. There is something inexpressibly beautiful about her and at the same time repulsive, fiendish' (Tarkovsky 1996 [1986]: 108). And Tarkovsky attests to the same kind of contradictory response in relation to the image that begins and structures his last film, *The Sacrifice*. Leonardo's unfinished undersketch for the *Adoration of the Magi* (c. 1481–82) provides the background for the film's opening credits, and hangs as a print in the house of the film's protagonist, Alexander. Indeed this picture provides the structure for much of the film. Mary sits at the centre with Jesus on her lap, while around her are the faces of the three magi, and then an ever-widening group of angels and other onlookers. The faces that surround the mother and child emerge strangely and just a little threateningly from the sepia background, and being half-sketched are like half-dreamed, ghostly figures. The opening credits do not show the entire picture but remain in close-up on the exchange at the picture's centre: where the leaning infant touches the gift offered by the wise man kneeling in the foreground. At the end of the credit sequence, the camera pans up the picture plane to show the tree that is growing behind and above the Madonna. A tree opens and closes the film. Indeed a tree is the first thing we see at the beginning of *Nostalghia*, at the centre of the screen. But at the beginning of *The Sacrifice*, Alexander and his young son are planting a dead tree in the hope that it will one day come into leaf, and at the film's end we see the son—Little Man—lying beneath the tree that he has just laboriously watered. As he looks up at the tree he speaks for the first time in the film: 'In the beginning was the Word. Why is that papa?' In between these two moments, the film unfolds its story of a fearful gift exchange; a retelling of the exchange at the heart of Leonardo's painting, as humanity reaches out to the divine, and the divine touches humanity.[1] Leonardo's picture seems to capture something of what is truly awful in the coming of God among us.

At one point in the film, Alexander looks at Leonardo's painting with Otto, the local part-time postman and philosopher. Here and at other points we are reminded that they are looking at a print of the painting, with the picture obscured to varying degrees by reflections in the glass, sometimes of trees outside the house, and always of its viewers. They are at the same time caught in the picture's mystery and excluded from its comprehension. Looking at the picture, Otto finds it 'sinister' and admits that he has always found Leonardo terrifying.[2] Later he tells Alexander that he prefers Piero della Francesca. But as we have seen, Piero is also terrifying for some, and both pictures in both films are deeply disquieting for their onlookers.

---

1. See further Loughlin 2008.
2. In a somewhat bizarre article, C. Marchetti and E. Panconesi (1970) argue that the painting is not unfinished but is as intended by Leonardo, and depicts suffering humanity in the faces of those clustered around the infant Jesus, their flesh displaying (for those who know what to look for) a variety of skin diseases.

Both Madonnas—Piero's and Leonardo's—are pictures of birth. But in Piero's the pregnant mother is about to give birth, while she has just given birth in Leonardo's. In both pictures she promises life, but as we have seen this is also the promise of death, so that hope is inextricably mixed with fear. And it is this duality in the act of bringing forth that is elaborated in Tarkovsky's films. In the screenplay we are told that Eugenia finds herself praying with the women in the church. But in the film she seems incapable of prayer; she cannot bend her knee in adoration or supplication. But the women can and do so in the form of a ritual, an action of desire. And later in the film, both Gorchakov and the 'madman' Domenico will pray through ritualized actions, both of which remind us of the candles burning before the Madonna at the beginning of the film. Gorchakov will complete the action Domenico could not complete: the carrying of a lighted candle across the pool of St Catherine without it going out; while Domenico will become a lighted candle when he sets fire to himself in Rome. Here supplication for a new life—for a rebirth of humanity—is performed through death, and in *The Sacrifice*, Alexander prays to exchange his life for the life of his family, and seals his promise by sleeping with Maria, whom Otto is convinced is a witch, and whose house is filled with images of the Virgin Mary. But what most commentators ignore in their readings of these films is the way in which the inchoate longings of their protagonists are embedded within the Christian drama of the divine incarnation, of a life and death that is more than itself, that escapes the boundaries of birth and death, but is not other than them: birth gives rise to death and death to life. The picture of the magus offering his gift to the child is terrifying because in return he will be offered the gift of the child's death, the very gift that brings the tear to the eye of the Madonna del Parto.

BIBLIOGRAPHY

Deleuze, Gilles
    1986   *Cinema 1: The Movement Image* (trans. Hugh Tomlinson and Barbara Habberjam; London: Athlone Press).
    1989   *Cinema 2: The Time-Image* (trans. Hugh Tomlinson and Robert Galeta; London: Athlone Press).
Guerra, Tonino, and Andrei Tarkovsky
    1999   'Nostalghia', in Andrei Tarkovsky, *Collected Screenplays* (trans. William Powell and Natasha Synessiosm; London: Faber & Faber): 463-503.
Johnson, Vida T., and Graham Petrie
    1994   *The Films of Andrei Tarkovsky: A Visual Fugue* (Bloomington: Indiana University Press).
Le Fanu, Mark
    1987   *The Cinema of Andrei Tarkovsky* (London: BFI Publishing).

Loughlin, Gerard
    2008   'Tarkovsky's Trees', in Nathan Dunne (ed.), *Tarkovsky* (London: Blackdog Publishing): 80-95.
MacGillivray, James
    2002   'Andrei Tarkovsky's Madonna del Parto', *Canadian Journal of Film Studies* 11.2: 82-99.
Marchetti, C., and E. Panconesi
    1970   'Leonardo da Vinci: Beauty or Human Suffering in the World—Notes on Pathological Cuteneous Alterations in The Adoration of the Magi', *Journal of the European Academy of Dermatology and Venereology* 8: 101-11.
Tarkovsky, Andrei
    1996   *Sculpting in Time: Reflections on the Cinema* (trans. Kitty Hunter-Blair; Austin: University of Texas Press [1st edn 1986]).

MARY MAGDALENE IN MOTION

Caroline Vander Stichele

Over the past ten years, interest in Mary Magdalene has increased almost exponentially, as one can witness in both the scholarly and more popular works either devoted to her or in which she plays a more or less prominent role.[1] The majority of this growing body of literature is written by women and puts Mary in a favourable light, reclaiming her as a prominent disciple with whom Jesus had a close relationship. Views differ, however, when it comes to defining the nature of that relationship. In general, scholarly based studies tend to stress the significance of Mary Magdalene among the followers of Jesus, while popular works often elaborate on the potentially romantic character of her intimate relationship with Jesus. Notwithstanding this difference in focus, in both cases a shift has taken place, away from the traditionally dominant representation of Mary Magdalene as a penitent prostitute.

In this study I want to explore the image of Mary Magdalene that is reproduced in three recent films, more specifically *The Passion of the Christ* (2004), *The Da Vinci Code* (2006) and *Mary* (2005). I will also compare the image of Mary Magdalene in these films with her representation in *The Last Temptation of Christ* (1988), the last major film of the twentieth century about Jesus.[2] If *The Last Temptation* caused commotion because of its 'sex scenes', Mel Gibson's *The Passion of the Christ* attracted large crowds, at least in the US, and received a lot of media attention due to its

---

1. Scholarly based works since 1998 listed in chronological order: Maisch 1998; Jansen 2000; Mohri 2000; Apostolos-Cappadona 2002; Ruschmann 2002; Schaberg 2002; Brock 2003; King 2003; De Boer 2004; Hearon 2004; Meyer and de Boer 2004; Chilton 2005; Schaberg and Johnson-Debaufre 2006; Thompson 2006; and De Boer 2007. For an overview of earlier research, see Thimmes 1998. Some recent popular works and fiction include: Fredriksson 1999; Curtis Higgs 2001; George 2002; Brown 2003; Picknett 2003; Bellevie 2005; Clare Prophet and Booth 2005; Gardner 2005; Starbird 2005; Burstein and de Keijzer 2006; Malarkey 2006; McGowan 2006; Nahmad and Bailey 2006; Longfellow 2007; and Roberts 2007.

2. For an analysis of the role of Mary Magdalene in *The Last Temptation*, see Kennedy 2005. For a comparison of her role in other films about Jesus, see Schaberg 1996 and Apostolos-Cappadona 2006.

violence and allegations of anti-Judaism [3] Gibson's truth claims also triggered scholarly debates about historical inaccuracies and misrepresentations, as well as deviations from the biblical passion accounts.[4] Popular works often make such claims and thus in a way attract such criticism. However, this is not my interest here. Rather, I want to focus on the portrayal of Mary Magdalene: how is she represented and on what sources is this image based?

The second film under discussion here is Ron Howard's *The Da Vinci Code*, released in 2006 and based on Dan Brown's bestseller by the same title, which was published in 2003. The film is further proof of the immense success of the novel, which generated a whole body of literature criticizing or endorsing the views put forward within it.[5] Here again, my concern is not with the accuracy of the portrayal of Mary Magdalene, but rather with the way she is represented, as well as her importance for the novel/film. Although I focus on her portrayal in the film, I occasionally refer to the novel where relevant.

Abel Ferrara's *Mary*, which came out in 2005, one year after *The Passion* and two years after Brown's novel, is the third film I will discuss. The title is somewhat misleading in that it refers to Mary Magdalene, not Jesus' mother. The film received several awards at the 2005 Venice Film Festival, but otherwise went largely unnoticed. Interesting, however, is that Mary Magdalene plays a more prominent but also very different role in the plot than is the case in both Gibson's *Passion* and *The Da Vinci Code*.

In what follows, I analyze the role of Mary Magdalene in each film from a gender-critical perspective. A core issue here is to what extent her depiction supports or challenges traditional gender roles. Of related interest to me is the interplay between the representations of Mary Magdalene in these films and their respective contemporary religious and ideological agendas. I also try to determine how this portrayal reflects as well as shapes different views on the role of women in religion and society.

1. SILENT SUPPORTER?

Mary Magdalene makes her entry early in Gibson's *The Passion of the Christ*. She is introduced together with Mary, Jesus' mother, who suddenly wakes up when Jesus is arrested in the Garden of Gethsemane (scene 4).

---

3. For a discussion of the issue of anti-Judaism in Gibson's *Passion*, see especially the essays in: Landres and Berenbaum 2004: 173-278; Plate 2004: 3-52; Fredriksen 2006: 1-30; and Garber 2006. For the issue of violence, see Crossan 2004: 8-27; Beal and Linafelt 2006; and Fredriksen 2006: 127-45.

4. See, for instance, Corley and Webb 2004; Fredriksen 2006; and Garber 2006.

5. For example, issues related to Da Vinci himself, the Holy Grail, Opus Dei, the Priory of Sion, Early Christian history and Mary Magdalene.

Mary Magdalene, who is with her, wakes up as well and asks: 'What Mary? What is it?', to which Jesus' mother replies: 'Why is this night different from every other night?' Mary Magdalene in turn answers: 'Because once we were slaves…and we are slaves no longer…' This evocation of the famous words from the Pesach liturgy is one of the few instances in which the two women actually speak in the film. The second time is shortly thereafter in scene 6, when Jesus is brought before the high priest. Here Mary Magdalene appears again together with Jesus' mother, but this time also with John, who had informed the women of Jesus' arrest. When two Roman soldiers pass by, Mary Magdalene exclaims: 'In there! Stop them! They've arrested him! In secret! In the night! To hide their crime from you! Stop them!' When the soldiers inquire what is going on, a temple guard appears and tells her to shut up. This is the only time that Mary Magdalene is depicted as proactive and also the last time in the film that she actually speaks. In what follows, she is almost always following Jesus' mother around silently, dressed alike, looking like her younger sister and shadow.[6]

The most important scene in terms of the way Mary Magdalene is depicted in this film, however, is the one in which the two women wipe off Jesus' blood from the pavement after his scourging (scene 18). Sitting on her knees, Mary Magdalene remembers her encounter with Jesus. The event evoked in this flashback is the story about the woman caught in adultery, narrated in Jn 8.2-11,[7] but that is never made explicit in the film. No words are spoken in this scene. We only see Jesus writing in the sand and a number of men who drop the stones they hold in their hands, then turn around and walk away. Next, we see the face of Mary Magdalene as she is crawling towards Jesus, touching his foot and him extending his hand toward her. Only biblically informed viewers can figure out what this scene is all about.

In another scene, closer to the end of the film, Mary Magdalene is focalized in a similar position, as in the earlier scene, sitting on her knees (scene 27). Here, she becomes the sole witness to a remarkable event. After Jesus has been nailed to the cross, it is turned over, leaving him suspended instead of smashed, face down under the weight of the cross. Mary appears to be the only one actually to notice this extraordinary event and the expression on her face is one of amazement.

6.   For the depiction of the two women in the film, see also the stills in *The Passion* (Duncan and Gibson 2004: 17, 21, 27, 65). For a discussion of the role of women in *The Passion*, see further Corley 2004; Ortiz 2004; Thistlethwaite 2006: 131-34; and Vander Stichele and Penner 2006: 29-30.

7.   In John, the woman is anonymous, but later Church tradition associated her with Mary Magdalene.

Apart from the scenes just mentioned, Mary Magdalene appears as a silent and passive witness to the events taking place before her and our eyes. As Ortiz notes, she is 'so passive as to be almost invisible' (2004: 112). Together with Jesus' mother and John, she follows him around from his arrest to his crucifixion. Although she is shown to empathize with Jesus' pain and suffering, there is no indication that she was close to Jesus apart from her relationship to his mother. Instead, she appears as a woman, and a beautiful one at that, who was saved by Jesus and therefore follows him around. Moreover, the fact that she is shown several times with loose hair and on her knees evokes the traditional image of the penitent Magdalene, the former prostitute, who radically changed her way of life after meeting Jesus.[8] Apart from the flashback in which she appears with long hair, earrings and make-up, in the film her hair is covered, until she uses her veil to wipe off Jesus' blood. As we will see, this image of the repentant sinner may well have been inspired, among other things, by Gibson's literary sources.

One of Gibson's most important sources of inspiration for his interpretation of the Passion was the meditations of Anne Catherine Emmerich (1774–1824), an Augustinian nun living in Germany. Her visions were recorded and published some ten years after her death, under the title *The Dolorous Passion of Our Lord Jesus Christ*. In these meditations, Jesus' mother plays a prominent role and often appears together with Mary Magdalene. The scene of Jesus' mother and Mary Magdalene both wiping Jesus' blood after his scourging, which is absent from the Gospel accounts, is clearly based on this work:

> I soon after saw Mary and Magdalen approach the pillar where Jesus had been scourged; the mob were at a distance, and they were partly concealed by the other holy women, and by a few kind-hearted persons who had joined them; they knelt down on the ground near the pillar, and wiped up the sacred blood with the linen which Claudia Procles had sent (2003: 138).

In the film, that is indeed what happens. Jesus' mother is handed the linen by Pilate's wife, Claudia, while Mary Magdalene uses her veil to wipe the blood and that in turn triggers the flashback of her earlier encounter with Jesus. This flashback, which does not appear in Emmerich's book, but was inserted here by Gibson, identifies Mary Magdalene with the anonymous woman caught in adultery. This is one of the traditional identifications of Mary Magdalene with anonymous women in the Gospels. In his comments on this scene, Bartunek concedes that

---

8. For a discussion of the image of the penitent Magdalene, see, e.g., Maisch 1998: 62-81 and Jansen 2000: 199-244.

> there's nothing to say for sure she was the woman who was going to be
> stoned, but then again there's nothing to say for certain that she wasn't.
> Literally speaking, it could have been her. The film makes the connection,
> however, because in one way or another Jesus did save Magdalene, just as
> He saved the adulterous woman (Bartunek 2005: 103-104).

The result, however, is that in saving this girl from a certain death, Jesus'
heroic credentials are established and this in turn leaves her no other
option but to be grateful (Thistlethwaite 2006: 133). The resultant depiction of Mary Magdalene as a sinner saved by Jesus is consonant with
Emmerich's depiction, as she stresses on several occasions Mary Magdalene's feelings of repentance. Emmerich, however, identifies her with the
anonymous woman anointing Jesus' head in Mark 14: 'The holy and
boundless love she felt for our Lord prompted her to cast herself at his
feet, and there pour forth the feelings of her heart (as she once poured the
precious Ointment on his head as he sat at table)...' (Emmerich 2003:
121). This is again an example of the identification of Mary Magdalene
with anonymous women elsewhere in the Gospels, but also of the process
of conflation between the anointment stories in the four Gospels (Mt.
26.1-13; Mk 14.1-11; Lk. 7.36-50; Jn 12.1-8).

For the miraculous scene of the suspended cross at the end of the film,
Gibson appears inspired by the work of another nun, Mary of Agreda,
who lived in Spain during the seventeenth century (1602–1665). She
wrote an extensive work entitled *The Mystical City of God*, which was
published in 1670, five years after her death. An abridged version of this
work was published in English under the title *The Divine Life of the Most
Holy Virgin*. The passage from this work that corresponds to Gibson's
scene reads as follows:

> After having thus crucified the Lord, those monsters of cruelty began to
> fear that the nails would be loosened and the Sacred Body fall to the
> ground; therefore, they determined to prevent it. Raising the Cross, they
> turned it over in such a manner that our Saviour lay upon His face on the
> ground, and whilst He was in this position, they riveted the nails. At the
> sight of this new excess of barbarity the beholders shuddered, and many of
> the crowd, being excited to compassion, raised a great tumult. Mary had
> recourse to the Eternal Father and prayed Him not to allow this incon-
> ceivable cruelty to be accomplished, according to the intention of those
> executioners, and she commanded the Angels to assist their Creator (Mary
> of Agreda 1997: 187).

In *The Passion*, when the cross is turned over, Jesus is shown to be suspended rather than crushed into the ground, the suggestion being that
this was prevented from happening. In the film, the sole witness of this
miracle is Mary Magdalene. As Bartunek notes, 'She looks at her battered
Lord and sees the miraculous suspension of the Cross... She glances

around—no one else sees it (except the audience who sees through her eyes, shares her experience)' (2005: 143). Again, Mary Magdalene is pictured on her knees and this is also how Emmerich presents her when Jesus is dying on the cross: 'Magdalen was crouched to the ground in a perfect frenzy of grief behind the Cross' (Emmerich 2003: 189).

None of these scenes derives from the biblical passion accounts. The words Mary Magdalene speaks in scenes 4 and 6 were scripted and Gibson inserted the flashback to a story based on John 8 into a scene based on Emmerich's vision (scene 18). He also turned Mary Magdalene into the sole witness of a miraculous event mentioned by Mary of Agreda (scene 27). Both nuns therefore appear to have been important sources of inspiration for the roles attributed to Jesus' mother and Mary Magdalene in *The Passion*. As Morgan observes, 'Generally speaking, Gibson leans on Emmerich for her heartfelt sympathy with women. For him, as for Emmerich, men are heartless or weak, women are empathic and powerless' (Morgan 2004: 92). However, in both Emmerich's and Gibson's views, Mary Magdalene clearly appears as the less important character of the two. It is rather the strong emotional bond between Jesus and his mother that is foregrounded in the story. Of course, the prominent presence of Jesus' mother throughout the film does nothing to upset the boundaries of traditional gender roles. Women consistently appear as caretakers, with their role firmly located in the domestic sphere, while men dominate the public arena and most often aggressively so. They are also the ones inflicting violence on Jesus. He, for his part, 'takes it like a man', while the women follow him around with compassion and devotion. Indeed, this is 'the feminine genius that the film frequently characterizes: compassion, understanding, peacemaking' (Bartunek 2005: 97). In other words, as Schaberg notes, 'Bad man kill and good men are killed, and women mop up the blood' (2006: 78-79).

This image of Jesus as the male martyr, who can be beaten, but whose will cannot be broken, is also remarkably similar to that of William Wallace in Gibson's earlier film *Braveheart* (1995).[9] Here too, the female protagonists are supportive of the suffering hero, but are equally domesticated, as the first becomes his wife and the second the mother of his child. Both films thus replay a well-known type-scene; that of the tragic death of a hero in the presence of a woman who loves him, a trope already available in antiquity, as Linafelt demonstrates. In *The Passion*, the key elements of this type-scene are all in place: the violent death of Jesus, the presence of loving but passive women, their solidarity and the association of his mother with the domestic sphere (Linafelt 2006: 35).

9.   For a discussion of the male hero image in *Braveheart* and *The Passion*, see Vander Stichele and Penner 2006: 31-34.

When compared with *The Last Temptation*, it is immediately clear that Mary Magdalene is reduced from a major to a minor character in *The Passion*. She has changed places with Mary, the mother of Jesus, as the most important woman in his life. Although in both films a contrast is set up between Mary Magdalene's sinful past and her conversion to a follower of Jesus, she is explicitly identified as a prostitute in *The Last Temptation* (scenes 3 and 7). In both films, moreover, she is identified with the woman caught in adultery from John 8.[10] The two films also have in common that the 'conversion' of Mary Magdalene is marked with a change in her appearance. She no longer wears jewellery and is dressed in black, often with her head covered. *The Last Temptation* thus reproduces the image of Mary Magdalene as the penitent prostitute, who changed her way of life and followed Jesus. In comparison to *The Last Temptation*, however, in *The Passion* she is both de-sexualized and silenced. The result is that she appears as neither the prominent disciple nor as the one with whom Jesus had a close relationship, because Gibson reserved that place of honour for Jesus' mother.

2. SACRED VESSEL?

In the film *The Da Vinci Code*, Mary Magdalene plays a more central role than in Gibson's *Passion*. However, she does so not as a character, but as a key element in the development of the plot, which centres around the search for the Holy Grail. The importance of Mary Magdalene is revealed to the two protagonists of the novel/film, Robert Langdon and Sophie Neveu, by Leigh Teabing, a former British royal historian.[11] Teabing uses Leonardo Da Vinci's painting of the *Last Supper* and quotes from the *Gospel of Philip* and the *Gospel of Mary* to support the claim that Mary Magdalene was Jesus' companion/spouse. He first points out that the figure Da Vinci painted in the place of honour at Jesus' right hand is in fact a woman and more specifically Mary Magdalene. He continues to explain that she was Jesus' wife and quotes the *Gospel of Philip* as proof: 'And the companion of the Saviour is Mary Magdalene. Christ loved her more than all the disciples and used to kiss her often on the...'[12] When Neveu objects that nothing is said about them being married, Langdon

---

10.   The motive given for her stoning in *The Last Temptation*, however, is that she has broken the law by working on the Sabbath (scene 7).

11.   Scene 12 in the film. The corresponding chapters in the novel are Chapters 55–56, 58 and 60.

12.   In the novel, the quote is longer and continues as follows: '...on the mouth. The rest of the disciples were offended by it and expressed disapproval. They said to him, "Why do you love her more than all of us?" ' (Brown 2006: 266).

points out that the word 'companion' used here literally meant 'spouse' at that time. Teabing then goes on to read a quote from the *Gospel of Mary*: 'And Peter said: "Did he prefer her to us?" And Levi answered: "Peter, I see you contending against a woman like an adversary. If the Saviour made her worthy, who are you, indeed, to reject her"'.[13] Jesus, Teabing adds, also told Mary Magdalene that she is to continue his church. Not only that, Mary Magdalene herself is the Holy Grail. She is the chalice, which, in this case, is not a cup, but the ancient symbol of the female womb. Mary Magdalene is thus identified as the one who carried Jesus' royal bloodline. Moreover, far from being a prostitute as claimed later in a smear campaign by the Church, Mary Magdalene was of royal descent herself and pregnant at the time of the crucifixion. No longer safe in Jerusalem, however, she fled to France where she gave birth to a daughter named Sara.

In both the novel and the film, Teabing backs up his interpretation of Mary Magdalene with a number of sources. First of all, he explicitly refers to extra-canonical writings, more specifically the *Gospel of Philip* and the *Gospel of Mary*, which Teabing believes to offer more trustworthy evidence than any of the canonical accounts (under the presumption that these have been manipulated by the Church and therefore cover up some aspects that are evidenced elsewhere in early Christian literature). The *Gospel of Philip* (logion 63) is quoted in support of the idea that Mary Magdalene was Jesus' wife,[14] while the *Gospel of Mary* is claimed to provide evidence that Jesus chose Mary Magdalene rather than Peter to carry on his Church.[15]

---

13. Again the quote is more extensive in the novel. The additional elements are italicized: 'And Peter said: *"Did the Saviour really speak with a woman without our knowledge? Are we to turn about and all listen to her?* Did he prefer her to us?" And Levi answered, "Peter, *you have always been hot-tempered.* Now I see you contending against the woman like an adversary. If the Saviour made her worthy, who are you indeed to reject her? *Surely the Savior knows her very well. That is why he loved her more than us"'* (Brown 2006: 268).

14. The quote (GM 17–18) seems to be taken over from *Holy Blood, Holy Grail* (Baigent, Leigh and Lincoln 1983: 382), which refers to the English translation of the Nag Hammadi Library in Robinson 1988: 148: 'And the companion of the…Mary Magdalene. […loved] her more than [all] the disciples [and used to] kiss her [often] on her…' The text, however, is closer to the translation given by Pagels (1981: 77), who also fills in the blanks.

15. The quote largely corresponds with the one given in Pagels (1981: 77-78), but the translation is closer to Robinson's (1988: 526-27). However, some relevant changes have been made. First, the response of Mary to Peter is left out; second, the singular 'adversary' is used instead of the plural 'adversaries' and third, the articles have been changed: 'the woman' has become 'a woman' and 'the adversaries' 'an adversary'. As a

The 'truth' about Mary Magdalene, then, is an alternative story to the one officially put forward by the Church, which proclaims the divinity of Jesus in contrast to his humanity and presents itself as the only way to salvation. In the novel, Teabing explains:

> The threat Mary Magdalene posed to the men of the early Church was potentially ruinous. Not only was she the woman to whom Jesus had assigned the task of founding the Church, but she also had physical proof that the Church's newly proclaimed *deity* had spawned a mortal bloodline. The Church, in order to defend itself against Magdalene's power, perpetuated her image as a whore and buried evidence of Christ's marriage to her, thereby defusing any potential claims that Christ had a surviving bloodline and was a mortal prophet (Brown 2003: 274).

In the novel, Teabing also lists the titles of some of his other sources: *The Templar Revelation*, *The Woman with the Alabaster Jar*, *The Goddess in the Gospels* and, most important of all, *Holy Blood, Holy Grail* (Brown 2003: 273-74). Two of these books, *The Woman with the Alabaster Jar* (1993) and *The Goddess in the Gospels* (1998), were written in the 1990s by Margaret Starbird and were highly influenced by *Holy Blood, Holy Grail*, which was published in 1983. *The Templar Revelation*, published in 1997, was inspired by both that book and Starbird's first book. A closer look at these books makes it clear that Brown used elements from all four of them for his portrayal of Mary Magdalene.

Rather than being the cup used by Jesus at the Last Supper or the cup in which Joseph of Arimathea caught Jesus' blood at the crucifixion, as often believed, *Holy Blood, Holy Grail* claims that the Holy Grail refers to Jesus' royal bloodline, which was carried on by Mary Magdalene, who was Jesus' wife and pregnant at the time of the crucifixion (Baigent, Leigh and Lincoln 1983: 313). She was not a prostitute, as often believed in popular tradition, but can be identified with the anonymous woman anointing Jesus in Lk. 7.36-50. Because the Gospel of John identifies this woman with Mary of Bethany (Jn 11.1-2; 12.1-3), these two Marys may well be one and the same person referred to under different names (Baigent, Leigh and Lincoln 1983: 333-38). She was probably (in their view) from royal descent, most likely from the tribe of Benjamin. According to the authors of *Holy Blood, Holy Grail*, the marriage between Jesus and Mary Magdalene would thus have reunited the tribes of Judah and Benjamin. The political significance of this marriage, however, would also have turned Jesus and his descendents into a serious threat for the political regime established by the Romans (Baigent, Leigh and Lincoln 1983:

---

result, the statement becomes more specific, with Peter appearing to be a more direct opponent to Mary Magdalene.

346-47). The canonical gospels have obscured this fact, because they have been revised in view of a Roman audience. The Nag Hammadi collection, which did not undergo such censorship, therefore offers a more authentic picture of the issues at stake. Important documents in this collection are especially the *Gospel of Philip* and the *Gospel of Mary*, the former because it reveals that Mary Magdalene was Jesus' 'companion', meaning 'spouse', and the latter because it gives evidence of the ongoing antagonism between Peter and Mary, thus reflecting the tensions between the adherents of Jesus' message and those of his bloodline.

In *The Woman with the Alabaster Jar* and *The Goddess in the Gospels*, Margaret Starbird largely subscribes to this picture of Mary Magdalene as wife of Jesus and royal bride. She also identifies Mary Magdalene with Mary of Bethany, arguing that 'Magdalene' has nothing to do with the town of Magdala in Galilee. Rather, Magdalene alludes to Mic. 4.8 where the expression 'Magdal-eder' is used, meaning 'tower of the flock'. The term Magdala more specifically means 'elevated, great' and is used in the Gospels as an epithet for Mary as wife of the Messiah, indicating that the prophecy in Mic. 4.8 ('the former dominion will be restored to you') is fulfilled (Starbird 1993: 50-51). The marriage between Jesus and Mary was explicitly a Sacred Marriage (*hieros gamos*), symbolically enacted through the anointing of Jesus' head by his royal bride (Mt. 26.12; Mk 14.8). After the crucifixion, the pregnant Mary probably fled to one of the Jewish communities in Alexandria and continued from there to France. The child to whom she gave birth was possibly Saint Sarah the Egyptian, who is venerated in Les Saintes-Maries de la Mer, where Mary is believed to have gone ashore (Starbird 1993: 60-61).

The Templar Revelation in turn builds further on the insights of both *Holy Blood, Holy Grail* and *The Woman with the Alabaster Jar*, but adds some elements of its own to the interpretation of Mary Magdalene. First of all, the suggestion is made that the person sitting at Jesus' right hand in da Vinci's 'Last Supper' is not Jesus' beloved disciple John, but a woman (Picknett and Prince 1997: 20), identified later in the book as Mary Magdalene. In line with both *Holy Blood, Holy Grail* and Starbird's work, she is believed to be one and the same woman as Mary of Bethany, who anointed Jesus (1997: 253). This particular ritual identifies Jesus and Mary as partners in a sacred marriage. Again, a more authentic picture of their relationship than the one from the canonical gospels is believed to be offered by the Gnostic Gospels (1997: 295). They reveal that Mary Magdalene was Jesus' consort and that she rather than Peter was meant to be Jesus' successor. *The Templar Revelation*, however, goes one step further than the other books in suggesting that Mary Magdalene was a pagan priestess and 'sexual initiatrix' (1997: 258) and that she initiated Jesus in the mysteries of Isis and Osiris through the rite of sacred sex (1997: 302).

As can be noted, the portrayal of Mary Magdalene in all four works is remarkably similar. Mary Magdalene is first identified with the nameless woman who anoints Jesus' feet in Lk. 7.36-50 and then with Mary of Bethany, the sister of Martha and Lazarus, mentioned in Luke 10 and John 11–12. On the basis of both the *Gospel of Mary* and the *Gospel of Philip*, Mary Magdalene is further claimed to have been Jesus' wife. Through her, Jesus' royal bloodline could continue. Moreover, she, rather than Peter, was supposed to be his successor. Apart from this general picture reproduced by *The Da Vinci Code*, the importance of quotes from the *Gospel of Philip* and the *Gospel of Mary* seem to be taken from *Holy Blood, Holy Grail*. The focus on the figure of Mary Magdalene, rather than Jesus, is also a common point of interest with Starbird's work. The idea that Mary bore a child in France named Sarah likewise comes from Starbird. Finally, the use of Da Vinci's work and the identification of the person at Jesus' right hand as Mary Magdalene in his *Last Supper* are clearly inspired by *The Templar Revelation*.

Notwithstanding the importance of her character, the Mary Magdalene thus presented to us by Brown is silent. In *The Da Vinci Code*, she rather is the one 'talked about'. In the film, we catch a fleeting glimpse of her in a flashback, which first shows her heavily pregnant and then giving birth. This image aptly captures the impression we get of her, in so far as her significance is seen mostly in her relationship to Jesus, as his wife and the mother of his child. She is further reclaimed as the Divine Mother, the Rose, the Holy Grail, the sacred feminine which was lost, but now redeemed. These images reflect a positive appreciation of Mary Magdalene that is placed in sharp contrast with her vilification in the past (by the Church). In her discussion of the novel, Jennie Knight suggests that the popularity of *The Da Vinci Code* may well be related to the fact that it allows 'readers from a Christian background to image the divine as feminine through icons of their own tradition, rather than through goddesses from traditions perceived as alien to Christianity' (Knight 2005: 56). Popular fiction, moreover, makes it possible to engage alternative representations on an imaginative rather than a purely rational level. According to Knight, such images are appealing to feminist Christian women, who question the exclusively male imagery used in their churches, but the absence of the divine feminine is especially striking in Protestant churches, in so far as there are no such female figures available as the figure of Mary, the mother of Jesus, or female saints deemed worthy of devotion as is the case in the Catholic Church.

In addition, I would suggest that Mary Magdalene is an attractive alternative to the figure of Mary, the mother of Jesus, for *both* Protestant and Catholic Christians, because she is not tainted by confessional disputes between the two churches. Moreover, the traditional asexual image of

Mary, as both virgin and mother, is highly problematic for Catholic feminists. The figure of Mary Magdalene is clearly less problematic in this respect. The irony, however, is that, no less than Mary before her, the image of Mary Magdalene recast in *The Da Vinci Code* novel and its predecessors also affirms traditional female gender roles and essentialist notions of female and male identity, firmly grounded in biological difference. Robbed of her historicity, Mary Magdalene thus becomes the archetypal female, the 'other' to the male self, the chalice for *his* holy bloodline. Her significance is related to that of Jesus, not as his mother, but as his bride. Her identity is derived from his. Even when the suggestion is made that she also is to continue his church, we never get a sense of what that could have been like or what the content of her message was. Thus, by 're-sexualizing' Mary Magdalene, as Nancy Calvert-Koyzis puts it, Brown

> actually serves to perpetuate the tradition in which Mary's sexuality takes precedence over her apostleship and, in effect, contributes to the diminish-ment of her role as apostle to the apostles in a way similar to members of the Early Church that he condemns so severely (Calvert-Koyzis 2006: 15).

It is telling in this respect that the Gnostic Gospels are highly valued, but that apart from the information offered about the relationships between different characters, no attention is paid to the particular content of these other sources. The only quotes used in *The Da Vinci Code* and its sources are *about* Mary Magdalene, but never *from* her. In both the novel and the film, her response to Peter is even omitted from the quote taken from the *Gospel of Mary*. As de Boer notes, Dan Brown explicitly refers to the *Gospel of Mary*, but 'he does not allow her to say anything in his book. In Dan Brown's plot Mary Magdalene is important only as a female body' (de Boer 2007: 3).

What still appeared as the ultimate temptation in *The Last Temptation*, that is, to have a wife and family, is turned into reality in *The Da Vinci Code*. In the novel, explicit reference is made to the commotion caused by *The Last Temptation*, which, as Sophie Neveu remembers, 'was about Jesus having sex with a lady called Mary Magdalene'. At that time, she had asked her grandfather: '"Did Jesus have a girlfriend?" Her grandfather was silent for several moments. "Would it be so bad if He did?" Sophie considered it and then shrugged. "I wouldn't mind"' (Brown 2006: 267).[16] In both *The Da Vinci Code* novel and the film, Mary Magdalene is claimed to be the wife of Jesus, a fact obscured by the Church in an effort to erase

---

16.   References to *The Last Temptation* also occur in Starbird (1993: xxi) and Pick-nett and Prince (1997: 60-66), providing further evidence of the impact of the movie, especially its representation of the sexual relationship between Jesus and Mary Magdalene.

the humanity of Christ in favour of his divinity. Christ's humanity is embraced and Mary Magdalene is acknowledged as an incarnation of the divine feminine, albeit in the safe role of wife and mother. As in *The Passion*, her sexuality thus appears 'tamed' and her relevance circum-scribed by traditional gender roles. It is mostly her relationship with Jesus that is elaborated upon. Different from both *The Last Temptation* and *The Passion*, however, the suggestion is made that she also was a spiritual leader, but unfortunately this aspect is never explored beyond her conflict with Peter.

3. SPIRITUAL GUIDE?

Abel Ferrara's *Mary*, the third film under discussion here, starts with a scene from a film about Jesus entitled *This is My Blood*, in which the figure of Mary Magdalene plays a prominent role. When the shooting of this film within a film is over, Marie Palesi (Juliette Binoche), who plays the role of Mary Magdalene in *This is My Blood*, is so absorbed by her character that she leaves for Jerusalem instead of going home, while the director Tony Childress (Matthew Modine), who himself also plays the role of Jesus, goes back to New York to edit his film. One year later, at the official presentation of *This is My Blood* to the press, Théodore Younger (Forest Whitaker), who hosts a TV talk show entitled 'Jesus, the Real Story', is so impressed by Marie Palesi's performance that he wants to invite her to his show. However, when Younger's personal life unexpec-tedly takes a dramatic turn and he experiences an existential crisis, he calls her for advice instead.

Ferrara's film starts where Gibson's *Passion* ends, with the resurrection. The opening scene shows two women visiting the tomb, thus taking as its point of departure the Synoptic account, where several women are said to visit the tomb rather than just Mary Magdalene, as is the case in the Gospel of John. The scene is more specifically based on Luke's version, in which the women meet two men inside the tomb, who ask them 'Why do you look for the living among the dead?' (Lk. 24.5). It is preceded by Mary's dialogue with two angels, from Jn 20.13: 'They said to her, "Woman, why are you weeping?" She replies to them, "They have taken away my Lord, and I do not know where they have laid him"'. At that point in John's story and the film, Mary turns around and sees Jesus standing outside. The dialogue that follows between Mary Magdalene and Jesus is based on Jn 20.16-17. It ends with Jesus sending Mary to his male disciples with the good news of his ascension. This opening scene simul-taneously introduces both the film *Mary* and *This is My Blood* as well as two of their main characters, Marie Palesi playing Mary Magdalene and Tony Childress in his role as Jesus.

Several other scenes of *This is My Blood* appear in what follows. One shows the washing of the disciples' feet during the last supper in Jn 13.4-5 (scene 11), another one is based on Jesus' farewell speech in John 14–16 (scene 10 using Jn 14.27, 28b; 16.32; 15.20b, 25; 16.1-2; 14.29; 16.4). Both scenes are taken from the Gospel of John and include Mary Magdalene among the disciples witnessing these events. The other scenes from *This is My Blood* are based on the *Gospel of Mary* and show us Mary Magdalene telling the disciples what she has learned from Jesus, her teacher. In these scenes, the text of the *Gospel of Mary* is reproduced almost verbatim.[17] It is never made explicit, however, that these words come from the *Gospel of Mary*.[18] In addition to these scenes that are based either on the canonical Gospels or the *Gospel of Mary*, there are also two scenes in which Mary Magdalene is shown leaving and coming back in a fishing boat together with other women (scenes 7 and 12), suggesting that she may well have been a fisherwoman herself.

If Mary Magdalene appears as a character in *This is My Blood*, several characters in *Mary* also comment on her significance. Thus, Marie Palesi tells TV host Younger: 'I played the role of Mary Magdalene in Tony's movie and I became fascinated and inspired by her' (scene 10). She also notes: 'Jesus helped Mary Magdalene, she's helping me now' (scene 6). We also see Younger watch a video in which Elaine Pagels, author of *The Gnostic Gospels*, explains:

> The Gospel of Thomas, the Gospel of Philip, the Gospel of Mary Magdalene, these were apparently buried nearly two thousand years ago... What you find in ancient legend history, she was a prostitute. Modern fiction turns her into a lover and wife of Jesus, but what you find in these early texts is that she is neither a prostitute, nor a lover. She's one of the disciples and one of the most important (scene 6).

Moreover, in the next scene Younger asks Jean-Yves Leloup, who makes an appearance as a guest in his show on Jesus, if Peter has a problem with Mary because she is a woman or because she is putting herself in the primary position as the number one disciple, or both. Leloup answers that it is both, but probably mostly because she is a woman (scene 7).

The Mary Magdalene thus presented to us by Ferrara is a woman who received spiritual insights from Jesus, which she shares with his other disciples after his death. Her knowledge (*gnosis*) in turn becomes a source of inspiration for Marie Palesi, who breaks with her past to follow in Mary Magdalene's footsteps. Ferrara also shows us Marie Palesi turning to Mary

17. The translation used is the one of Jean-Yves Leloup (2002).

18. The passages from the *Gospel of Mary* quoted are GM 9-14 and 17-18 (scene 3), GM 15 (scene 5) and GM 16-17 (scene 12).

Magdalene for spiritual guidance and Younger next turning to Marie for help. However, just as Mary Magdalene's testimony is discredited by Peter, but defended by Levi in *This is My Blood*, so is Marie rejected as having gone crazy by Tony, but taken seriously by Younger in *Mary*.

Ferrara's Magdalene thus is decidedly different from both Gibson's silent witness as well as *The Da Vinci Code*'s sacred vessel. Ferrara gives Mary a voice. She relates to Jesus as her teacher and she becomes a teacher herself. Her relationship with Jesus is portrayed as a spiritual one. This image is largely and consciously based on the *Gospel of Mary*. In an interview, Ferrara himself relates that the *Gospel of Mary* opened his eyes to a different perception of the gospel story.[19]

Nevertheless, a closer comparison with both *The Passion* and *The Da Vinci Code* also reveals some remarkable similarities. Thus, in both *Mary* and *The Passion*, Mary Magdalene is presented as a 'natural beauty', but her sexuality is hidden under a long dress. Moreover, in both films, she appears sometimes with her head covered, but other times with loose, long and flowing black hair. To a certain extent, this similarity in appearance strengthens the contrast between Mary Magdalene's role in both movies: virtually silent in *The Passion*, while speaking 'words of wisdom' in *Mary*. One can, of course, wonder to what extent this film is Ferrara's response to *The Passion*, as some critics suggest.[20] Some elements may point in that direction. Like Gibson, Tony Childress is both an actor and director. The title *This is My Blood* for Ferrara's 'film within the film' applies very well to the bloody gore of *The Passion*. Further, just as Gibson's film was met with protest, so is *This is My Blood*. Moreover, one of the issues raised on that occasion is the film's purported anti-Semitism.[21] A further indication that Ferrara had *The Passion* in mind is that he originally asked Monica Bellucci (in 2002), who played the role of Mary Magdalene in *The Passion*, to play the role of Mary and wanted to use material from *The Passion* for the embedded Jesus film in question.[22]

---

19. See the interview with Abel Ferrara and Frank DeCurtis in the Press Documentation, available (in French) online at: http://www.mary-lefilm.com/presse/dp.pdf (p. 23, accessed 6 January 2007).

20. See, for instance, the review of Jeremy Heilman at http://www.moviemartyr.com/2005/mary.htm (accessed 7 January 2007).

21. In the interview, Ferrara himself states that he would not have been able to find the necessary finances for his film without *The Passion*, suggesting that it created a more positive perception of Bible movies as profitable (http://www.mary-lefilm.com/presse/dp.pdf (p. 23). In *Mary*, Tony Childress replies jokingly to Younger's question about why he made a movie about Jesus: 'Cause that Gibson movie made like a million dollars' (scene 10).

22. This relates to an earlier version of the script, listed under 'Unrealised Projects', in Stevens (2004: 348-49).

Apart from these links with *The Passion*, Ferrara's film also has some features in common with Dan Brown's novel. In both cases, the story of Mary Magdalene serves as an element in the plot of a present-day story. Moreover, in both films, the *Gospel of Mary* is used as a prominent source for the reconstruction and reclaiming of the 'true' Mary. The same text from the *Gospel of Mary*, with Peter questioning Mary Magdalene's testimony, is also adduced as evidence for a conflict about the importance of these two disciples in the early Christian Church, with academic experts serving as sources of authority in support of its interpretation. As Beal observes with respect to *The Da Vinci Code*:

> Part of what makes this alter-history believable to so many readers is not only Brown's prefatory claim (reiterated in interviews) to historical accuracy but also the fact that all this material is placed in the mouths of scholars who, though fictional, are identified with actual institutions of higher education and research (Beal 2006: 2).

If, in the case of *The Da Vinci Code*, the experts (Robert Langdon and Leigh Teabing) are fictional, in 'Mary', the 'religious experts' in question, as they are called in the credits, are 'real'. They are Dr Amos Luzzato, introduced as 'President of the Italian Jewish Communities', Ivan Nicoletto, introduced as a 'Benedictine Monk', Jean-Yves Leloup introduced as a 'theologian' and Elaine Pagels (who is only mentioned in the credits). Both Leloup and Pagels are well-known scholars who have published on the *Gospel of Mary*.

However, the most striking similarity between *Mary* and the film version of *The Da Vinci Code*, which came out after *Mary*, is that the story centres on the spiritual quest of the male protagonist: Robert Langdon in the case of *The Da Vinci Code* and Ted Younger in *Mary*.[23] The importance of Mary Magdalene is related to the needs of these male protagonists and the female characters play supportive roles as 'mediums' (Sophie Neveu in *The Da Vinci Code* and Marie Palesi in *Mary*). Notwithstanding Ferrara's revision of Mary's role and the reappraisal of her character, she is valued for what she means to Younger rather than as a person in her own right.[24] An important difference between *The Da Vinci Code* and *Mary*,

---

23. As Beal notes, a shift takes place here between the novel and the film version of *The Da Vinci Code*: 'Dan Brown's literary narrative of apocryphal religious revelation becomes Ron Howard's cinematic narrative of personal transformation and coming to faith, starring Tom Hanks as the Harvard religious symbologist Robert Langdon, a scholarly skeptic who, in the end, remembers how to pray' (Beal 2006: 3). In *Mary*, Ted Younger undergoes a similar process of transformation.

24. This theme also occurs in *Bad Lieutenant* (1992), an earlier film by Ferrara, in which the main character is a police officer who is addicted to drugs, money, sex and

however, is that Mary is kept silent in the former. Her reply to the criticism of the male disciples in the *Gospel of Mary* is omitted, while her
words are given prominence in *Mary*.

If Gibson's *Passion*—and maybe *The Da Vinci Code* novel as well—
somehow 'informed' the making of *Mary*, so did Scorsese's *The Last Temptation of Christ*, which is explicitly mentioned in *Mary* by director Tony
Childress in his interview with Younger, when he states that 'Religious
films are always subject to criticism. Look what they did to Scorsese with
The Last Temptation of Christ' (scene 10). Moreover, Barbara Hershey's
comment that she failed to capture the spirit of Mary Magdalene in *The
Last Temptation* seems to have inspired Ferrara to make a film about an
actress who, after playing the role of Mary Magdalene, goes on a spiritual
quest to Israel (Stevens 2004: 348). One element the Marys in both films
do have in common, though, is that both are present at the Last Supper.
Other than that, their roles are very different. Far from being a (former)
prostitute, Ferrara's *Mary* clearly reflects the image of Mary as a spiritual
teacher put forward in feminist scholarship. [25] As such, it offers an
alternative to the still popular perception of her as a woman of the flesh
rather than the spirit. Nevertheless, Ferrara does not escape the either/or
dialectic between body and mind in that the focus shifts from Mary's body
to her mind, which is visualized in the close ups of her head while she is
speaking. Thus, while Mary speaks her mind, her body disappears from
view.

CONCLUDING OBSERVATIONS

If Gibson's portrait affirms the traditional role of women as caretakers,
devoted to the men they follow, *The Da Vinci Code* portrays Mary Magdalene as an incarnation of the divine feminine, worthy of worship, while
Ferrara's *Mary* affirms the role of women as spiritual guides. As a result, in
all three films the role of Mary Magdalene is negotiated, but resolved
differently. This is clearly the case when compared with the role of Mary
Magdalene in *The Last Temptation of Christ*. What the four films have in
common, however, is that Mary Magdalene appears as the 'other' of a
male protagonist. She is there for his sake and while *she* changes roles and
faces in these films, *his* identity remains securely positioned at the centre.

violence, but experiences a moral crisis and undergoes a change of heart. Similarly, in
this earlier film, the catalyst in the process of transformation of the male protagonist is
a religious woman, in this case a nun.

25.   In an interview, Ferrara himself calls the history of Mary 'a feminist history'
and relates the re-evaluation of her role to the birth of feminism in the seventies. Cf.
http://www.mary-lefilm.com/presse/dp.pdf (p. 23).

In *The Last Temptation*, she represents Woman to Jesus as the Universal Man. In Gibson's *Passion*, she is there to offer moral support to Jesus. In *The Da Vinci Code*, she is the sacred vessel for Jesus' bloodline and the answer to Langdon's quest for the Holy Grail. In Ferrara's *Mary*, she, through Marie Palesi, becomes the spiritual guide of Ted Younger.

What makes these representations of the Christian past so attractive and convincing to people today? And, to what extent do these reinterpretations reflect present-day concerns and interests? In my view, the two questions are related: these representations are attractive and convincing precisely *because* they reflect present-day concerns and interests. Still, different views appeal to different people. Both Scorsese's *Last Temptation* and Gibson's *Passion* affirm traditional gender roles and confirm the views of theologically conservative Catholics and Protestants alike. *The Da Vinci Code*'s 'subversive' interpretation of early Christianity, with its suspicious attitude towards the Catholic Church and Opus Dei, no doubt attracts a different type of believer, more suspicious of institutional religion, especially the Catholic Church. And Ferrara's existentialist take on issues of faith is more likely to appeal to those few souls searching for enlightenment of a different, more gnostic kind. An intriguing question that remains is if this change also represents a shift to a different understanding of the role of Mary Magdalene and, by implication, the role of women more generally.

Films clearly play their part in this debate, but as Laura Mulvey in her analysis of narrative cinema so pointedly observes, 'In a world ordered by sexual imbalance, pleasure in looking has been split between active/male and passive/female. The determining male gaze projects its phantasy on the female form which is styled accordingly' (Mulvey 1975: 11). Set against this larger background, the way in which Mary Magdalene appears on screen not only reflects the views of these male directors, but also manifests issues at stake in culture at large, in that Mary Magdalene has become a discursive site to negotiate gender (and religious!) issues in Western culture. Despite claims to the contrary, who she 'really' was is not 'really' the issue. The quest for the historical Jesus has turned into a quest for the historical Mary Magdalene. In both cases, however, the quest for the past reflects the questions of the present.

BIBLIOGRAPHY

Apostolos-Cappadona, Diane
  2002   *In Search of Mary Magdalene: Images and Traditions* (New York: American Bible Society).
  2006   'The Saint as Vamp: Mary Magdalene on the Silver Screen', in Burstein and de Keijzer 2006: 252-59.

Baigent, Michael, Richard Leigh and Henry Lincoln
1983   *Holy Blood, Holy Grail* (New York: Dell Publishing).
Bartunek, John
2005   *Inside* The Passion: *An Insider's Look at* The Passion of the Christ (Westchester: Ascension Press).
Beal, Timothy K.
2006   'Romancing the Code', *The Chronicle of Higher Education: The Chronicle Review* 6.9, http://www.timothybeal.com/Beal-RomancingtheCode-CHE.pdf (accessed 17 August 2007).
Beal, Timothy K., and Tod Linafelt (eds.)
2006   *Mel Gibson's Bible: Religion, Popular Culture and* The Passion of the Christ (Chicago: University of Chicago Press).
Bellevie, Lesa
2005   *The Complete Idiot's Guide to Mary Magdalene* (New York: Alpha Books).
Boer, Esther de
2004   *The Gospel of Mary: Beyond a Gnostic and a Biblical Mary Magdalene* (Journal for the Study of the New Testament Supplement Series, 260; London: T.&T. Clark International).
2007   *The Mary Magdalene Cover-Up: The Sources Behind the Myth* (London: T.&T. Clark International).
Brock, Ann Graham
2003   *Mary Magdalene, the First Apostle: The Struggle for Authority* (Harvard Theological Studies, 51; Cambridge, MA: Harvard University Press).
Brown, Dan
2003   *The Da Vinci Code* (New York: Doubleday).
2006   *The Da Vinci Code* (New York: Anchor Books).
Burstein, Daniel, and Arne J. de Keijzer (eds.)
2006   *Secrets of Mary Magdalene: The Untold Story of History's Most Misunderstood Woman* (New York: CDS Books).
Calvert-Koyzis, Nancy
2006   'Re-sexualizing the Magdalene: Dan Brown's Misuse of Early Christian Documents in *The Da Vinci Code', Journal of Religion and Popular Culture* 12.1, http://www.asask.ca/relst/jrpc/art12-resex-print.html (accessed 5 January 2007).
Chilton, Bruce
2005   *Mary Magdalene: A Biography* (New York: Doubleday).
Clare Prophet, Elizabeth, and Annice Booth
2005   *Mary Magdalene and the Divine Feminine: Jesus' Lost Teachings on Woman* (Gardiner, MT: Summit University Press).
Corley, Kathleen E., and Robert L. Webb (eds.)
2004   'Mary and the Other Women Characters', in Kathleen E. Corley and Robert L. Webb (eds.), *Jesus and Mel Gibson's* The Passion of the Christ: The Film, the Gospels and the Claims of History (London: Continuum): 79-88.
Curtis Higgs, Liz
2001   *Unveiling Mary Magdalene* (Colorado Springs, CO: WaterBrook Press).

Duncan, Ken, and Mel Gibson
    2004   *The Passion: Photography from the Movie* 'The Passion of the Christ' (Carol Stream, IL: Tyndale House).

Emmerich, Anne Catherine
    2003   *The Dolorous Passion of our Lord Jesus Christ* (El Sobrante, CA: North Bay Books).

Fredriksen, Paula (ed.)
    2006   *On* The Passion of the Christ: *Exploring the Issues Raised by the Controversial Movie* (Berkeley: University of California Press).

Fredriksson, Marianne
    1999   *According to Mary Magdalene* (Charlottesville, VA: Hampton Roads Publishing).

Garber, Zev (ed.)
    2006   *Mel Gibson's* Passion: *The Film, the Controversy, and its Implications* (West Lafayette, IN: Purdue University Press).

Gardner, Laurence
    2005   *The Magdalene Legacy* (London: HarperElement).

George, Margeret
    2002   *Mary Called Magdalene* (London: Pan Books).

Haskins, Susan
    1993   *Mary Magdalene: Myth and Metaphor* (New York: Viking Books).

Hearon, Holly E.
    2004   *The Mary Magdalene Tradition: Witness and Counter-witness in Early Christian Communities* (Collegeville, MN: Liturgical Press).

Jansen, Katherine Ludwig
    2000   *The Making of the Magdalen: Preaching and Popular Devotion in the Later Middle Ages* (Princeton, NJ: Princeton University Press).

Kennedy, Tammie
    2005   '(Re)Presenting Mary Magdalene: A Feminist Reading of *The Last Temptation of Christ*', *Journal of Religion and Popular Culture* 9.1, http://www.usask.ca/relst/jrpc/art9-scorsesemisogynist-print.html, accessed 5 January 2007.

King, Karen
    2003   *The Gospel of Mary of Magdala: Jesus and the First Woman Apostle* (Santa Rosa, CA: Polebridge Press).

Knight, Jennie S.
    2005   'Re-Mythologizing the Divine Feminine in *The Da Vinci Code* and *The Secret Life of Bees*', in Bruce David Forbes and Jeffrey H. Mahan (eds.), *Religion and Popular Culture in America* (Berkeley: University of California Press, 2nd rev. edn): 56-74.

Landres, J. Shawn, and Michael Berenbaum (eds.)
    2004   *After* The Passion *is Gone: American Religious Consequences* (Walnut Creek, CA: AltaMira Press).

Lawler, Michael G.
    2004   'Sectarian Catholicism and Mel Gibson', *Journal of Religion and Film* 8 (Special Issue 1), http://www.unomaha.edu/jrf/2004Symposium/Lawler.htm, accessed 5 January 2007.

Leloup, Jean-Yves
    2002   *The Gospel of Mary Magdalene* (trans. J. Rowe; Rochester, VT: Inner Traditions).

Linafelt, Tod
    2006   'Tragically Heroic Men and the Women Who Love Them', in Beal and Linafelt 2006: 29-37.

Longfellow, Ki
    2007   *The Secret Magdalene* (New York: Crown Publishers).

Maisch, Ingrid
    1998   *Mary Magdalene: The Image of a Woman through the Centuries* (Collegeville, MN: Liturgical Press).

Malarkey, Tucker
    2006   *Resurrection* (New York: Riverhead Books).

Mary of Agreda
    1997   *The Divine Life of the Most Holy Virgin: Being an Abridgment of The Mystical City of God* (Rockford: Tan Books).

McGowan, Kathleen
    2006   *The Expected One* (New York: Simon & Schuster).

Meyer, Marvin, and Esther A. de Boer
    2006   *The Gospels of Mary* (San Francisco: Harper).

Mohri, Erika
    2000   *Maria Magdalena: Frauenbilder in Evangelientexten des 1. bis 3. Jahrhunderts* (Marburger theologische Studien, 63; Marburg: N.G. Elwert Verlag).

Morgan, David
    2004   'Manly Pain and Motherly Love: Mel Gibson's Big Picture', in Landres and Berenbaum 2004: 149-57.
    2005   'Catholic Visual Piety and *The Passion of the Christ*', in Plate 2005: 85-96.

Mulvey, Laura
    1975   'Visual Pleasure and Narrative Cinema', *Screen* 16.3: 6-18.

Nahmad, Claire, and Margaret Bailey
    2006   *The Secret Teachings of Mary Magdalene* (London: Watkins Publishing).

Ortiz, Gaye W.
    2004   '"Passion"-ate Women: The Female Presence in *The Passion of the Christ*', in Plate 2004: 109-20.

Pagels, Elaine
    1981   *The Gnostic Gospels* (New York: Vintage Books).

Picknett, Lynn
    2003   *Mary Magdalene: Christianity's Secret Goddess* (London: Robinson).

Picknett, Lynn, and Clive Prince
    1997   *The Templar Revelation: Secret Guardians of the True Identity of Christ* (New York: Touchstone).

Plate, S. Brent (ed.)
    2004   *Re-Viewing the Passion: Mel Gibson's Film and its Critics* (New York: Palgrave Macmillan).

Roberts, Michèle
    2007   *The Secret Gospel of Mary Magdalene* (London: Vintage Books).

Robinson, James M. (ed.)
  1988   *The Nag Hammadi Library* (Leiden: Brill, 3rd edn).
Ruschmann, Susanne
  2002   *Maria von Magdala im Johannesevangelium. Jüngerin—Zeugin—Lebens-botin* (Neutestamentliche Abhandlungen, NF 40; Münster: Aschendorf Verlag).
Schaberg, Jane
  1996   'Fast Forwarding to the Magdalene', in Alice Bach (ed.), *Biblical Gla-mour and Hollywood Glitz* (Semeia, 74; Atlanta: Scholars Press): 33-45.
  2002   *The Resurrection of Mary Magdalene: Legends, Apocrypha, and the Chris-tian Testament* (New York: Continuum).
  2006   'Gibson's Mary Magdalene', in Beal and Linafelt 2006: 69-79.
Schaberg, Jane, and Melanie Johnson-Debaufre
  2006   *Mary Magdalene Understood* (New York: Continuum).
Starbird, Margaret
  1993   *The Woman with the Alabaster Jar: Mary Magdalen and the Holy Grail* (Rochester, VT: Bear & Co.).
  2005   *Mary Magdalene: Bride in Exile* (Rochester, VT: Bear & Co.).
Stevens, Brad
  2004   *Abel Ferrara: The Moral Vision* (Surrey: FAB Press).
Thimmes, Pamela
  1998   'Memory and Re-vision: Mary Magdalene Research since 1975', *Currents in Research: Biblical Studies* 6: 193-226.
Thistlethwaite, Susan
  2006   'Mel Makes a War Movie', in Fredriksen 2006: 127-45.
Thompson, Mary R.
  2006   *Mary of Magdala: What The Da Vinci Code Misses* (New York: Paulist Press, rev. edn).
Vander Stichele, Caroline, and Todd Penner
  2006   'Passion for (the) Real? *The Passion of the Christ* and its Critics', *Biblical Interpretation* 14: 18-36. Also in J. Cheryl Exum (ed.), *The Bible in Film: The Bible and Film* (Leiden: E.J. Brill, 2006): 18-36.

MORE PAIN, MORE GAIN! ON MEL GIBSON'S FILM, *THE PASSION OF THE CHRIST**

Arnfríður Guðmundsdóttir

He was wounded for our transgressions,
crushed for our iniquities;
by his wounds we are healed.

This citation, taken from the book of Isaiah ch. 53, appears on the screen at the beginning of Mel Gibson's film entitled *The Passion of the Christ*. With this citation, Gibson makes clear his understanding of Jesus Christ as the suffering servant, which is an important key to his interpretation of Christ's passion. As the suffering servant, Christ is 'like a lamb that is led to the slaughter' and silently meets its death. This Christ is the victim of evil, which is incarnated in the movie as the devil in a woman's body, but also in the Roman solders, the Jewish leaders and last but not least in the crowd, which demands Jesus' death. The violence is limitless, and Christ's immense suffering raises critical questions about his 'true' humanity. Can this person really be *vere homo*? In the background looms God the father, who seems to be in favour of it all, if not the mastermind behind it.

Gibson's movie, *The Passion of the Christ*, not only proved highly controversial, but also opened up a lively discussion about plausible interpretations of the suffering and death of Jesus Christ. Among other important issues, it triggered questions of authenticity, interpretation and the use of sources. My aim in this article is twofold: first of all, to examine Gibson's use of sources, of biblical as well as extra-biblical origin; secondly, to provide a theological reading of Gibson's interpretation of the passion story.

Despite Gibson's claim that his film is a literal representation of the New Testament passion stories, the script clearly depends to a great extent on extra-canonical sources. Gibson's most important non-biblical

* I would like to extend my gratitude to Professor Anna Carter Florence, at Columbia Theological Seminary, Decatur, GA, USA, for her helpful editorial comments and critique.

source comes from Anne Catherine Emmerich, a nineteenth-century Roman Catholic nun, whose meditations on the passion of Christ were written down and later published with the title *The Dolorous Passion of our Lord Jesus Christ*. Gibson's attempt to sell his movie as a 'documentary' was therefore far fetched, and his claim of 'literal interpretation' was an important part of the marketing of the film. What I consider troubling about Gibson's film is not his use of extra-biblical materials *per se*. Rather, it is his claim that he strictly followed the biblical narratives, when the evidence is clear that he did not. Gibson's uncritical use of sources, particularly Emmerich's visions, is, furthermore, problematic. An obvious example is Gibson's emphasis on the violence Christ experienced on his way to the cross. While the Gospel writers briefly mention a violent treatment of Jesus Christ after his arrest, Emmerich's visions include detailed descriptions of the beatings and brutal treatment by the Roman soldiers, as well as the crucifixion itself. I do think that Gibson's focus on violence poses a problem, not simply because it goes way beyond what is in the Gospel narratives, or for that matter, what is biologically plausible, but first and foremost for theological reasons. *The Passion of the Christ* is a clear example of what has been labelled 'a glorification of suffering', where Christ's suffering is not only understood as God's will, but also as valuable in itself. Such an understanding of suffering is theologically questionable, not only for the implied understanding of God, but also because it provides a potential justification of all kinds of violently inflicted suffering and pain.

Even if Gibson's interpretation is not really his own, but based on particular readings from the Christian tradition, he still has to be held accountable for what he did. Making a movie about the passion of Christ calls for a sensitivity regarding the material one is presenting as well as the historical context of the prospective audience. I think Gibson's movie expresses limited sensitivity to both. For one thing, Gibson should have paid more attention to a critical evaluation submitted to him in May 2003 by a group of prominent Catholic and Jewish scholars. In their evaluation, the scholars criticized Gibson's 'shooting script', among other things for 'significant historical errors', 'a partial and skewed' portrayal of the person and mission of Jesus and for disregarding 'Catholic principles of Biblical interpretation' in the use (or ignorance) of texts from the New Testament (Ad Hoc Scholars Report 2004: 230-36). Gibson could have avoided a lot of the criticism he got later, had he followed the scholars' advice. Most importantly, his film could have improved drastically. A passion movie, in which violence and abuse is applauded and given spiritual significance, not only presents a very questionable reading of the

Gospel stories, but also is insensitive to the historical setting of its audience. The reason being, first of all, the preoccupation with violence within Western societies, and secondly, the growing awareness of all the suffering and pain that has been, and still is, inflicted upon people (be they victims of domestic violence or abuse by worldly or spiritual authorities), and then excused or even justified by Christ's example. Therefore, I think Gibson's message of 'more pain, more gain' is rightly questioned, as well as its significance for the ongoing explication of the passion of Christ.

A 'LITERAL' PORTRAYAL OF THE GOSPEL STORIES?

In interviews associated with the premiere of his movie, Gibson repeatedly referred to the Gospels as 'eyewitness accounts' (Boys 2004: 150). Thus, it became obvious that he did not make any distinction between the Gospels and other contemporary sources available (Reinhartz 2004: 175). But even if Gibson maintained that his movie was first and foremost complying with the accounts of those who had been present with Christ during his trial and execution, he made no attempt to deny that he consulted other sources as well (Crossan 2004: 12).[1] Still, when Gibson was accused of not being true to the Gospels, he is quoted to have responded: 'It's a movie, not a documentary!', which seems to indicate his ambivalence regarding the true nature of his film (Fredriksen 2004: 31-32).

For Gibson, it seems to make no difference that the Gospels were written several decades after the fact. The aim of the Gospels—namely, to distribute the good news about the crucified One to Jewish and non-Jewish readers alike—apparently makes no difference to him, either. Gibson also seems to ignore the fact that during the writing period, Roman authorities were constantly threatening their citizens, which is why it became crucial for the newly established religious group to try everything to earn the goodwill of the Romans, or at least not to offend them. This is probably why the Gospel writers chose to downplay the role of the Romans, while they emphasized the key role of the Jews. For this same reason, they indicated that Pilate, against his own will, did not dare but to obey when the Jews insisted on Christ's execution (Ad Hoc Scholars Report 2004: 233-34).[2] It is also important to keep in mind that

1. Gibson includes material from all four Gospels, without any apparent pattern (Cunningham 2004: 62-63).
2. An example is from the Gospel of John, which states: 'When the chief priests and the police saw him, they shouted, "Crucify him! Crucify him!" Pilate said to

the Gospels were written after the Jewish revolt, 66–73 BCE, when the Jewish temple was destroyed. For some gospel writers, the destruction of the temple was considered God's punishment to the Jews for being responsible for Christ's death. The most obvious example of this is the crowd's response, in the Gospel of Matthew, when Pilate declared his innocence by washing his hands, and '...the people as a whole answered, "His blood be on us and on our children!"' (Mt 27.25).[3] These words were later used to inflame anti-Semitic propaganda in support of the persecution of the Jews, which gradually increased, reaching a peak by the High Middle Ages (Fredriksen 2004: 45).

ANTI-SEMITIC?

Gibson's depiction of the Jews has been harshly criticized in light of the long history of anti-Semitism. Such criticism is, for example, presented in the so-called 'Ad Hoc Scholars Report'.[4] In this report, Gibson is warned not to repeat the mistake of classical passion plays, which often emphasized the Jews as Christ's arch enemies (Ad Hoc Scholars Report 2004: 226). The authors cite repeated warnings from the Vatican concerning 'erroneous and unjust interpretations of the New Testament regarding the Jewish people and their alleged culpability [for the crucifixion]...' (2004: 246). This is the case, for example, in the well-known *Nostra Aetate* (1965) from the second Vatican Council. The authors also call Gibson's attention to the 'Guidelines on the Presentation of Jews and Judaism in Catholic Preaching' from 1988, a document originating from the Bishops' Committee for Ecumenical and Interreligious Affairs, within the Roman Catholic Church in the United States, which states that 'Christian reflection on the Passion should lead to a deep sense of the need for reconciliation with the Jewish community today' (2004: 250-51; Plate 2004).

In terms of concrete examples, the authors of the report criticize Gibson for portraying the Jews as bloodthirsty and full of hate, posing a

them, "Take him yourselves and crucify him; I find no case against him". The Jews answered him, "We have a law, and according to that law he ought to die because he has claimed to be the Son of God". Now when Pilate heard this, he was more afraid than ever' (19.6-8).

3. As a response to the harsh criticism of his portrayal of the Jews, Gibson decided to remove the English translation of this phrase from his movie.

4. Gibson received the report in May of 2003, or a little less than a year before the opening of his movie, but it was not made public until after the premiere of the movie in February of 2004.

real threat to Pilate. In the movie, only Caiaphas is able to control the mob, which pays no attention to Pilate's orders (Ad Hoc Scholars Report 2004: 242-44). Caiaphas is portrayed as 'smug' and 'arrogant', and wearing the 'richest robes', while Pilate is sympathetically described as well-meaning but apprehensive (2004: 244-45). Gibson's interpretation of Pilate is in stark opposition to contemporary sources, where he is described as a 'ruthless tyrant' known for his use of violence to maintain his control—for instance, by ordering 'hundreds of Jews crucified without proper trial under Roman law...' (2004: 253). Therefore, the authors of the report consider it implausible to have Pilate fearing the crowd and its leader, Caiaphas. They point out that Pilate was Caiaphas's superior, and could only serve as high priest with Rome's assent. As an 'appointee' of Rome, it was Caiaphas's responsibility to maintain peace in Jerusalem, while Pilate, who resided on the coast, came to Jerusalem during the Jewish festival in order to prevent a riot. During Jewish festivals like Passover, Pilate used the crucifixion as a tool to avoid uproar in the city (2004: 236-38; Cunningham 2004a: 61).

FOLLOWING CHRIST TO THE CROSS

The traditional *passion play* is clearly an important prototype for Gibson's work, but no less significant is the well-known tradition of the Stations of the Cross. Already in the time of the early church, pilgrims travelled to the Holy Land to walk the *via dolorosa* ('the way of sorrow'), through the city of Jerusalem and up to Golgotha. On the way, the pilgrims stopped and reflected on certain events from the passion story, based either on the Gospels or on later sources. This particular way of commemorating Christ's passion has continued to play a significant role in the observance of Lent, particularly within the Roman Catholic Church. Gibson uses the Stations of the Cross to frame a structure for his passion story, where Jesus' mother escorts the viewer from one Station to another (Boulton 2004: 20).

The number and content of the Stations was not fixed until the seventeenth century, but since then the following events are represented at the fourteen Stations:
1.   Pilate's hall of judgment, where Jesus is condemned to death;
2.   Jesus receives his cross;
3.   Jesus falls for the first time;
4.   Jesus meets his mother;
5.   Simon of Cyrene is compelled to carry the cross;
6.   Veronica wipes the face of Jesus;

7. Jesus falls a second time;
8. Jesus meets the women of Jerusalem and pronounces his lament;
9. Jesus falls a third time;
10. Jesus is stripped of his garments;
11. Jesus is nailed to the cross;
12. Jesus dies on the cross;
13. Jesus' body is taken down from the cross;
14. Jesus' body is laid in the tomb (Evans 2004: 128-29).

The fifteenth Station, devoted to the resurrection of Christ, is sometimes added to the traditional fourteen.

Most of the celebrated events in the Stations of the Cross are reported in all four Gospels, but not without exceptions. The story of Simon of Cyrene is, for example, only in the synoptic Gospels, while the Gospel of John has Christ carry his cross himself. In addition, Luke is the only one who tells of the meeting of Jesus and the women of Jerusalem. Moreover, five out of fifteen Stations are based on extra-biblical sources: the three Stations that pay tribute to Jesus' repeated falls on the way to the cross, and the two which describe his meetings with his mother and with Veronica. One can imagine that the pilgrims may have figured that Jesus was so exhausted by the time he started his walk that he had a hard time standing on his feet. John's story of Mary present by the cross may similarly have evoked the idea that she was also there, close to him, on his way from Pilate's hall to the place where they crucified him. In writings from the second century, there is a story about a woman named Veronica (believed to be the same woman Jesus cured of a blood disorder in Mt. 9:20-22), who came to Pilate in order to testify to Jesus' innocence (Hoagland 2002). From the Middle Ages, there are references to Veronica's veil, a cloth she is believed to have used to wipe Jesus' face on his way to Calvary, and upon which the image of his face was preserved. An image is kept in St Peter's Church in Rome, which has been claimed to be the original veil (Evans 2004: 131).

ACCORDING TO EMMERICH

As in Gibson's movie, the Stations of the Cross provide a framework for the nineteenth-century work *The Dolorous Passion of Our Lord Jesus Christ*.[5] In this work, which was recorded and published by Klemens

5. See Emmerich's mystical writings, recorded and published by Brentano: http://www.jesus-passion.com/DOLOROUS_PASSION_OF_OUR_LORD_JESUS_CHRIST.htm.

Brentano, the Roman Catholic mystic Anne Catherine Emmerich describes her visions of the events surrounding Christ's suffering and death (Webb 2004: 160-61).[6] Emmerich died in 1824 and was beatified in October of 2004, which was the year *The Passion of the Christ* premiered (see Cunningham 2004b). When Gibson's movie is compared, on the one hand, to the gospel narratives and, on the other hand, to Emmerich's visions, Emmerich's extensive influence on Gibson becomes obvious.[7] Some have even remarked that if Gibson was to win an Oscar for his movie, it should have been for 'Best Adapted Screenplay' (Corley and Webb 2004a: 176).

An example of Emmerich's influence is the emphasis on violence and blood in the movie. Contrary to the Gospels, Gibson makes violent beatings the focal point of Christ's passion.[8] Given the amount of violence and blood in Gibson's passion movie, it might be hard to believe that Emmerich's descriptions are bloodier and more graphic than Gibson's. Thus, his reported statement that he did indeed tone the violence down from what is described in Emmerich's visions, surprisingly enough, proves to be true (Webb 2004: 169). Emmerich's anti-Semitism is another example of her influence on Gibson. The bribes used to encourage the mob to show up at the hearings, Satan's presence in the midst of the crowd and the Jewish leaders showing up on Golgotha are all ideas borrowed from Emmerich, which contribute extensively to the negative impression of Jews in Gibson's movie. For this reason, Gibson proves himself guilty of a serious lack of judgment, by allowing himself to copy Emmerich's negative portrayal of the Jews, even if he does not go nearly as far as she does. In this sense, Gibson ignores the history of centuries of anti-Semitism and hostility towards Jews, which has often been justified by their participation in the death of Christ. I think Robert Webb is right on target when he writes:

> Thankfully, Gibson chose not to use many of the more obviously anti-Semitic elements from Emmerich, but I fear that he did not exercise sufficient critical discernment in some of what he did choose to use. Neither artistic licence nor Christian faith justify a lack of critical discernment concerning the highly charged issue of anti-Semitism (Webb 2004: 172).

6.   For biographical information, see *New Advent 2005* and *jesus-passion.com*.

7.   See, for example, Crossan 2004: 12; Fredriksen 2004: 32; Webb 2004: 161.

8.   The Gospel writers do not dwell on the violence, while Emmerich gives detailed descriptions of the violent treatment Christ suffered by the Jews as well as the Romans. Gibson is obviously relying on Emmerich's graphic depictions of the violence in his movie.

Once again, the problem is not that Gibson consults other sources besides the New Testament; rather, the problem is *how* he does it.

THE CROSS: THE POLITICAL POINT OF VIEW

The Gospels as well as other contemporary sources provide limited access to information about the praxis of crucifixion. What is known for sure is that crucifixion was a common criminal, as well as political, punishment during antiquity. In the Roman Empire, it was most often used for dangerous criminals and members of the lower class. Martin Hengel maintains in his book, *Crucifixion*, that the main reason for its use was 'its allegedly supreme efficacy as a deterrent', and for that reason it was exercised in public, 'usually associated with other forms of torture, including at least flogging'. Crucifixion was an especially harsh punishment, which Hengel sees as a clear sign of the cruelty of those in charge, and the maximum humiliation of the victim, who frequently was left on the cross, 'served as food for wild beasts and birds of prey' (Hengel 1977: 86-88). For Jews, God's curse was furthermore believed to be on those who were crucified, as Paul reminds his readers in his letter to the Galatians, where he writes, citing the book of Deuteronomy (21.23): '...for it is written, "cursed is everyone who hangs on a tree"' (Gal. 3.13).

It is crucial that Christ's crucifixion is understood in its religious and historical context. Both religious and world leaders believed Christ to be a real threat to the peace in Jerusalem during the Passover. The fact that Christ was arrested at night, and that Pilate even bothered to crucify him, seems to indicate that Christ had significant support among the crowd. From Gibson's portrayal of the 'crowd' as being the enemies of Christ, it is easy to assume that Gibson does not take those historical realities into account (Fredriksen 2004: 39). Furthermore, there are no historical grounds for the massive violence that precedes Christ's crucifixion. It was a custom to scourge those who had been sentenced to death on the cross. In his movie, Gibson makes the most of this scourging in Jesus' case, leaving hardly a dry spot on his body, while the other two men crucified with him get away with only a few scars. The uniqueness of Christ's crucifixion plays a key role in Gibson's interpretation, as he looks to Emmerich for detailed descriptions of the procedure. According to contemporary sources, those who had been sentenced to death on the cross 'would carry only the crossbeams to the crucifixion site, where the upright beams would be permanently mounted' (Cunningham 2004a: 62). In Gibson's movie, those who were crucified with Christ carry the crossbeams, contrary to Christ who is made to carry a huge cross, with both beams, which he then turns out to be too weak to manage.

THE CROSS FROM THEOLOGICAL PERSPECTIVES

When it comes to a theological interpretation of the cross event, there is no single version that has been predominant within the Christian tradition. In his now classic book, *Christus Victor: An Historical Study of the Three Main Types of the Idea of the Atonement* (1970 [1931]), the Swedish theologian Gustav Aulén maintains that within the Christian tradition there have been, from the beginning, 'three main types' or ways to interpret the meaning of Christ's suffering his death on the cross. Even if Aulén's typology (like most typologies) is considered with its shortcomings, it can nevertheless be a helpful tool for studying this particular area within the theological tradition. A closer look at Aulén's typology will therefore provide important information about the theological background of Gibson's representation of the passion story.

The first type in Aulén's typology is what he calls *the classic type*, where Christ 'fights against and triumphs over the evil powers of the world, the "tyrants" under which mankind is in bondage and suffering, and in Him God reconciles the world to Himself' (Aulén 1970: 4). Based on Christ's complete victory over evil powers, this type is often labelled *the Christus-Victor theory*. The second type, identified by Aulén as *the Latin type*, originates from the medieval period, and is based primarily on images and analogies from the court of justice. As Christ, the sinless human being, pays the debt on behalf of sinful humanity with his death, Christ 'satisfies' the demand of God's justice, something sinners cannot do. For this reason the Latin theory is commonly known as the *satisfaction theory* (1970: 146). In the third type, the *moral example theory*, the focus is on Christ as the perfect example, or the great teacher, who through his teaching and behaviour makes known God's endless love to humanity. The proper response by human beings is to imitate Christ's example, or practice his teachings, in their daily lives (1970: 95-97).

In his book, Aulén argues for the prominence of the *Christus-Victor* theory. He maintains that it was the dominant theory from early on, or until Anselm of Canterbury and Peter Abelard presented their reinterpretations of the meaning of the cross in the late eleventh and early twelfth centuries. According to Aulén, the classical theory about the victorious Christ was later reintroduced by Luther in the sixteenth century, and again after the First World War, following a growing pessimism regarding the human ability to restrain the power of evil. In Gibson's interpretation of Christ's passion, the *Christus-Victor* motive is certainly strong, which still does not exclude ideas of Christ's death as a satisfactory payment for human sin, or the compelling influence of his example.

CHRIST THE CONQUEROR

The focus of the *Christus-Victor* theory is the victory Christ accomplished by his own death, over evil, sin and death. The assumption is that humanity 'fell into sin' in the Garden of Eden, as a consequence of Adam and Eve's disobedience to God (Gen. 3), and thereafter remained under the power of Satan. Thus, Christ's commission was to rescue humanity from that power, by becoming a ransom paid to Satan in order for humanity to become free again. The image of a baited hook has often been used to explain what was going on between Christ and the devil, the bait representing Christ's humanity and the hook his divinity. According to this image, the devil, 'like a great sea monster', snapped at the bait, only to discover the hook, but too late. Despite the great influence of the *Christus-Victor* approach, from its inception it has not been considered without its problems. First of all, the image of God hiding behind humanity and from there luring the devil into a trap implied the idea of God as a trickster. The second subject of dispute had to do with the notion that God owed the devil something. For many, the idea that the devil had earned the right to control humanity was regarded as highly problematic (McGrath 2001a: 415-16).

An example of the way *Christus-Victor* is used in *The Passion* is evident in the opening scene, set in the garden of Gethsemane, where Christ is trembling with fear in the presence of Satan, who keeps questioning him: 'Who is your Father? Who are you?' A snake appears in Satan's nose, as well as from underneath his cloak, making the resemblance to the Garden of Eden obvious. Christ is certainly not simply somebody who is afraid of his enemies. His disciples have never seen him like this, and they are worried, because they do not understand. What becomes clear to the audience, although it is hidden from Christ's disciples, is that this is indeed a battle between good and evil, a war between life and death. When Christ finally crushes the snake with his heel, the final outcome becomes evident. Goodness will eventually win, but the power of evil is nevertheless not to be underestimated. Satan's presence among the crowd is a sign of that power. The ultimate victory of good over evil is finally accomplished on Calvary, when Christ commends his spirit into the hands of his Father, and Satan screams in Hell, indicating his defeat.

THE GOD-MAN PAYS THE PRICE

Anselm, archbishop of Canterbury (c. 1033–1109), was one of those who was uneasy with the prerequisites of the *Christus-Victor* model. In his attempt to solve its shortcomings, he used images from the feudalistic system of his own time to respond to the ever-pressing question '*Cur deus homo?*' or 'Why did God become human?' The main point in Anselm's theory is that the honour of the lord of the manor (for Anselm, God) has been offended by the people and their sin. According to Anselm's satisfaction theory, God's justice has to be met, no matter what. There are two options: either a proper penalty, which means eternal destruction, or an act of satisfaction, where the God-man, without sin, substitutes himself for a sinful humanity. The God-man, or the perfect sacrifice, satisfies God's justice with his death, which demands a proper penalty, and at the same time rescues humanity from eternal destruction (Teselle 1992: 42). In Gibson's movie, we run across two issues that have become controversial in Anselm's atonement theory. First is the focus on Jesus' death, which seems to imply that his death is much more important than his life and work, even his resurrection (Ray 1998: 56). Second is the transcendent perspective, which is also the case with the *Christus-Victor* model, where the fight between good and evil seems, first and foremost, to take place outside of this world.

'SEE WHAT LOVE…'

Anselm's satisfaction theory incited strong reactions, for example from Peter Abelard (1079–1142), who is the best known of Anselm's early critics. Abelard criticized Anselm for what he saw as an overemphasis on Christ's death, which easily undermines the importance of his life and work. A primary emphasis on his death, furthermore, suggested that Christ was simply born to die (Ray 1998: 56). The priority given to God's justice, rather than love, was another reason for Abelard's disagreement with Anselm's approach. By giving prominence to God's justice, Abelard worried that Anselm was undermining the importance of God's love, which became the focus of Abelard's interpretation of Jesus' life and death. For Abelard, the incarnation should be considered a declaration (or revelation) of the creator's infinite love for the creation. The high point of this revelation was reached in Christ's suffering and death on the cross. According to Abelard's theory, Christ's salvific act consisted first and foremost of the impact Christ's life and death has on us, especially the humility, obedience and self-sacrificial behaviour he exercised, over and against limitless cruelty and pain (McGrath 2001b: 343). Because of this subjective impact of Christ's life and death, Abelard's theory is often called the *subjective atonement theory* (in distinction to Anselm's *objective* theory) or simply the *theory of Christ's moral example*.

Abelard's theory existed, for the longest time, in the shadow of Anselm's satisfaction theory. An interest in Jesus Christ as a moral example increased radically in the period of the Enlightenment, following a growing uneasiness about any 'supernatural' meaning of Jesus' person and work. A critical evaluation of ancient doctrines was common at that time, including 'the two nature, one person theory', eventually giving way to a new understanding of Christ's difference from other human beings in terms of degree rather than nature. Subsequently, the classical interpretation of Jesus' death in terms of payment or satisfaction of human sin was seriously questioned. A more plausible way of understanding the meaning of the life and death of Christ is to take into account the impact Christ made with his life as well as his sacrificial death. Thus, the key is Christ's ability to impress and encourage people to follow in his footsteps, or to 'lure' them to become 'like him' (*imitatio Christi*). Thus, the emphasis on Christ's powerful example became a way to respond to the challenge Christianity was confronted with by the philosophy of the Enlightenment, to come up with a religion which exists within 'the limits of reason alone'.[9]

Seen from the perspective of Abelard's subjective theory, Gibson is clearly convinced by the power of Christ's example to impress his observers. Like those few who are moved by watching Jesus being tortured by his adversaries, Gibson expects the audience to be moved by what they see. The prototype is Malchus, the high priest's slave, whose ear Simon Peter cuts off in the garden of Getsemane. When Jesus 'touched his ear and healed him' (Lk. 22.51), Malchus recognized who his healer was and was unable to follow Jesus' enemies anymore. Malchus had been transformed by what he had seen and experienced.

CHRIST AS THE SUFFERING SERVANT

Ever since Paul wrote his First Letter to the Corinthians, other theologians have repeated his emphasis on the significance of the cross, as well as the danger of forgetting 'the harsh reality of crucifixion in antiquity' (Hengel 1977: 89-90). The terror of Christ's passion is certainly in focus

---

   9.   A classic example is Kant's book on *Religion within the Limits of Reason Alone* (1793).

in Gibson's movie. Gibson seemingly uses the terror to underscore not only the value of Christ's sacrifice, but also the depth of his love 'for us' (Webb 2004: 162). For Gibson, the amount of Christ's suffering is a clear sign of Christ's love, namely: 'more pain, more gain'. Gibson himself claims that this is why he uses what he calls the 'shock and scare' method in his interpretation of Christ's passion (Bucher, Barrett and Dawson 2004: 19). The citation from Isaiah's song about the Suffering Servant is obviously meant to justify the use of violence. The violence in Gibson's passion movie not only exceeds the violent treatment Christ suffers in the gospel stories, but is also over and above what could be expected to be withstood by any human being. It has, for example, been pointed out that the amount of blood Christ loses during the beatings is way beyond what any human being can tolerate. Compared to other movies of the twentieth century concerning Jesus, the contrast is striking. In many of the earlier movies, the suffering and pain seem unreal, and Christ is withdrawn and unaffected by what is going on. In his portrayal of Christ, Gibson, on the other hand, chooses the *Übermensch* as a model, very similar to the superheroes in many of Gibson's previous movies. It is safe to say that to some extent Gibson's Christ seems to have more in common with William Wallace, the hero of Gibson's multi-awarded *Braveheart* (1995), than to the key figure of the New Testament's passion stories. Thus, it is only fair to ask if Gibson's interpretation is in any way more authentic (for example, in regard to Christ's humanity) than the distant, and in many ways not very human, Jesus figure in movies like *The King of Kings* (1927) or *The Greatest Story Ever Told* (1965). Could it be that the pendulum has swung too far from the docetic interpretation of the older Jesus movies, over to the superman, who has very little in common with the rest of us? I think so. I will argue that Gibson has indeed gone too far in his attempt to make Jesus' suffering and pain real. At least it is clear that the excessiveness of the violence does call for somebody 'more than' human, somebody who is able to survive what any 'normal' human being could not. Given Gibson's historical record within the film industry (most often working with action movies of some sort), it is not far fetched to think that he assumed the audience needed all this violence in order to 'get the point'. Whether Gibson was using the violence in order to 'sell' the message, because he did not think the Gospel stories would be enough, is another question.[10]

10. Massive marketing of Gibson's movie took place, both before and after the movie's premiere. A number of homepages were created in support of the movie, with some advertizing souvenirs, including bracelets with 'the passion nail' and a crown of thorns. See http://www.thepassionofchrist.com/splash.htm; www.supportMelGibson.

Regardless of any possible marketing motives, it is clear that Gibson wanted his movie to be perceived as a testimony of his faith. By choosing the suffering servant as a hermeneutical key for his interpretation of the cross, Gibson follows a long and widely accepted tradition of interpreting Christ's passion in light of this powerful figure from Deutero-Isaiah. The citation that appears on the screen at the beginning of Gibson's movie is taken from Isa. 53.5, which reads as follows: 'But he was wounded for our transgressions, crushed for our iniquities; upon him was the punishment that made us whole, and by his bruises we are healed'.[11] This particular verse is a key verse in Isaiah 53, which tells the story of one who suffers on behalf of others. The suffering one is an outcast from society, who has been appointed by God to carry the punishment (on 'our' behalf), in the form of suffering (53.6). This is a passively accepted suffering. The one who suffers walks silently, 'like a lamb that is led to the slaughter, and like a sheep that before its shearers is silent, so he did not open his mouth' (53.7).

The image of the suffering servant is a logical prerequisite to another leading image in Gibson's movie, namely that of the paschal lamb. The suffering servant is afflicted, yet does not 'open his mouth'. This is clearly true for Jesus, who in the garden of Gethsemane is terrified by what is coming, yet whose obedience to his father is, in the end, stronger than his fear. Christ decides to face his destiny, the destiny of the paschal lamb, focused and perfectly calm. The images of the paschal lamb, as well as references to Isaiah's depiction of the suffering servant, are also borrowed from Emmerich's visions. In a chapter describing Jesus being brought to the high priest, there is the following description:

> The streets in the vicinity of Caiphas's tribunal were brightly illuminated with lamps and torches, but, as the crowds gathered around it, the noise and confusion continued to increase. Mingling with these discordant sounds might be heard the bellowing of the beasts which were tethered on the outside of the walls of Jerusalem, and the plaintive bleating of the lambs. There was something most touching in the bleating of these lambs, which were to be sacrificed on the following day in the Temple—the *one* Lamb alone who was about to be offered a willing sacrifice opened not his mouth, like a sheep in the hands of the butcher, which resists not, or the lamb which is silent before the shearer; and that Lamb was the Lamb of

com; www.SeeThePassion.com; and www.thepassionoutreach. com. For more on this issue, see Caldwell 2004.

11. Gibson leaves out the follwoing part of the sentence: '...upon him was the punishment that made us whole...'

God—the Lamb without spot—the true Paschal Lamb—Jesus Christ
himself (Emmerich 1994: 149).

Gibson's focusing on the blood is yet to be understood, not only in light
of the image of the paschal lamb, but also in light of the Roman Catholic
understanding of communion, where the bread and wine are actually
transformed into Christ's body and blood.[12] Gibson reinforces his understanding with a series of flashbacks from the Last Supper during Christ's
crucifixion. A scene from the time the bread is taken out of the cloth is,
for example, shown during the time Christ is stripped of his garments.
This also explains why the two Marys are so preoccupied with cleaning
up Christ's blood, which appears in abundance following the continuous
floggings. Gibson's conception on the key role of Christ's blood is furthermore apparent from Veronica's bloody face, after she kisses the cloth she
used to wipe Christ's face, and Mary's kissing of the bloodstained feet of
the crucified One.

I maintain that Gibson's depiction of Christ's suffering and pain can
be seen as a classic example of what is often called a *glorification of suffering*. In his movie, violence is not only justified as being the will of God,
but it is also a necessary prerequisite for the good that is expected to come
out of it. In other words, violence is desirable, and suffering is valuable in
itself, regardless of its historical context. This certainly raises questions in
our contemporary situation, where violence is evaluated according to its
entertainment qualities, as well as marketing value. When push comes to
shove, our understanding of Christ and his death on the cross cannot
simply be based on theoretical concerns, but has to be evaluated in light
of our experience. We have to ask: What does this emphasis on violence,
suffering, sacrifice, obedience and submission to authorities mean within
a context of violence, abuse and oppression (Ray 1998: 21)? But we also
have to ask about the underlying understanding of God: Who is God, in
such a context? In other words, what does the passion story teach us
about God *vis-à-vis* violence and unjustifiable suffering and pain?

Christ's passion story, in the context of his own life and work, is a
strong witness to resistance against injustice and evil. Not only did Christ
side with victims of injustice and evil, but furthermore he encouraged
them to stand up and resist. Those who take on the great task of enacting
Christ's passion have to take Christ's religious and historical context, as
well as their own context, into consideration. There is a great responsibility that follows such an execution. The image of the lamb, which is

12. This understanding is based on the doctrine on *transubstantiation*, formally
defined by the Fourth Latern Council in 1215 (McGrath 2001a: 524-25).

silently led to the slaughter, too often has served, even today, as a justification for the suffering of the innocent. Gibson's passion movie leaves us with pressing questions, such as how to interpret the harsh reality of evil, suffering and violence, without making it desirable or valuable in itself. The vital theological task is to figure out how it is possible to interpret the paradoxical message of the cross, about the good that may come out of evil, without making God the *primus motor* of the whole thing and turning Christ into a passive victim.

BIBLIOGRAPHY

Ad Hoc Scholars Group
    2004   'Ad Hoc Scholars Report', in *Perspectives on the Passion of the Christ: Religious Thinkers and Writers Explore the Issues Raised by the Controversial Movie* (New York: Miramax Books): 225-54.

Aulén, Gustaf
    1970   *Christus Victor: An Historical Study of the Three Main Types of the Idea of the Atonement* (London: SPCK [1931]).

Boulton, Matthew Myer
    2004   'The Problem with the Passion', *Christian Century* (March 23): 18-20.

Boys, Mary C.
    2004   'Seeing Different Movies, Talking Past Each Other', in *Perspectives on the Passion of the Christ: Religious Thinkers and Writers Explore the Issues Raised by the Controversial Movie* (New York: Miramax Books): 147-63.

Bucher, Gregory S., Brian Barrett and Michael Dawson
    2004   'When the Passion Has Cooled', *Journal of Religion and Society* 6, http://moses.creighton.edu/jrs/2004/2004-16.html, accessed 27 April 2008.

Caldwell, Deborah
    2004   'Selling Passion', in *Perspectives on the Passion of the Christ: Religious Thinkers and Writers Explore the Issues Raised by the Controversial Movie* (New York: Miramax Books): 211-24.

Corley, Kathleen E., and Robert L. Webb
    2004a   'Conclusion: *The Passion*, the Gospels and the Claims of History', in Corley and Webb 2004b: 173-77.

Corley, Kathleen E., and Robert L. Webb (eds.)
    2004b   *Jesus and Mel Gibson's The Passion of the Christ: The Film, the Gospels and the Claims of History* (New York: Continuum).

Crossan, John Dominic
    2004   'Hymn to a Savage God', in Corley and Webb 2004b: 8-27.

Cunningham, Philip
    2004a   'Much Will Be Required of the Person Entrusted with Much: Assembling a Passion Drama from the Four Gospels', in *Perspectives on the Passion of the Christ: Religious Thinkers and Writers Explore the Issues Raised by the Controversial Movie* (New York: Miramax Books): 49-64.
    2004b   'Commentary: The Beatification of Anne Catherine Emmerich', Center for Christian-Jewish Learning at Boston College, http://www.

bc.edu/research/cjl/meta-elements/texts/cjrelations/topics/
commentary_emmerich.htm, accessed 30 January 2006.

Emmerich, Anne Catherine
1994   *The Dolorous Passion of our Lord Jesus Christ* (repr., Rockford, IL: TAN
        Books & Publishers).
2002   *The Dolorous Passion of our Lord Jesus Christ*, http://www.jesuspassion.
        com/DOLOROUS_PASSION_OF_OUR_LORD_JESUS_CHRIST.h
        tm, accessed 25 August 2004.

Evans, Craig, A.
2004   'The Procession and the Crucifixion', in Corley and Webb 2004b: 128-
        37.

Fredriksen, Paula
2004   'Gospel Truths: Hollywood, History, and Christianity', in *Perspectives
        on the Passion of the Christ: Religious Thinkers and Writers Explore the
        Issues Raised by the Controversial Movie* (New York: Miramax Books):
        31-47.

Hengel, Martin
1977   *Crucifixion* (trans. John Bowden; Philadelphia: Fortress Press).

Hoagland, Victor
2002   'The Stations of the Cross and Other Devotions to the Passion', http://
        www.cptryon.org/prayer/xstations/index.html, accessed 30 August 2006.

Johnston, Robert K.
2004   'The Passion as Dynamic Icon: A Theological Reflection', in S. Brent
        Plate (ed.), *Re-viewing the Passion: Mel Gibson's Film and its Critics*
        (New York: Palgrave Macmillan): 55-70.

McGrath, Alister E.
2001a   *Christian Theology: An Introduction* (Oxford: Blackwell, 3rd edn).
2001b   *The Christian Theology Reader* (Oxford: Blackwell, 2nd edn).

Musser, Donald W., and Joseph L. Price (eds.)
1992   *A New Handbook of Christian Theology* (Nashville: Abingdon Press).

Nostra Aetate
1965   'Declaration on the Relation of the Church to Non-Christian Relig-
        ions', http://www.ewtn.com/library/COUNCILS/v2non.htm, accessed
        30 January 2006.

Plate, S. Brent
2004   'Criteria for the Evaluation of Dramatizations of the Passion', in
        Bishops' Committee for Ecumenical and Interreligious Affairs (National
        Conference of Catholic Bishops, 1988): 180-90.

Ray, Darby Kathleen
1998   *Deceiving the Devil: Atonement, Abuse, and Ransom* (Cleveland: Pilgrim
        Press).

Reinhartz, Adele
2004   'Jesus of Hollywood', in *Perspectives on the Passion of the Christ: Religious
        Thinkers and Writers Explore the Issues Raised by the Controversial Movie*
        (New York: Miramax Books): 165-79.

Richardson, Alan, and John Bowden (eds.)
    1983   *Westminster Dictionary of Christian Theology* (Philadelphia: Westminster Press).
Teselle, Eugene
    1992   'Atonement', in Musser and Price 1992: 41-43.
Webb, Robert L.
    2004   'The *Passion* and the Influence of Emmerich's *The Dolorous Passion of our Lord Jesus Christ*', in Corley and Webb 2004b: 160-72.

JESUS AND JOSEPHINE:
THE BIBLE IN DANISH POPULAR CULTURE*

Jesper Tang Nielsen

The Bible does not hold a central position in the everyday life of the Danes, not even in the religious life of regular churchgoers. Yet, biblical stories and imagery have always been transmitted to the public through other media. The most striking example is the *Hymn Book* of the Danish Church, which is used more frequently than is the Bible. For this reason, Danish popular culture has seldom referred directly to the Bible. But in the last decade this has changed. The Bible, biblical stories, language and imagery seem to be playing a more prominent role in everyday life and popular culture. This development is almost certainly a reaction to the fact that in recent decades, Danes have been confronted with another religious tradition with Holy Scriptures, namely Islam. Given this situation, it is urgent that we discuss the contemporary use of the Bible and the underlying interpretation of its message. A striking example of a creative way of reception of the Bible is *Jesus and Josephine*, a television mini-series.

TV CHRISTMAS CALENDARS: THE GENRE

In 1962, the Danish National Television (*Danmarks Radio*) initiated a Danish Christmas tradition that has grown increasingly in popularity. Every night from 1–24 December, a televised series called the *TV Jule-kalender* (*TV Christmas Calendar*) is broadcast. For Danish children and childlike persons, it is fixed ritual during Advent to watch the yearly *TV Christmas Calendar*. Until 1988, Denmark had only one TV channel, which made the year's *Christmas Calendar* a national event and a part of the collective memory. With the introduction of commercial TV, several competing *Christmas Calendars* have been broadcast, including some for adults. Consequently, none of them is able to attract the attention of the

---

* I am grateful to Michael Perlt for invaluable technical assistance.

entire nation, as the *Christmas Calendar* used to do—unless, of course, the production is of extraordinary quality. This was the case with *Jesus and Josephine* in 2003.

Every year the story depicted in the *TV Christmas Calendar* is completely new and different. One year it was a puppet-show and the storyline was about three friends who found a treasure map and had to solve a riddle to find the treasure.[1] Another year, the setting was a small town in the 'good old days'. The mayor's family members were the principal characters along with two pixies living in the attic. The main premise of the series was the mayor's worry about his ship 'The Hope', which had not returned from a voyage. He feared it had foundered and his fortune was lost. For that reason he constantly told the children that Christmas would be cancelled. But every time he said this, the pixies teased him by taking some of his things. In the end, the ship returned, and they all celebrated Christmas.[2] Yet another year, the main characters were Santa Claus' helpers. Five of them were sent on a special mission because Santa Claus had lost the spirit of Christmas. After several failures, they retrieved the true spirit of Christmas just in time for the Christmas Eve celebration.[3] A final example is a *Christmas Calendar* that was set in a time so long ago that nobody can remember it. The scene is a fairytale castle; the king had lost a war and was to give his daughter to the prince of his enemies. The princess, however, was more interested in the new gamekeeper. In this series as well, the pixies tried to keep up the spirit of Christmas despite the dire situation. In the end, everything worked out because it was revealed that the gamekeeper was the prince of the hostile country.[4]

Although the various televised Christmas Calendars have entirely different storylines, they often have the same plot structure: in the beginning something goes wrong and a lack occurs. It looks like Christmas will not be celebrated at all. In the episodes that follow, the characters try to solve the problem and restore what is lacking. In the end they are successful and everybody celebrates Christmas after all.[5] While counting down to

1. *Jullerup Færgeby* (Danmarks Radio 1974), directed by Per G. Nielsen.
2. *Jul i Gammelby* (Danmarks Radio 1979), directed by Hans Christian Ægidius.
3. *Nissebanden* (Danmarks Radio 1984), directed by Per Pallesen.
4. *Jul på slottet* (Danmarks Radio 1986), directed by Finn Henriksen.
5. There was one exception to this: in one televised *Christmas Calendar* two people were seeking the missing Santa Claus in a subterranean labyrinth. They became lost in the labyrinth and met several mysterious creatures, but not Santa. After 23 days in the cave, they found the exit, gave up and went home. Only in the very last scene did the viewers catch a glimpse of Santa crossing the road (*Jul og grønne skove*, Danmarks Radio 1980, director unknown). When it was broadcast, it provoked a

Christmas Eve, the *Christmas Calendar* creates suspense by questioning if Christmas will ever arrive.

If the structure of *TV Christmas Calendars* is reminiscent of fairytales, the characters are as well. Santa Claus, his helpers and other legendary figures have played key roles in the most popular series. In particular, pixies have been important because they represent the original childlike joy and anticipation of Christmas, which adults allegedly tend to lose. In these stories, pixies and children are typically collaborators in the struggle for Christmas, which has been endangered because of adults' mistakes, worries and fears. In this way, most of the series are connected to folk-loristic beliefs, but they never refer directly to a religious universe. Everything in the series is focussed on Christmas, without ever mentioning God, Jesus, the Bible or any other religious phenomenon. It is almost paradoxical that a Christmas tradition is formed by folkloristic mythology and never explicitly influenced by Christianity.[6]

This changed in 2003 when a very bold producer from a commercial Danish TV channel (TV2) decided to make a *TV Christmas Calendar* that actually had something to do with Christmas. The result was *Jesus and Josephine*.[7] In this series, Christianity and the biblical story take up a hitherto unseen central position. This was an innovation not just in the history of *TV Christmas Calendars*, but also in the entire history of Danish children's television.

JESUS AND JOSEPHINE: THE STORY

The main character of *Jesus and Josephine* is a 12-year-old Danish girl, Josephine. She lives with her nuclear family, including her little brother, Lucas, her mother, who is a newly ordained minister in the Danish Church, and her father, who is on sick leave from his job as a school teacher. Apart from her family, we also meet her friend, Oscar. Minor characters are Josephine's female school teacher, Jytte, and her school friends. Besides the characters that belong in Denmark of 2003, the 12-year-old Jesus and his friends, Simon and Judas, have major roles.

---

public outcry, and although it has never been rerun and half the episodes have been erased, it has gained status as a 'cult'. It was a forerunner to the very popular satirical adult *TV Christmas Calendars* of the 1990s.

6. Of course, the plot structure invites Christian interpretations, as many Christmas sermons testify. But the stories never explicitly refer to Christianity. The closest connection is made in *Jul i Gammelby*, when the ship 'The Hope' returns safely on Christmas Eve.

7. *Jesus og Josefine* (Cosmo Film/TV2 Drama 2003), directed by Carsten Myllerup. The manuscript was by Nikolaj Scherfig and Bo Hr. Hansen.

Josephine hates Christmas because she was born on 24 December and does not want to share her birthday with Jesus. In the beginning that is the main problem. The first episodes are about Josephine's struggles to get her birthday for herself. She even writes to the Danish Minister of Ecclesiastical Affairs and proposes to cancel Christmas or at least move it to Midsummer Day. Her argument is that Jesus was not really born on 24 December. She receives a polite ministerial refusal.

At this point in the narrative, Josephine seems vain and selfish. She claims that Jesus has stolen her birthday, and she has no concern for people, like her younger brother, who are looking forward to Christmas. At the same time, however, she is a quite pious girl and every night she says her prayers. Almost every episode ends with a scene of Josephine praying. In the beginning of the series she even asks God to move Christmas.

But all her efforts are futile until she meets another person who dislikes Christmas: Thorsen, a mysterious antiquities trader. He tells Josephine that he was once cast out from home by his father on Christmas Eve and has not returned ever since. For that reason he detests everything about Christmas. Josephine visits Thorsen frequently. In the back of his shop she discovers an old Christmas crèche. It turns out that the crèche has magical powers: it is a time-travel device that enables Josephine to go back and forth between Denmark, year 2003, and Nazareth, year 12.

In Nazareth, Josephine meets Jesus, Simon and Judas. She and Jesus become friends and she visits him almost daily. She discovers that, at the age of 12, Jesus is not aware of his divine identity and extraordinary powers, although Mary insists that Joseph is not Jesus' real father, and Joseph enjoys Jesus' ability to change water into wine.[8] During their encounters, Josephine teaches Jesus to use his unusual talents, for example he learns to walk on water and multiply bread. When Josephine wants him to heal a blind man on a Shabbat, Jesus refuses. But Josephine convinces him by saying: 'It doesn't matter what day it is!'

Before long, Josephine realizes that her influence on Jesus is a powerful weapon in her fight against Christmas. Testing her feminine powers of persuasion, she wants Jesus to forbid the boiling of rice and milk in a pot. He promises to make this prohibition, if he one day becomes a great prophet. Josephine then tells Jesus about pizza. When she returns to Denmark, she finds that the traditional Danish Christmas dish, rice pudding, has been replaced by 'Christmas Pizza'.

---

8.   The characters of Mary and Joseph are very Lucan. Mary is a confident, God-fearing woman, who runs her house with a firm hand. Joseph is rather fond and timid, trying to stay out of trouble while attending to his carpentry business. But Joseph is also under divine guidance, being directed through dreams, as is the case in the Gospel of Matthew.

As a consequence of Josephine's adventures in Galilee, more things in Denmark change. Christmas beer is replaced by 'Nazareth Juice' (apple juice) and suddenly a certain kind of roll is called a 'Nazareth Bun'. Soon Josephine even finds herself appearing in the Bible as 'The Girl from North' who gives advice to Jesus.

The relationship between Jesus and Josephine grows closer and the two 12-year olds are attracted to each other. Josephine starts wondering what would have happened if Jesus had led a normal life and had not founded Christianity. She asks two people and gets two different answers. Her mother, theologian and minister, answers that if we were lucky, we would have another religion to make sense of our lives; otherwise, life would be meaningless. Josephine's female teacher, Jytte, on the other hand, answers that without Christianity we would be in Hell, devoid of hope. Josephine does not get any further in her inquiry; she is interrupted because Jesus arrives in Denmark. He has found the other end of the time-travel device and wants to see where Josephine lives.

It is not easy being Jesus in Denmark of 2003. He is sent to a psychiatric hospital; but Josephine rescues him and he returns to Galilee. Before he goes back, he visits a Danish church and sees something that he at first does not understand: a cross with a dead man on it. When he comes home to Nazareth, he has a mystic experience that explains it to him: he is the Son of God and it is his Father's will to let him die on the cross. But Jesus refuses! He does not want to die a disgraceful death at a young age and does not care about being the Son of God. He tells Josephine that he will run away to Caesarea and join a school for gladiators. That is what he wants to do: be a famous gladiator and fight in the Coliseum in Rome.

At this point in the story things go to Hell! When Josephine returns from Nazareth, Denmark has literally changed into Hell. And if we did not know already, we now discover the true identity of Thorsen, whose name derives from the old Nordic God, Thor. He is Satan and he now rules over a grim and ugly world where there is no God and therefore everybody is god (although not as much god as Thorsen), and there is no telling right from wrong. Nobody in this world has names, only numbers; everybody must work in Thorsen's boiler rooms and no-one is allowed to go up into the apparently polluted air. Christmas and Christianity are non-existent and neither hope nor compassion has a place. When Satan rules, everybody takes care of themselves.

Josephine confronts Thorsen and accuses him of having used her. He admits it. She was just what he needed: a naïve girl who was far too concerned about herself. He tells her that Jesus became a famous gladiator, triumphant in Rome, taking the laurel wreath, and died as an old man with many children. Is it really right, Thorsen asks Josephine, to take this happy life away from Jesus and make him die a terrible painful death on the cross?

Resisting Thorsen's temptation, Josephine realizes that she must try to convince Jesus to take on his identity as Son of God and so she travels back to Galilee. The turning point happens when Jesus has a revelatory dream and sees the present state of Denmark in 2003. In the dream, he meets Christ and the following dialogue takes place.[9]

Jesus:	Who are you?
Christ:	I am nothing! The one I should be, I will never be!
Jesus:	Why not?
Christ:	Why do you ask such a stupid question? I am you as an adult! I am Jesus! The Jesus who is the Son of God. But I will never exist.
Jesus:	Are you me?
Christ:	Yes! You had the whole world in your hand; but look what happened. The world looks like this just because you wanted to be a gladiator.
Jesus:	I don't want to die on a cross!
Christ:	And then humans have to live without hope for salvation in a world that looks like this!... Take heed, young Jesus. Sometimes you have to make sacrifices.
Jesus:	What shall I do?
Christ:	You know the answer.

After this, Jesus leaves the gladiator school and travels back to Nazareth with Simon, Judas and Josephine. On their way back, they spend the night in the desert. Jesus tells Josephine always to trust in God and together they recite the Lord's Prayer.

When Josephine returns to Denmark, everything is back to normal. 'The Girl from the North' is not in the Bible; the Danes eat rice pudding, drink Christmas beer and have not heard of 'Nazareth Juice', 'Christmas Pizza' or 'Nazareth Buns'. But Thorsen and Josephine have one final confrontation, when Josephine casts Thorsen to Hell by trusting God and reciting the Lord's Prayer.

Finally, on Christmas Eve everybody celebrates Christmas in the traditional Danish manner; and Josephine does not mind sharing her birthday with Jesus. Compared to the beginning of the series, her character is changed. She is neither selfish nor inconsiderate. On the contrary, she seems loving and compassionate. In the end, Jesus himself comes one last time to visit her and congratulate her on her birthday. During this final meeting, Josephine asks him if he will be okay, now that he knows what he is going to face. Jesus answers yes, because now he knows for whom he must die.

9. Translations from *Jesus and Josephine* are the author's.

In this way, *Jesus and Josephine* ends where a *TV Christmas Calendar* must end: with a good-old, traditional Danish Christmas. Denmark went to Hell along the way, but was saved and restored to its original state. That is a real Danish Christmas carol!

JESUS AND JOSEPHINE AND CONTEMPORARY UNDERSTANDING OF RELIGION

Jesus and Josephine is great TV. It not only has a brilliant script, wonderful direction, and superb acting performances; it is also first-class testimony of popular understanding of religion and particularly of Christianity.

First and foremost, *Jesus and Josephine* shows that the era of public critique of religion, or even outspoken anti-religion, is over. Religion is not conceived of as an ancient relic or as a repressive ideology. On the contrary, it is presented as a very real and concrete phenomenon with immense consequences for both personal and social lives. It was almost shocking (especially for someone raised on the 'politically correct' TV of the 1970s and 1980s) to see a 12-year-old girl earnestly praying on national TV. Twenty to thirty years ago, it would probably have been called indoctrination and would have provoked a left-wing chorus of disapproval; but in 2003, the criticism was very restrained.[10] In the series, Christianity is not just accepted as a part of Danish culture, it is presented as an important part of the daily life of the characters. On the level of Danish society as a whole, the consequences of Christianity are even more fundamental. Any changes to its formative period have immediate corresponding changes in Denmark of 2003. Christianity is portrayed as the reason that Denmark is what it is. Remarkably, this presentation of the massive personal and cultural influence of Christianity does not involve any kind of ideological criticism. The role of Christianity is entirely positive.[11] But exactly because there is no explicit criticism of religion, it is important to examine how the religion is presented.

10. *Jesus and Josephine* was almost unanimously well received. A few atheists were critical of the promotion of religion and some conservative Christian parties criticized the free play with the biblical story, but otherwise it was only praised. The ratings speak for themselves: an average of 1 million people watched the daily episodes—almost 20% of Denmark's population.

11. In a film that followed up on the success of *Jesus and Josephine*, the manuscript writers of *Jesus and Josephine* presented a critical view of the role of Christianity in the middle ages. However, the involvement of the Christian Church in witch hunts was clearly presented as a deviation of the true interpretation of Christianity. See *Oskar og Josefine* (Cosmo Film 2005), directed by Carsten Myllerup.

One salient aspect of the presentation of Christianity is its remarkably mythological character. Christian faith is apparently associated with a literal belief in the Virgin Birth, Jesus' miracles, Satan and angels.[12] Mary insists that Joseph is not Jesus' father; Jesus walks on water, heals the handicapped and performs other miracles; God communicates through angels, dreams and mystic experiences; and Satan was originally one of the sons of God but was thrown out of his heavenly home by his father. These depictions of the main religious characters are taken directly from the biblical and apocryphal literature, and their mythological status is maintained.

The mythological understanding of religion is not surprising in a children's series, but it is noteworthy that this rather naïve exegetical view is combined with a quite undeveloped theological understanding of religion. Two examples show how the mythological Christianity basically functions as a magical protection against evil. At one point, Josephine is given a feather by her schoolteacher. It turns out that it came from an angel, and Josephine uses it to protect herself and her friends against Satan. The other example is apparent in two interconnected episodes. On Josephine's last night in Galilee year 12, Jesus tells her always to trust in God and together they recite the Lord's Prayer. Back in Denmark, she has a final showdown with Thorsen. He tries to drive Josephine and her friend into Hell, but because they trust in God and recite the Lord's Prayer, Thorsen himself is cast into Hell. These separate events demonstrate an apotropaic understanding of Christianity and confirm the mythological universe of *Jesus and Josephine*.

Another striking feature is the age and gender of the Danes interested in religion. Besides Thorsen, Josephine's father is the only male adult among the main characters. He explicitly states that he does not know as much about Jesus as does Josephine's mother; nevertheless, he introduces to an interested Josephine the theory that Jesus was not born at Christmas time. Later he commits Jesus to a psychiatric hospital. Contrary to Josephine's mother, he insists that it is a sign of mental instability to claim to be Jesus. At the psychiatric hospital, Jesus is interviewed by a male psychologist, who thinks Jesus has troubles at home. Apparently, men do not consider religious phenomena real.

Only the two women take religion seriously and react to Josephine's questions about Jesus and Christianity. Josephine's mother has the role of a liberal Christian. She is, as Josephine expresses it, a modern minister. According to Josephine, this means that she does not really believe in the biblical stories. Her mother disagrees and claims that she certainly believes

---

12. While Denmark is Hell, the schoolteacher, Jytte, leads a secret group of children and tells them about angels.

in them, but interprets them symbolically. The other religious person is
Josephine's schoolteacher, Jytte. Her belief is almost pre-modern. In a
very uncritical way, she believes in God, Jesus and angels. She is the simple Christian believer. In two episodes the two women are contrasted,
because Josephine asks them both the same question. Early in the series,
she asks whether they believe that Jesus was the Son of God. Jytte replies
without hesitation 'yes', and when confronted with the question of how
she can be sure, she answers that an angel has told her so. Josephine's
mother is much more reluctant to answer clearly. This is illustrated in the
following dialogue, which is supposed to be characteristic of a modern
minister:

Josephine: What are you writing?
Josephine's mother:
               I'm writing my sermon for Sunday.
Josephine: Why don't you just write that we don't know if Jesus was the
               Son of God?
Josephine's mother:
               Huh, I think some people will be disappointed. Anyway, it
               isn't true.
Josephine: Can you guarantee it? That Jesus was the Son of God!
Josephine's mother:
               Guarantee and guarantee, I can guarantee it, but in the end I
               don't *know* it.
Josephine: So, you're lying in Church!
Josephine's mother:
               No, I agree 100 % with what Jesus is saying. For example,
               that we should be nice to each other and accept that we are
               different!

As mentioned above, the women are contrasted a second time, when
Josephine asks them how the world would be without Christianity. Also
in this case, Josephine's mother appears as the academic but vague theologian, whereas the schoolteacher is unreflective but firm in her conviction.
In both cases, the series sides for the plain, almost naïve belief of the
schoolteacher. In other episodes, angels do communicate with humans
and even intervene for their sake; and the story shows that Jytte is right
about the result of Christianity's disappearance. In this way, the series
takes a stand against a 'modern' Christianity that focuses on Jesus' ethical
demands. According to *Jesus and Josephine*, Christianity changed the
world because Jesus literally was the Son of God.

In combination, these characteristics of the presentation of religion in
Jesus and Josephine describe Christianity as a mythological, irrational and
magical religious phenomenon. It is only endorsed by women and children; and the more naïve, the more insight they have. Religion belongs to
the stereotypically uncritical children and women; men do not belong in

the mysterious universe of angels, magical feathers and apotropaic prayers. In this way, *Jesus and Josephine* promotes a traditional dualistic view on gender: masculinity stands for rationality, critique and logic; femininity equals emotion, naivety and mysticism. Hence, religion belongs to the sphere of women and children (just like Christmas belongs to pixies and children in other *TV Christmas Calendars*).

These traits describe the narrative surface of the series. For a complete evaluation of the understanding of Christianity, its role in the narrative structures and function in the development of the plot are more fundamental. These underlying basic structures generate the overall understanding of religion.

METHODOLOGICAL FRAMEWORK

Although the plot structure of *Jesus and Josephine* on one level is similar to other *TV Christmas Calendars*, it is more complicated. To pinpoint the difference and locate the narrative function of Christianity, it is helpful to establish a methodological framework. A promising starting point is the analysis of folktales in structuralism, because ordinary *TV Christmas Calendars* obviously have structural traits in common with this genre.

W. Propp's formalistic analysis, from 1928, of Russian folktales became unwillingly the pioneering work of structuralism (Propp 1958). Propp located 31 different narrative functions belonging to seven spheres of action in the material he examined. The French-Litauien structuralist and semiotician A.J. Greimas formalized his results further and raised them to a much higher level of abstraction.[13] On the basis of Propp's narrative functions, Greimas defined a limited number of *actantial* roles, namely, formalized narrative functions that on the text's surface emerge as various narrative characters, which Greimas named actors. Furthermore, he defined the relation between the different *actantial* roles in his well-known *actantial* model. This model operates with the following actants: *Sender, Object, Receiver, Subject* (the protagonist), *Helper* and *Opponent*. This model has been 'invested' in the following way in a *TV Christmas Calendar*: a chief from the 'Secret Pixies' Intelligence' sends (*Sender*) his special pixies agents (*Subject*) to find two magical stones (*Object*) and give them to Santa Claus (*Receiver*). The mission almost fails because somebody (*Opponent*) steals the stones and pretends to be Santa Claus. But then everything goes wrong (*Helper*) for the opponent, and in the end the pixies retrieve the stones and return them to the real Santa.[14]

13. See, e.g., Greimas 1966, but references to Propp abound in Greimas's works.
14. *Nissebanden i Grønland* (Danmarks Radio 1989), directed by Per Pallesen, and Flemming Jensen.

Using his actantial model, Greimas is able to present a formalized structure of the narrative course of the *Subject*, that is, the narrative trajectory (Greimas and Courtés 1976a). It has four phases: (1) the phase of *manipulation*, when the *Sender* presents a task (to acquire an *Object*) to the *Subject*; (2) the phase of *competence* where the *Subject* gains ability to perform the task; (3) the phase of *performance*, when the task is solved (the *Object* is taken in possession) and the opposition from the *Opponent* is overcome; and (4) the phase of *sanction*, when the *Object* is presented to the *Receiver* and failure or success of the phase of performance is evaluated by the *Sender*, and the *Subject* is rewarded or punished. Through this process, the *Subject* is transformed from one status of being to another, for example from not being a hero to being a hero. In the technical terminology of Greimas' semiotics, this course is called the canonical narrative schema.

On the basis of the canonical narrative schema and on other abstract semiotic models, it is possible to present a universal narrative structure, which has four core elements: Harmony, Negation of harmony, Disharmony and Negation of disharmony. The initial harmony is negated when a lack occurs and produces disharmony. But in the course of the narrative, the disharmonic situation is negated and harmony is re-established. Using this basic model, innumerable variations are possible. Many narratives take their starting point in the disharmonic state, in other words, the lack has already occurred and the task of the *Subject* is to restore harmony, but the state of disharmony only makes sense if a broken harmony is presupposed. Almost all fairytales and ordinary TV Christmas Calendars match this model.

Although stories of great complexity can be composed on the basis of this fundamental structure, in this form it is a model of simple narratives, because it only describes one narrative dimension. Greimas, however, distinguishes a pragmatic dimension from a cognitive one (Greimas and Courtés 1976b). The pragmatic dimension concerns concrete changes in the life world of the narrative characters. The described course from harmony to disharmony and back to harmony and the *Subject*'s narrative trajectory take place in the pragmatic dimension. If a given narrative only holds pragmatic changes, the story is categorized as 'simple', which means that the status of the involved characters and parties is not complicated concerning truth and lies. In Greimas' terms, their veridictory status is definitely true; everything *is* what it *appears* to be (Greimas and Courtés 1976b).

It may happen that something *appears* to be something it *is* not, or *is* something it does not *appear* to be. In this case, three different possible combinations of *being* and *appearance* can be deduced: correspondence between *being* and *appearance* is *truth*; *being* without corresponding *appearance* is *secrecy*; *appearance* without corresponding *being* is *lie* (Greimas and Courtés 1976b). When some narrative elements are not definite *truth*, the cognitive dimension of the text emerges. It consists of the narrative characters' understanding and evaluation of the people, events and changes in the pragmatic dimension. With a manifest cognitive dimension, the characters not only go through a pragmatic narrative trajectory, which transfers them from one status of being to another, but they also go through a narrative trajectory concerning a cognitive development from not knowing to knowing, or more precisely, from a false understanding to a true one.

When narratives only manifest a pragmatic dimension, they are denoted as 'simple' in Greimas' terminology. Others that have both the pragmatic and the cognitive dimension are denoted as 'complex'.[15] Some complex stories place all the importance in the cognitive dimension, so that the pragmatic dimension is only a pretext for exploring the cognitive trajectory. However, it is not possible to leave the pragmatic dimension out. Whereas it is both possible and common to construct stories without a cognitive dimension, a narrative with just the cognitive dimension cannot work. The cognitive dimension needs the pragmatic dimension to refer to, otherwise the complicated relation between *being* and *appearing* is not possible. In this way, the pragmatic dimension functions as the internal reference of the cognitive dimension (Greimas and Courtés 1976). The cognitive status and the changes in the cognitive trajectory are always related to pragmatic conditions. For that reason, the pragmatic dimension is narratologically superior to the cognitive one.

ANALYSIS

With this theoretical basis, the narratological difference between *Jesus and Josephine* and other *TV Christmas Calendars* can be defined. Ordinary *TV Christmas Calendars* are simple stories that take place in the pragmatic dimension and follow the universal narrative structure. They begin in or presuppose a state of harmony, which is followed by a crisis and a state of disharmony (Christmas is endangered). But when the protagonists overcome the crisis, the state of harmony is restored (Christmas is saved). In the harmonious end situation, everybody celebrates Christmas once again. In a way, the *TV Christmas Calendar* stories can be compared to mythological dramas. They challenge the order of the year and destabilize the known universe, but only to re-establish it and affirm the known order.

---

15. The narratological distinction between simple and complex narrative derives from Aristotle (*Poet.* 1452a11-17). Greimas's definition, however, does not correspond to the Aristotelian concepts.

The story of *Jesus and Josephine* is complex because it manifests both a pragmatic and a cognitive dimension. For that reason, the narrative structures are more complicated than they are in ordinary *TV Christmas Calendars*. The initial state of harmony is not endangered by a crisis but by a pseudo-crisis: Josephine must share her birthday with Jesus. However, at this point Josephine does not know that it is a pseudo-crisis.

An apparently ordinary narrative trajectory begins. In the phase of *manipulation*, Josephine acts both as *Sender* and *Subject*, giving herself the task to move or remove Christmas (*Object*). This is the beginning of an ordinary narrative trajectory, which continues in the phase of *competence* when Thorsen (*Helper*) provides the magical instrument that can help her solve the task. But in the phase of *performance*, when she tries to overcome the pseudo-crisis, a real crisis occurs: Christianity disappears and a real state of disharmony emerges.

At this point, Josephine discovers that her endeavour has been a *lie*: it *appeared* as if she was solving her task, but she *was*, in fact, helping Thorsen, who is the real *Opponent*. Her trajectory was a pseudo-trajectory in the status of *lie*, because it *appeared* as something it *was* not. Josephine was a *Pseudo-Sender*, because she was in fact Thorsen's *Helper*, the *Object* was a *Pseudo-Object*, and the *Helper* was a *Pseudo-Helper* or the *Opponent*.

Now another trajectory begins. Josephine is again her own *Sender* when she decides to fight Thorsen and bring back Christianity (*Object*). Her *Helper* in this trajectory is not only the magical crèche, the angel feather and her trust in God, it is first and foremost Christ, who convinces Jesus to take on his identity. Through her endeavour to solve the real crisis, Josephine actually solves the pseudo-crisis too. In the final phase of *sanction*, when the state of harmony is restored, Josephine's critique of Jesus stealing her birthday has ceased, and with her newly won insight, she has turned into a pleasant and considerate girl. Corresponding to the fact that Josephine is her own *Sender*, she is also the *Receiver*, and the *sanction* is that she herself is satisfied with the final situation. In this way, the initial harmony is not only restored, it is confirmed, because Josephine accepts it as a state of harmony.

To sum up, the story has several narrative structures: one in the cognitive dimension and one in the pragmatic one. Josephine's development from hating to loving Christmas is the cognitive level, whereas Denmark's course, from harmony with Christianity to disharmony without Christianity back to harmony with Christianity, constitutes the pragmatic level. Josephine's cognitive trajectory begins in misunderstanding and disliking Christmas, because she thinks it is a *lie*: *appearing* to be a joyous celebration of Jesus' birthday but in fact *being* a theft of her birthday. However, it turns out that the struggle for her birthday is a *lie*: *appearing* to benefit

Josephine, but in fact *being* a part of Thorsen's plan. Finally, Josephine ends in accepting and enjoying Christmas, when she realizes that it *is* a *true* occasion for celebration. According to the narratological theory, this cognitive course is dependent on Denmark's pragmatic trajectory from 2003 to Hell and back to 2003. Cognitive changes always relate to pragmatic conditions. Josephine's cognitive change is provoked by the fact that Denmark goes to Hell without Christianity. When she sees the difference between Denmark with and without Christianity, she understands its importance and cannot hate Christmas.

There is parallel story on the cognitive level: Jesus' acknowledgment of his role as the Son of God. Jesus also makes a cognitive change in the narrative. At one point he thinks his destiny is a *lie: appearing* to be God's will but actually *being* a disgraceful misfortune; but in the end, he realizes that it is a *secret: appearing* to be a disgrace but *being* the salvation of humanity. It is significant that Jesus' and Josephine's cognitive courses are dependent on the same pragmatic course, that is, Denmark's change to Hell without Christianity. When he realizes that Denmark will be Hell if he refuses to be the Son of God and die on the cross, he comes to terms with his duty.

Both Josephine's and Jesus' cognitive trajectories show that the pragmatic story has priority over the cognitive ones in the narrative construction. It is Denmark's pragmatic trajectory that produces the cognitive changes, not the other way around.[16] But the cognitive level confirms the pragmatic one. Harmony in Denmark is not just disturbed and re-established; it is also affirmed by Josephine's acknowledgment of Christianity's role in Denmark. Through the changes in Denmark's situation, Josephine is brought to accept the situation in Denmark of 2003 and even celebrate Christmas. Because the result of Josephine's adventures is that the situation in Denmark cannot be separated from the status of Christianity, Josephine accepts that when she understands that Denmark will be Hell without Christianity. Moreover, Jesus accepts it when he realizes that his duty is to save humans from the Hell that Denmark would be without his sacrifice.

Through this narrative analysis, the overall message of the story is apparent. Jesus takes on his divine role *in order to* save Denmark from Hell

---

16. In a DVD recording about the production of *Jesus and Josephine*, the authors claim that the story is about a girl who tries to be God; and Jesus who tries to be human. Both of them realize that they are wrong and accept respectively their human limitations and divine calling. See *Alt om Jesus og Josefine* (Cosmo Film 2003), directed by Ole Stenum. The authors repeated this point in a response to a newspaper article I wrote on the one-year anniversary of the series (see Scherfig and Hansen 2004). The authors, however, neglect the narratological fact that these cognitive developments were impossible without the pragmatic changes.

and make it what it is today. Consequently, Josephine cannot hate Christmas or dispute Christianity *because* it is the reason that Denmark is what it is today. In short, Jesus dies voluntarily on the cross to establish a state of harmony in Denmark of 2003; and because the state of harmony in Denmark of 2003 is the result of Christianity, its position should not be challenged.

EVALUATION

Jesus and Josephine is in many ways revolutionary in Danish television history. The Bible has never before been presented as foundational to Danish culture without any kind of critical edge. *Jesus and Josephine* obviously belongs to a new epoch of Danish cultural history. But it is also evident that the objective of *Jesus and Josephine* is conservative. It depicts Christianity and the Bible as the foundation of Danish culture; in fact, according to *Jesus and Josephine*, Christianity was meant to constitute Danish culture and the biblical story leads directly to Danish society. For that reason, the Bible cannot be changed; otherwise, Denmark will go to Hell. The provocative and revolutionary force of the Bible has been removed. We are left with Denmark of 2003 as the end of biblical history and Danish culture as the summit of Christianity: The Heavenly Jerusalem!

Of course, it is very problematic theologically and exegetically to connect the Bible and a certain culture, as is done in *Jesus and Josephine*. Even more problematic is when this use of the Bible is seen within the cultural milieu in Denmark, at a time when there is a political trend to defend traditional Danish values against the challenge of Islam. Note that the first step towards Hell is when Josephine makes Jesus prohibit a certain dish! Even though Josephine's theologically minded mother opens the possibility that another religion could replace Christianity, the narrative contradicts her. Without Christianity we would be in Hell: it is the Devil that challenges our good-old Danish Christmas.

FINAL REMARKS

Jesus and Josephine is indeed a fascinating phenomenon. The ideological criticism above should not hide the fact that narratologically, creatively and technically it is world-class children's television. Seen from the perspective of cultural history, it shows clearly that any reluctance to deal with religion has disappeared. Yet it also shows how Christianity is conceived of in contemporary culture. It is basically seen as the foundation of Danish, or even Western, culture and for that reason it should not be changed. And this also works the other way around: because the contemporary culture should not be changed, Christianity must remain what it is. According to this conception, Christianity cannot be but conservative.

The *Wirkungsgeschichte* of *Jesus and Josephine* confirms this interpretation. Since 2003, there have been two *TV Christmas Calendars* that use material from Danish cultural history to establish and present Danish cultural identity.[17] One of the series used old Nordic mythology, the other used Danish history, but in both cases the purpose was to show the deep roots and long tradition of contemporary Danish culture. By using the biblical story, *Jesus and Josephine* not only shows the ancient heredity of Danish culture, it provides this culture with a religious foundation and divine recognition. According to the interpretation of Jesus' motive to take on his identity and willingly suffer death on the cross, Danish culture and Denmark of 2003 are, in fact, the will of God.

Admittedly, in *Jesus and Josephine*, the simple believer, Jytte, also describes Christianity as giving hope, but her statement is contradicted by the actual presentation of Denmark in 2003. In this world, there is nothing to hope for; it is complete harmony. The only conflicts stem from selfish misunderstandings (Josephine) and external attacks on the state of harmony (Thorsen). The role of Christianity has been to establish this state and its current function is to protect it from evil, as Josephine demonstrates when she casts Thorsen to Hell by means of the Lord's Prayer. Christianity conserves the culture it has established itself; there is no room for hoping for changes.

Jesus and Josefine removes the revolutionary and critical potential of the Bible. It merges completely with Danish culture and is not able to present a radical alternative that can be the basis for Christian hope. We are left with the divinely founded Danish society and culture of 2003. Theologically, this cannot be criticized too severely, but artistically *Jesus and Josephine* cannot be praised too much.

BIBLIOGRAPHY

Greimas, Algirdas Julien
    1966   *Sémantique structurale* (Paris: Larousse).
Greimas, Algirdas Julien, and Joseph Courtés
    1976a   *Sémiotique: Dictionnaire raisonné de la théorie du langage* (Paris: Hachette).
    1976b   'The Cognitive Dimension of Narrative Discourse', *New Literary History*
            8: 433-47.

17. *Jul i Valhal* (Cosmo Film/TV2, 2004), directed by Martin Schmidt; *Absalons hemmelighed* (Danmarks Radio 2006), directed by Morten Køhlert, Trine Piil and Malene Vilstrup.

Nielsen, Jesper Tang
    2004   'Jesus og Josefine—et år efter', *Kristeligt Dagblad*, 12 May: n.p.
Propp, Vladimir Jákolevic
    1958   *Morphology of the Folktale* (Bloomington: Indiana University Press).
Scherfig, Nikolaj, and Bo Hr. Hansen
    2004   'Jesus og Josefine er tænkt som dramatik', *Kristeligt Dagblad*, 22 December: n.p.

FILMOGRAPHY

Alt om Jesus og Josefine (Cosmo Film 2003), directed by Ole Stenum.
Oskar og Josefine (Cosmo Film 2005), directed by Carsten Myllerup.

TV CHRISTMAS CALENDARS

Jullerup Færgeby (Danmarks Radio 1974), directed by Per G. Nielsen.
Jul i Gammelby (Danmarks Radio 1979), directed by Hans Christian Ægidius.
Jul og grønne skove (Danmarks Radio 1980), director unknown.
Nissebanden (Danmarks Radio 1984), directed by Per Pallesen.
Jul på slottet (Danmarks Radio 1986), directed by Finn Henriksen.
Nissebanden i Grønland (Danmarks Radio 1989), directed by Per Pallesen and Flemming Jensen.
Jesus og Josefine (Cosmo Film/TV2, 2003), directed by Carsten Myllerup.
Jul i Valhal (Cosmo Film/TV2, 2004), directed by Martin Schmidt.
Absalons hemmelighed (Danmarks Radio 2006), directed by Morten Køhlert, Trine Piil and Malene Vilstrup.

TREKKIES, JEDI-KNIGHTS AND POP WITCHES: FANTASY AND SCIENCE FICTION AS RELIGION

Britt Istoft

Religion does not only appear in churches, temples and sacred sources; it also appears in, for instance, fantasy novels, pop music and science fiction films, all part of popular culture, transmitted through mass media. Though often using traditional religious themes and imagery, popular culture has taken on a life of its own, creating its own stories and myths through which people find meaning and identity.[1] Popular culture thus has become an influential force in many areas of society and it seems that the entertainment industry is also capable of creating meaning that functions as religion for—at least some—consumers of popular culture. When fans virtually organize their lives around a film or television series, this activity could be regarded as religious or at least as analogous to religious activity.

In the following, I focus on how popular *fantasy* and *science fiction* movies and television series may constitute a religion for their most devoted fans. My main example concerns the 'ur-cult' television show *Star Trek*, but I also consider the rival *Star Wars* fandom, which has been in existence since the late 1970s, and discuss how television series about witches and magic, exemplified by *Charmed* (1998–2006) and *Buffy the Vampire Slayer* (1997–2003), have influenced Wicca groups.

Religion can be defined in many ways. Substantive definitions of religion focus on the essence of religion. They tend to emphasize a relationship with higher beings or a transcendental realm. Functional definitions of religion stress the systems of meaning-making that religion provides. Formal definitions of religion include typically religious forms such as myths, rituals and moral codes. In the following, I discuss the religious aspects of the two fan phenomena and the impact of fantasy television series on the religious practices of viewers, by combining these definitions of religion: the uses of myth, ritual, moral codes, institution building and the possible use of transcendental imagery.

---

1. See the Introduction to Forbes and Mahan's (2000) *Religion and Popular Culture in America* (pp. 1-20).

STAR TREK

From its start as a television show in 1966, *Star Trek* embodied progressive and liberal social values such as inter-racial equality, represented by the multi-cultural crew on the starship *U.S.S. Enterprise*, and the idea of fighting for freedom against injustice even when it meant disobeying orders. The tales of 'The Original Series', as it is affectionately known, featuring the Earthlings, or Terrans, Captain Kirk and Doctor McCoy, the Vulcan Mr Spock, and supporting characters such as Chekov, Sulu, Uhura, Scotty, and Nurse Chapel, are continued in the next six films, including a new crew in the second television series and the seventh film, which were both placed in the twenty-fourth century, a century later than the original shows.

The fan phenomenon has been in existence since the original *Star Trek* was first broadcast, but it became apparent when the original series was threatened with cancellation in 1968. Fans of the series organized a letter-writing campaign to keep *Star Trek* on the air, which resulted in one million letters of protest. The network, NBC, decided to renew the program for one more year, but finally cancelled it after its third season. Though the show had stopped, the fans remained active: the first *Star Trek* convention was held in New York in 1972, and by then *Star Trek* fan magazines and manuals were being published for fans all over the world who wanted to know more about the *Star Trek* universe.

Fan activities to revive *Star Trek* continued for years. An animated series was made from 1973 to 1974, and in 1979 the first of ten feature films was released (an eleventh is in pre-production). In 1987, *Star Trek: The Next Generation* (1987–94) was first shown on television and it quickly became a top-rated show in America among men as well as women (Jindra 2000: 166). This success has led to further spin-offs: *Deep Space Nine* (1992–99), *Voyager* (1995–2001) and *Enterprise* (2001–2005). Merchandise, novels, fan clubs, online computer groups, *Star Trek* role-playing and computer games, conventions, tourist sites and the many reruns of the series are also part of the fan phenomenon.

All this is not limited to science fiction fans; humanists of all kinds participate as well. From its start, *Star Trek* dramatized ideas of personal identity, gender relations, interspecies relationships and alternative political forms. Dedicated fans continue to fill out this utopian and mythological universe and keep it consistent through the formation of a canon of 'authentic' *Star Trek* events. In the following, I examine the worldview and 'beliefs' of fans as well as their rituals and organization.

MYTHOLOGY, WORLD VIEW AND 'BELIEFS'

Star Trek belongs to the category of science fiction, of which there are two main genres, the utopian and the dystopian. *Star Trek* falls into the utopian category with its central myth of progress and its faith in the power of science and the human mind. According to *Star Trek* history, war on Earth stopped after nations and planets in 2161 joined together in the *United Federation of Planets*, for which the later starship *U.S.S. Enterprise* is an ambassador. The legendary introduction to every episode of the original series stated the starship's purpose:

> Space…the Final Frontier. These are the voyages of the starship *Enterprise*. Its five-year mission: to explore strange new worlds, to seek out new life and new civilizations, to boldly go where no man has gone before.

The original series often reflected an interventionist American philosophy. *Star Trek: The Next Generation* has a more socially liberated message, and the *Federation* of *The Next Generation*'s time presents a utopian society; not a static paradise, but a constantly evolving society based on fundamental values such as tolerance, racial equality and inter-species understanding. Poverty, war and disease have all been eliminated on Earth, and social and technological problems are solved through the application of reason, science and technology:

> The acquisition of wealth is no longer the driving force in our lives. We work to better ourselves and the rest of humanity (Picard to Lily Sloan in *First Contact*, 1996).

The scientific and technical ideals of the twenty-fourth century are mixed with egalitarian ideology, to produce a progressive world where individuals of either sex and from all races and species work together to expand knowledge. National and racial equality, however, were important issues already in the original series. Though Captain Kirk was a White male, he had an Asian helmsman, Sulu, a Black female communications officer, Lieutenant Uhura, and an Alien, Mr Spock, at his side. There was even a Russian, navigator Pavel Chekhov, in the Starfleet in the midst of the Cold War, and in the famous episode 'Plato's stepchildren',[2] the first interracial kiss was shown on American television.

Though gender equality is stated as important, it may seem limited in the original series. Apart from Uhura,[3] few of the female mini-skirted

---

2. 'Plato's Stepchildren', *Star Trek: The Original Series*, season 3, episode 10 (1968/69).

3. Having a Black woman on a command bridge at a critical time in the Civil Rights Movement was important. When the actress who played Uhura, Nichelle Nichols, considered leaving the show after the first season, Martin Luther King

members of the *Enterprise* could be seen as alternative role models for women, although stronger female characters appeared in guest roles. That changed over the years, and with *Star Trek: The Next Generation*, the feminist vision of equality became apparent. The captain of the starship was still a man, Jean-Luc Picard, but several central characters were female, among others the medical doctor, Beverly Crusher, and the chief of security, Tasha Yar; and among the occasional female characters, we see judges, advocates, a general[4] and even an admiral.[5] In *Voyager*, the starship is commanded by a female captain, Kathryn Janeway.[6]

This positive view of the future is one of the most common reasons fans give for their attraction to *Star Trek*. For example, in the documentary film *Trekkies 2* (2004), Bosnian fans tell how they look to *Star Trek* as part of their dream of a future without starvation, war and killing.[7] But fans are also critical; in particular, gay fans have expressed discontent, because only a few gay characters have been written into the script.[8]

In the utopian world of *Star Trek*, religion in the human world seems to have faded away, as more enlightened secular humanist principles have taken over. This new age was initiated by the human professor Zefram Cochrane's invention of the 'warp drive' in the year 2061, which enabled a space ship to travel many times faster than the speed of light. This event was observed by a more developed species, the Vulcans, and was the reason that the humans/Terrans became members of the intergalactic community.[9] This *Federation of Planets* seeks to bring peace and harmony

persuaded her to stay on because she was a vital role model for young American Black women. It was also the character of Uhura that made a young Whoopi Goldberg realize that there were possibilities for African-American actresses. Goldberg later appeared as the god-like bartender Guinan in *Star Trek: The Next Generation*. According to Gene Roddenberry, the creator of the two first *Star Trek* series, Whoopi Goldberg almost forced him to cast her in *Next Generation*, no matter how small the role might be. See interview with Nichelle Nichols in the documentary *Trekkies* (1997).

4. 'The Measure of a Man', *Star Trek: The Next Generation*, season 2, episode 13 (1989).

5. 'Conspiracy', *Star Trek: The Next Generation*, season 1, episode 24 (1988).

6. On gender roles in *Star Trek*, see Lentz 2003.

7. *Trekkies 2* (2004) is a follow-up on the documentary *Trekkies* (1997). The focus in the first film is on the US, the content of the second is the rest of the world, especially Europe, but it also follows up on characters from the first film.

8. See 'Gay League—Gay Star Trek Timeline' (http://www.gayleague.com/forums/display.php?id=76, and 'Gay, Lesbian and Bisexual Characters on Star Trek—A 12-year Saga of Deceit, Lies, Excuses and Broken Promises' (http://www.webpan.com/dsinclair/trek.html).

9. The episode 'Metamorphosis' from the original series (season 2, episode 9, 1967) establishes a backstory for the invention of the warp drive, stating that it was

to the galaxy, though there is also a principle of non-interference in 'primitive' cultures, which are often characterized as having religious institutions. In the classic episode 'Who Mourns for Adonais?' from 'The Original Series', the message is that the era of myths is over; retreating into slavery to the gods of the past is not an option.[10] The movie *Star Trek V: The Final Frontier* dealt explicitly with the idea of God in a monotheistic sense: Spock's half-brother Sybok embarks on a search for God and takes the *Enterprise* to the centre of the galaxy. When the *Enterprise* arrives there, the crew finds a seemingly all-powerful being, but it is far from benevolent. It turns out that the being is simply a trapped alien power that wants to free itself by stealing the *Enterprise*.

There are many other powerful beings in the *Star Trek* universe. Such beings are sometimes taken for gods by less knowledgeable species.[11] But if 'God' means some kind of Western monotheist notion, then there is no ultimate God in the *Star Trek* Universe.[12] The difference between humans and seemingly divine beings may be of degree, not of kind.

Gene Roddenberry, the late creator of *Star Trek*, and his assistant writer Susan Sackett, both adhered to Humanism and *Star Trek* reflects this philosophy. In 1991, a few months before his death, an interview with Roddenberry was published in *The Humanist*, the official magazine of the *American Humanist Association*, to which Roddenberry belonged. Here he speaks of his conscious humanist philosophy (Alexander 1991). His intention was to express this philosophy in *Star Trek*, using futuristic situations and analogies for current problems on Earth, such as discrimination based on race and gender, and rectifying them; but the networks often intervened. Thus 'The Cage' (1965),[13] his first pilot programme, was rejected by NBC because it featured a female second-in-command, whose rank, borrowing from Naval terminology, is given as Number One.[14]

---

invented by Zefram Cochrane. After this episode, Cochrane is repeatedly referred to, but the details of his first warp drive were first described in the movie *Star Trek: First Contact* (1996).

10. 'Who Mourns for Adonais?', *Star Trek: The Original Series*, season 2, episode 2 (1967/1968).

11. Though the portrayal of religion in the *Star Trek* series is generally negative, in some *Deep Space Nine* and *Voyager* episodes a more positive approach is evident, especially through the spiritual experiences of the Native American Commander Chakotay. The approach to religion in *Voyager* is, however, rather 'New Age', a form of spirituality that is more comparable with the overall *Star Trek* worldview than are institutional and doctrinal forms of religion. See McLaren and Porter 1999.

12. On this subject see Kraemer, Cassidy and Schwartz 2001.

13. 'The Cage' is part of the special features of the box set: *Star Trek: The Original Series, season 3* (2004).

14. In 'The Cage', Number One was played by Majel Barrett, who went on to play Nurse Christine Chapel in the original *Star Trek*.

It was only after Roddenberry's death in 1991 that women were shown commanding their own ships (see Lawrence and Jewett 2002: 229).

By watching *Star Trek* and applying its lessons, *Star Trek* fans argue that one can make the world a better place. They emphasize the *Prime Directive* (forbidding interference in another culture), the cooperative governing structure of the *United Federation of Planets* and—in particular—the Vulcan philosophy of IDIC (Infinite Diversity in Infinite Combination) as values that are needed if we are to survive into the twenty-fourth century. IDIC was only discussed explicitly in one episode[15] of the original series, but has been turned into an entire worldview by fans, because they see the IDIC philosophy as summarizing the key messages of *Star Trek* (see Jindra 1999: 221). IDIC is thus the most central concept in *Star Trek* fandom. In itself, IDIC has no content. It is the particular interpretation of the concept made by fans that gives IDIC its meaning. The principle of diversity is, to fans, first and foremost symbolized by the ethnic and racial diversity of crewmembers. But many values are attributed by fans to IDIC—tolerance, vegetarianism, the fight against AIDS—and many fans trace their commitment to feminism, gay rights, pacifism or multi-culturalism to *Star Trek*'s IDIC philosophy (see, e.g., McLaren 1999: 234). Several of these issues are addressed in *Star Trek*, but only to a limited extent. In typical mythic fashion, the TV series and movies express such ideas through models and patterns more than through rules. *Star Trek* as a 'belief' system therefore must be understood in relation to those who hold and interpret these beliefs.

The future utopia of *Star Trek*, however, is not seen by fans as an inevitable state. The vision must be achieved. Fans encourage each other to make 'real' life more like *Star Trek* (Jindra 2000: 168), and they are often successful at that. Science fiction almost becomes science fact as fans work at making it true by becoming scientists and engineers. They have had an impact on the United States's space program, supporting increased funding and specific space programs. In 1976, they even managed to make NASA name the first space shuttle the *Enterprise* after the fictional starship. NASA also employed Nichelle Nichols, who played Uhura, in an attempt to recruit African-Americans and women to become astronauts.

In sum, *Star Trek* has affinities with a religious outlook: an underlying ideology and mythology that provide fans with an orientation to the world. *Star Trek* is set in the future, but it may nonetheless be seen as an origin myth,[16] as it shows how this future came into existence. It thus

15. 'Is There in Truth No Beauty', *Star Trek: The Original Series*, season 3, episode 5 (1968/69).

16. For a discussion of *Star Trek* as an origin myth, see McLaren 1999.

presents a myth about where we have come from and where we are going. Fans see the concept of IDIC as leading to a future utopia, and this encourages them to live the myth, to ensure that it comes into being. The present and the future are linked by living the myth.

Star Trek thus supplies models for human behaviour. It changes the way fans think about the world and encourages them to remake the world in the image of the myth. In this way, *Star Trek* has been inspiring fans to change the world for over forty years. *Star Trek* is a modern myth, but a secular one. Fans see *Star Trek* as a sign of hope for the future: not for personal salvation, but for the future of the collective 'we'. They want to participate in this vision and help to create it, and it is precisely the activities of fans that may give us a picture of potentially religious connotations of *Star Trek*.

COMMUNITY: CLUBS, CONVENTIONS AND PILGRIMAGES

From their more or less disorganized beginnings, fans of *Star Trek* became increasingly organized, gathering at *Star Trek* conventions to trade merchandise and meet stars from the show. *Star Trek* fans formed a group set apart from the rest of society. Fans married fans and raised their children to be fans. Therefore, third- and even fourth-generation fans are showing up at the many *Star Trek* conventions. These fans are often known as 'trekkies', though some fans consider this term derogatory and instead call themselves 'trekkers'. The term 'trekkie' became even less popular after 1986, when William Shatner, the iconic Captain Kirk, in an (in)famous national television parody, told the trekkies to 'get a life'.[17] Several self-described 'trekkers' have since been quoted as saying that they 'had a life' (in supposed contrast to 'trekkies').[18]

Fans have also formed organizations, among the largest being *Starfleet International*[19] and the *International Federation of Trekkers*.[20] *Star Trek* fan clubs, of which some are affiliated to the larger organizations, are now a diverse, worldwide phenomenon.[21] Some of the clubs are modelled after

17. William Shatner has since regretted this parody, most notably in his book *Get a Life* (1999).

18. This conflict is shown in several interviews with fans and cast characters in the two documentaries *Trekkies* (1997) and *Trekkies 2* (2004), which are in themselves considered controversial among fans, because of their odd mixture of ridicule of and respect for fans.

19. On the organization, see 'Starfleet: The International Star Trek Fan Association' (http://www.sfi.org).

20. See their webpage: http://www.iftcommand.com.

21. *Star Trek* fans in Denmark also have established a club of the more relaxed, non-hierarchical kind. They publish the magazine *Subspace*. See their homepage: http://www.trekkies.dk.

Star Trek ships and hierarchy is established by the titles given to leaders (Admiral, Captain, Lieutenant etc.). Other clubs have taken the alien Klingon warrior-culture to heart and have established 'Klingon Assault Groups' (KAG), but despite the intimidating name, the members of KAG also stress values such as tolerance, gender equality and cooperation.[22] *Star Trek* fans often describe their fellow fans as a 'family'; they stress community service projects and raise funds for charities, which show how seriously they take their beliefs about building a better world.

Trek identities can become very personal when Starfleet members take on specific ranks and titles and use them not only in the *Star Trek* groups, but also in the 'outside' world. During the *White Water* trial[23] in 1996, Barbara Adams, one of the alternate jurors, wore a red and black starfleet uniform to the court sessions. When CNN asked her why, she replied: 'I always wear my uniform to formal occasions'. Seemingly, the court had no problem with her unusual outfit, but when she gave an interview to the television programme *American Journal*, she was dismissed as a juror.[24] Adams' answer as to why she liked *Star Trek* enough to wear one of its uniforms to a serious legal hearing is significant. She said she found *Star Trek* an alternative to 'mindless television' because it promotes tolerance, peace and faith in humankind.[25]

However, much of *Star Trek* fandom revolves around communities that discuss *Star Trek* and remake it in various ways. These networks are more diffuse, and often deal with the more 'philosophical' issues of *Star Trek*. Privately published *Star Trek* novels are also popular. Fans write stories that continue the known narratives,[26] creating alternate endings and, frequently, suggesting romantic relationships not designated by the series or movies.[27] These stories focusing on the relationships of characters

22.   See their international homepage: http://www.kag.org.

23.   *White Water* concerned the real estate dealings of Bill and Hilary Clinton and their associates, James B. McDougal and Susan McDougal in the *Whitewater Development Corporation*, a failed business venture. An investigation resulted in criminal charges against the McDougals, but the Clintons themselves were never charged.

24.   The news media repeated that she was dropped as a juror for wearing her *Star Trek* uniform to the trial, and she herself noted that she was dismissed because she talked to reporters about her *Trek* uniform and not because she said anything about the trial.

25.   Barbara Adams is interviewed in the documentaries *Trekkies* (1997) and *Trekkies 2* (2004).

26.   The genre of fan fiction has been discussed also in relation to biblical scriptures. In Hellekson and Busse (2006), the Pseudepigrapha, as unauthorized derivative works, are seen as early examples of fan fiction.

27.   Series such as *Star Trek*, that is, not constrained by a linear narrative structure, over a period of time will establish back stories, parallel histories that may be

rather than on the more science and action aspects, not surprisingly, are mostly written by women.[28]

The different clubs and communities are often rather isolated from each other, but there are opportunities for them to gather at conventions and tourist sites, which also serve as locations where serious fans meet casual fans and where new club members can be recruited. There are nearly one hundred annual *Star Trek* conventions worldwide. Here one can find *Star Trek* literature, artwork, costume contests, rock music and appearances by *Star Trek* actors. Participation has been described in almost—at least in the *Star Trek* universe—mystical terms as a *time warp* (time travel faster than the speed of light) (Van Hise 1990: 90). One might argue that for some devoted fans, convention attendance represents a secular pilgrimage, where fans, like pilgrims in conventional pilgrimages, in a sense are 'out of time', liberated from everyday roles and hierarchies (see Porter 1999). The myths are lived; for instance, many couples are married *Star Trek*-style during conventions; possibly by an official dressed like Captain Kirk.[29]

For fans, *Star Trek* exhibitions and tourist sites have become popular places where they can experience the *Star Trek* universe more closely. *The Universal Studios* theme park in California has a *Star Trek* set in which tourists/pilgrims are filmed, in full uniform, taking on characters' roles and acting out a *Star Trek* plot, the closest thing actually to being on the show.

periodically revisited, and characters and peoples who appear in a single episode and disappear again into other possible futures. This allows fans to develop the *Star Trek* universe further. See Gwenllian-Jones and Pearson 2004: xxi.

28.   This fiction, often with homoerotic themes, is called slash-literature, named for the '/' that separates the character names, as in fiction about a homosexual relationship between Kirk and Spock. This fiction is written almost entirely by heterosexual women. They often state that they enjoy slash primarily for the intimacy between the male characters. Slash literature is also found in other fandoms. *Buffy* slash writers focus on the two male vampires Angel and Spike, and even among *Lord of the Rings* fan writers, one finds slash fiction, the most popular couple being Frodo and Sam. On *Star Trek* slash, see Bacon-Smith 1992. On *Buffy* slash, see Busse 2002. On *Lord of the Rings* slash, see Pullen 2006: 173, and Chen 2004.

29.   In the original series, the *Enterprise* had a chapel. In the episode 'Balance of Terror' (season 1, episode 9, 1966/1967), Captain Kirk performed a wedding ceremony for two of his crew members. Actually it was a podium rather than an altar, with no familiar religious symbols. The chapel seemed to be a kind of symbol of non-denominational ecumenism. The chapel does not return in future series. The network actually wanted a Christian chaplain on the *Enterprise*, but Roddenberry protested: 'How could you have a chaplain if you've got that many people of different and alien beliefs on your ship?' (David 1991: 6), and he protested again, when Spock was killed temporarily in one of the movies, and the producers wanted a Christian funeral for the alien Spock.

Sitting on the bridge in uniform and being filmed can be seen as a ritual act that allows the fan directly to participate in the *Star Trek* universe.

The *Star Trek* exhibitions and places of 'pilgrimage' are many, as various towns have taken up the *Star Trek* theme. Vulcan in Canada has thus turned itself into a *Star Trek* 'theme' town and built a thirty-one-foot replica of the *Enterprise* at the entrance to the city, and the town of Riverside, Iowa, holds annual Kirk festivals after having proclaimed the town the future birth place of Captain Kirk (the Kirk character does come from Iowa, born 22/3 2228).[30]

Fans also participate in the *Star Trek* universe when they buy *Star Trek* merchandise and collect episodes and movies, thus allowing them to enter that universe at any time. Religion points to another world: *Star Trek* does the same. In spite of *Star Trek*'s secularism, fan activities could be seen as 'symbolic communities', where exemplary models for human action are communicated symbolically, and the meaning of *Star Trek* is lived by fans to whom the stories have a mythic dimension. The *Star Trek* modernism could itself be seen as a faith practiced in the various types of communities that make up *Star Trek* fandom. When secular activities take on the forms of religion, they seem to take on the function of religion and become bearers and shapers of values and beliefs. Religion in *Star Trek* is mostly presented as outdated, and scientific humanism is offered as an alternative. Nonetheless, *Star Trek* fandom itself exhibits religious elements, from the *Star Trek* inspired ethical worldviews to the ritual practice of convention attendance, which often seem to represent a secular pilgrimage, where fans experience liberation from everyday roles, and myths become realized in an egalitarian *communitas* experience.

LINKING THE *STAR TREK* UNIVERSE TO THE PRESENT WORLD

The *Star Trek* universe is not seen by fans as a separate universe unconnected to the present. In various ways, it is 'linked' with the contemporary world. *Next Generation* episodes always begin with a close view of the Earth, then the camera runs through the other planets of the solar system, finally focusing on the *Enterprise*. This encourages the viewer to see the events as taking place in his or her own universe. Besides, the various TV series refer to historic events from the twentieth century, and occasionally time travel to the past occurs, which verifies that the world of *Star Trek* is the future we will have if we play our cards right. Also *Star Trek* fan literature links the world of *Star Trek* and the present. *Star Trek Chronology: The History of the Future* (Okuda and Okuda 1996) is a compilation

30. See *Trekkies* (1997).

of a history of the universe, incorporating both actual historical events and *Star Trek* history through the twenty-fourth century.

A huge amount of *Star Trek* material has developed through the years, even something approximating an 'orthodox' canon: the TV series, the 10 films, and a library of authorized commentary, including novels, audio materials and survey volumes with the Paramount[31] imprimatur. The aim of all this is to 'fill out' the *Star Trek* universe. Reference books, such as the *Star Trek Encyclopedia* (Okuda, Okuda and Mirek 1999) have proved popular. Dictionaries have been compiled for the languages of *Star Trek* alien species: *Klingon*, *Vulcan* and *Romulan*. The entire history, geography, philosophy and location of the fictional planets have been described (Johnson 1989; Mandel 2002). Even a *Star Trek Cookbook* has been published (Philips and Birnes 1999). Besides the above examples, there have been numerous non-canon novels and comic books published over the years or distributed on the Internet,[32] as mentioned earlier. *Star Trek* is thus an evolving universe of stories. It is part of television, but goes far beyond it. Also the concept of 'canon' is discussed among fans, and the idea of what is authentic *Trek* is not always clear, especially in the net-based communities. If new members/fans find some of the television series lacking in credibility, they may be encouraged to read the novels instead (Jindra 1994: 12).

The fans have taken the given universe of *Star Trek* and filled it out in order to make a consistent, utopian world. This fan creativity might be seen as a creation of mythology. One should not, however, eliminate the 'playful' aspect of *Star Trek*. There is certainly a mixture of fun and seriousness about *Star Trek* among fans, but this ambiguity is also present in the creation of many other mythologies. Here, too, reality and unreality, entertainment and mythology are often mixed. Participation in a religious performance, as in the *Star Trek* universe, often involves (serious) pretending, one might say. *Star Trek* fandom exists in a liminal area between entertainment and seriousness. In this respect, it might resemble Elvis Presley fans' pilgrimages to Graceland, often dressed in glittering garments, eating banana and peanut butter sandwiches and praising Elvis as the Redeemer. All tongue in cheek, but still these actions are considered meaningful and important by the people devoted to Elvis (see Plasketes 1997: 21-61).

Star Trek has been filled out to make it a full, consistent reality to enable fans to live within its universe, whether they are interested in the

31.   The Paramount Studio now owns the entire *Star Trek* franchise.

32.   The many Internet novels have led to increased legal action on the part of the studio, who view fan stories as infringing on their property. The ease of circulation on the Internet has also increased visibility. See Pullen 2006: 175-76.

technical details of the various starships, the supposed romantic escapades of the characters or the philosophy expressed in the series. The religious potential for the fandom is clear and the resemblance to religion obvious: the *Star Trek* fandom has myths, a belief set, a canon, rituals and devoted members. It has organization and a low-key recruitment system. Fans, however, do not consider their involvement with the *Star Trek* phenomenon religious, and the fandom does not adhere to the more restrictive, substantive definition of religion that posits belief in deities or in the supernatural. *Star Trek* fandom might rather be seen as sacralization of elements of modernist culture that expresses trust in science and hope in the future. However, the ritualistic behaviour of fans, their treatment of the *Star Trek* myth as a basis for transformative action and their structuring of their daily lives on the basis of the IDIC philosophy can be analyzed as religious at a functionalistic level.

STAR WARS

Star Wars fandom represents another long-term cult phenomenon. Although it is less organized, it seems to fit the substantive definitions of religion better than the *Star Trek* fan phenomenon does. The *Star Wars* movies are often considered science fiction, but events are actually ruled more by magic than by rational science and thus the *Star Wars* universe is nearer to the world of *fantasy* and more like a classical fairy tale. Further, the events do not take place in the future, but in the past, as the opening sentence makes clear: 'A long, long time ago in a galaxy, far, far away'.

In contrast to *Star Trek*'s band of explorers and diplomats, *Star Wars*, in the first trilogy, follows the tales of a group of rebels fighting against the evil Galactic Empire: Luke Skywalker, Princess Leia, Han Solo, Chewbacca, the robots R2-D2 and C-3PO and the hermit Obi-Wan Kenobi. The Empire's oppression is personified in the Emperor and in the black-armoured Darth Vader, who turns out to be Luke's father and is redeemed in the end. The second trilogy travels back in time to a period before the Empire, when Darth Vader was a child, and then a young man becoming a Jedi Knight—then known as Anakin Skywalker—tracing his fall from grace to evil.

The *Star Wars* canon—six films, including the first trilogy (1977–83)[33] and the prequel trilogy (1999–2005)[34]—is less complex and not nearly as

33. Consisting of the films *Star Wars: A New Hope* (1977), *The Empire Strikes Back* (1980), and *The Return of the Jedi* (1983).

34. Consisting of the films: *Episode I: The Phantom Menace* (1999), *Episode II: Attack of the Clones* (2002) and *Episode III: Revenge of the Sith* (2005).

large as the *Star Trek* canon, which so far consists of five television series[35] and ten films. But the tendency to create more or less religious societies based on the movies is also obvious with regard to *Star Wars*. According to rumour, Francis Ford Coppola suggested to George Lucas that he should turn the Jedi-philosophy he invented for *Star Wars* into a religious movement. Lucas declined.[36] But other fans of *The Force* have taken it upon themselves to organize something that resembles a religious canon, taking the film scripts as their scripture.[37] The central tenet of this Jedi Creed is that *The Force* is 'an energy field created by all living things. It surrounds us and penetrates us. It binds the galaxy together', as Obi-Wan Kenobi says in *Star Wars: A New Hope* (1977), the first of the movies.

It has been claimed that 'Jedism' has gained official recognition as a religion in England and Australia, but the fact is that this is based on replies to two censuses. In the 2001 UK census, 390,127 respondents listed their religion as 'Jedi', whereas in Australia, 70,509 people declared that they were followers of the Jedi faith, and that they believed in 'the force'. Most of the people who wrote Jedi on their census forms were suspected to have done so in response to an e-mail encouraging all *Star Wars* fans to get it recognized as an official religion.[38] But, of course, census data do not provide official recognition for a religion. The two censuses merely provide lists of the number of people in England and Australia that have given a particular answer to a particular question. As such, Jedism therefore is not officially recognized as a religion.

Yet it is interesting that many people do not see the fan phenomenon as *only* fun; instead, they invest a lot of time and serious dedication to their fandom. For many, the *Star Wars* saga has been a defining influence in their lives. As *Star Trek* has inspired people to become involved in astronomy, space programs and science in general, *Star Wars* seems to have inspired fans to become involved in, for example, technology, art, psychology and the military. It also informs fans' beliefs and ethics. Like *Star Trek* fans, they incorporate the films into their workplaces, homes and relationships. For many, *Star Wars* is not only a supplement that illustrates existing religion, but a persuasive ethical system in its own right. Many refer to the Jedi Knights forming a code of behaviour and

35.   The five TV series comprise a total of 703 episodes (*The Original Series*, 79 episodes; *Next Generation*, 178 episodes; *Deep Space Nine*, 176 episodes; *Voyager*, 172 episodes; *Enterprise*, 98 episodes).

36.   'The Gospel according to Luke (Skywalker)' (http://news.bbc.co.uk/2/hi/entertainment/1204829).

37.   See 'The Jedi Creed' website (http://www.jedicreed.org).

38.   See 'Jedi "Religion" Grows in Australia' (http://news.bbc.co.uk/hi/entertainment/film/2218456.stm), and 'Jedi Makes the Census List' (http://news.bbc.co.uk/1/hi/uk/1589133.stm).

belief based on the evidence of Yoda, Obi-Wan Kenobi, Qui Gong Jinn and Luke Skywalker (see Brooker 2002: 6). Some of these fans seem to have a Zen background, which is not surprising: the Jedi philosophy has strong resemblances with Zen philosophies (see, e.g., Bortolin 2005). One might even compare them to certain Buddhist warrior monks, like the Shaolin monks of China. But other similarities are also discernible—from Daoist (see Porter 2003) to Christian (see, e.g., Staub 2005).

Not all fans are delighted when the term 'religion' is used to describe their activities though. As one fan writes:

> Jedism is now a religion? I am saddened and horrified as it means another really good philosophy has been dragged down to the level of (yuk) RELIGION. It is now only a matter of time until 'they' show up...the pontificating pompous asses who will feel compelled to tell us dummies just what the REAL truth of Jedism is. Then there will come the disciples, then the rules... ('The Force is With ...Everyone', http://www.beliefnet.com/story/105/story_10570_5html#com).[39]

This fan sees himself as adhering to a philosophy, not a religion, a term that has very bad press in popular culture, because it rhymes with dogmatism, hierarchy and rules. But he seems to accept the term 'Jedism' as a description of his worldview. The spirituality in popular culture in general is unorganized, diffuse and ever changing, and many revolt at the idea of having their philosophy of life changed into something organized and pinned down for all eternity.

Although the *Star Trek* and *Star Wars* fan phenomena have much in common, one might say that the *Star Trek* phenomenon is organized to a greater degree than is the *Star Wars* phenomenon, which is more fragmented and diffuse. On the other hand, a transcendental aspect is more discernible among *Star Wars* fans than among those of *Star Trek*.

CHARMED AND BUFFY THE VAMPIRE SLAYER

The diffuse spirituality in popular culture is also discernible in other fantasy series, such as *Charmed* (1998–2006) and *Buffy the Vampire Slayer* (1997–2003), which have inspired many young pagans and Wiccans.

Wicca, or modern witchcraft, is an established religion, at least recognized as such in the United States. Wiccan Creeds are reflected in several fantasy or fantasy-inspired movies and television series from the mid-nineties up until the present day, most popularly in *Buffy the Vampire Slayer* and *Charmed*, a series about the three Halliwell sisters, Piper, Phoebe and Prue.[40] *Charmed* has explicit references to Wiccan expressions,

---

39. On this website one can find several responses to the Jedi question.
40. Prue is replaced by her half-sister Paige in season 4.

tools and so on (e.g. *The Craft, The Casting of a Circle* and the *Book of Shadows*). The first episode is even called 'Something Wicca this Way Comes'. The three sisters are initiated by a magic spell, and they have inherited their magical powers through the maternal lineage of the family. This matriarchal theme fits well with the Wiccan claim of reaching back to pre-Christian and pre-patriarchal times.

Various Wiccan websites have references to the Halliwell sisters, although there is some ambivalence as to how Wiccan they 'really' are.[41] Many teenage girls seem to have found the Wiccan sites interesting after having watched the series on television and wishing to learn more about how to become a Wiccan/witch.[42]

However, *Buffy the Vampire Slayer* probably has been the most influential media representation of witchcraft. The main character, Buffy Summers, is often taken as a spiritual guide (see, e.g., Riess 2004), but it is the character Willow that young witches claim to gain inspiration from— many actually adopt her name as their Witch name. Willow is Buffy's friend and is first characterized by her computer skills, but is portrayed increasingly on the show as a 'Wiccan'. Critics have—as in the case of the Halliwell sisters—pointed out that the depiction of Wicca on the show is inaccurate and Willow has been described as a 'Hollywood Witch' (see Golden 2003). Indeed, her initial interest in Wicca does seem to lie more in spell-casting than in the faith itself. Willow ends up as an extraordinarily powerful Wiccan, but after her first meeting with Wiccans at her college, she notes in disgust: 'Bunch of wanna blessed be's. Nowadays every girl with a henna tattoo and a spice rack thinks she's a sister to the dark ones.'[43] She expresses frustration that Wiccans have lost their connection with 'real' Witchcraft. This play with the boundaries of real world and fiction gives viewers the chance to laugh at any supposed connection between *Buffy* and real-life interests in alternative religion (see Schofield Clark 2003: 58). It inverts reality and fantasy, dramatizing Willow's 'Witchcraft' practises as real, while contemporary Wicca is treated with the same irreverent humour with which the show treats Christianity.[44]

41. See for instance *Pagan Today*'s homepage (http://www.pagantoday.com/wicca_faq.htm), which lists one 'frequently asked question' as being: 'Does the show *Charmed* represent an accurate portrayal of Wicca?', to which the answer is negative.

42. On the popularity of Wicca among teenagers, see also the many manuals for teen witches, the most popular being *TeenWitch: Wicca for a New Generation* (Ravenwolf 1998) and *The Real Witch's Handbook: A Complete Instruction for both Young and Old Alike* (West 2001).

43. From the episode 'Hush', season 4, episode 10 (1999).

44. The second episode of *Buffy* had en evil witch as the villain, which made many Pagans and Wiccans write off the show. However, they returned when a later

One characteristic of the show is an almost complete disinterest in organized religion. When references to religion turn up, they are approached with ambivalence. The only characters in *Buffy* that practice any sort of organized religion in churches, using altars and creeds, are the bad guys—the vampires. An overt reference to organized religion can be found in the episode 'What's My Line?', in which the vampire Spike performs a ritual in a chapel inside a gothic church. He chants, uses incense and performs what resembles a Christian communion ritual with blood as the symbol that restores, although in this case the purpose is to 'resurrect' a vampire.[45]

The humour, self-irony and the play between real world and fiction in *Buffy* is not far from the self-understanding of many modern witches. Wicca was created in post-war Great Britain by Gerald Gardner (1884–1964), who claimed direct historical lineage to a pre-Christian 'Old Religion' in Europe, which allegedly worshipped a Goddess and a God. In the United States, the English revivalist religion changed its focus, influenced by the women's movement. Characteristics of the new American movement, which was soon to be exported to the rest of the world, were feminism, decentralization, individualism, humour and a strong sense of self-irony. The fact that the basic rituals in Modern Witchcraft are built upon imaginary late medieval rituals—the sabbath, nocturnal gatherings and the circle or *coven* consisting of 12 members[46]—does not disturb modern witches, who claim to continually re-invent the Witch. Like *Star Trek* and *Star Wars* fans, Wiccans know that their myths are based on fiction, but at the same time, those myths convey a message that is taken very seriously and reworked in rituals and daily life.

CONCLUSION

In a society that has become more diverse, mass popular culture, especially television and film, in many ways has become a unifying element, taking the place of previous mythologies, such as Christianity, which

episode featured a good witch, who was a Wiccan, and the show introduced a new computer teacher at Sunnydale High School, Jenny Calendar, who was presented as a gypsy, a witch and a Techno-pagan. When Jenny is killed it is Willow who steps into the role of witch (Winslade n.d.). One can find many other interesting articles on themes related to the Buffy verse on 'Slayage: The Online International Journal of Buffy Studies' (http://www.slayageonline.com).

45. From the episode 'What's My Line?', season 2, episode 10 (1997).

46. There is also a substantial contribution from esoteric traditions from the nineteenth century, such as occult philosophy and ritual magic of brotherhoods, (e.g. the Freemasons and Rosicrucians). On the history of witchcraft see Hutton 2000 and Adler 1986.

traditionally have provided values and meaning and allowed people to make sense of the world and their place in it. Many popular culture phenomena have become modern myths on the basis of which people organize their lives. *Star Trek* fandom, the main example described in this article, not only has myths, but also a canon, rituals, devoted members and an organization. As such, it fits well with formal and functional definitions of religion. But the fans of *Star Trek* do not consider their participation in *Trek* fandom religious, and they do not operate with a transcendental realm; on the contrary, this fandom is highly modernist and secularistic in outlook. A consistent theme in the TV series is the presentation of scientific humanism as an alternative to religious faith. Nonetheless, fans' ritual participation in the *Star Trek* universe at convention sites as well as their attempt to make the future utopia of *Star Trek* come true by living the ideals of infinite diversity in infinite combination in their daily lives point to a longing for another world—though not a strictly transcendental one—which justifies analyzing the fan phenomenon in a religious framework. The *Star Wars* fandom is less organized, but may fit the substantive definitions of religion better in the sense that many fans find a transcendental core in the *Star Wars* myth: the all-embracing, universal concept of *The Force*. Unlike *Star Trek* fans, who do not consider their involvement with the fictional universe religious, *Star Wars* fans sometimes do. This belief, Jedism, informs fans' ethics and general orientation in life, but in common with *Star Trek* fans they do not find the concept of organized religion relevant, a trait that seems to bind together all of the studied phenomena. This links them to the general popular culture dislike of dogmatism, hierarchy and strict rules, which, however, does not rule out a more diffuse 'New Age'-like spirituality.

Only Wicca may fully live up to standard definitions of religion, having deities, a small-scale organization (the coven) and fully fledged rituals in the form of incantations and the creation of sacred spaces in the form of the circle. Nonetheless, the most popular form of Wicca spirituality is found on the Internet among solitary practitioners. All of the studied phenomena thus—in varying ways—may be said to represent religions, or religious border phenomena, well suited to modern secular societies. These cultural and spiritual expressions of popular culture have attained lives of their own and provide fans and practitioners with an overarching moral value system.

BIBLIOGRAPHY

Adler, Margot
    1986   *Drawing Down the Moon: Witches, Druids, Goddess-Worshippers, and Other Pagans in America Today* (Boston: Beacon Press [1st edn 1979]).
Alexander, David
    1991   'Interview with Gene Roddenberry: Writer, Producer, Philosopher, Humanist', in *The Humanist*, March/April (http://www.stjohns-chs.org/english/STAR_TREK/humanistinterview/humanist.html).
Bacon-Smith, Camille
    1992   *Enterprising Women: Television Fandom and the Creation of Popular Myth* (Philadelphia: University of Pennsylvania Press).
Bortolin, Matthew
    2005   *The Dharma of Star Wars* (Sommerville, MA: Wisdom Publications).
Brooker, Will
    2002   *Using the Force: Creativity, Community and Star Wars Fans* (London: Continuum).
Busse, Kristina
    2002   'Crossing the Final Taboo: Family, Sexuality, and Incest in Buffyverse Fan Fiction', in Rhonda V. Wilcox and David Lavery (eds.), *Fighting the Forces: What's at Stake in Buffy the Vampire Slayer* (New York: Littlefield Publishers): 207-17.
Chaires, Robert H., and Bradley Chilton (eds.)
    2003   *Star Trek Visions of Law and Justice* (Dallas: Adios Press).
Chen, Milly
    2004   'When Frodo Met Sam', *Sunday Times Style*, 18 July (http://www.theonering.net/scrapbook/view/13482).
Forbes, Bruce David, and Jeffrey H. Mahan (eds.)
    2000   *Religion and Popular Culture in America* (Berkeley: University of California Press).
Gwenllian-Jones, Sara, and Roberta E. Pearson (eds.)
    2004   *Cult Television* (Minneapolis: University of Minnesota Press).
Goldens, Christie
    2003   'Where's the Religion in Willow's Wicca?', in Glenn Yeffeth (ed.), *Seven Seasons of Buffy: Science Fiction and Fantasy Writers Discuss their Favorite Television* Show (Dallas: BenBella Books): 159-66.
Hellekson, Karen, and Kristina Busse (eds.)
    2006   *Fan Fiction and Fan Communities in the Age of the Internet: New Essays* (Jefferson, NC: McFarlane & Co.).
Hutton, Ronald
    2000   *The Triumph of the Moon: A History of Modern Pagan Witchcraft* (Oxford: Oxford University Press).
Jindra, Michael
    1994   'Star Trek Fandom as a Religious Phenomenon', *Sociology of Religion* (http://findarticles.com/p/articles/mi_m0SOR/is_n1_v55/ai_15383489/pg_1).
    1999   '"Star Trek to Me is a Way of Life": Fan Expressions of Star Trek Philosophy', in Porter and McLaren 1999: 217-30.

2000   'It's about Faith in our Future: Star Trek Fandom as Cultural Religion',
        in Forbes and Mahan 2000: 165-79.

Johnson, Shane
1989   *Worlds of the Federation* (New York: Pocket Books).

Kraemer, Ross S., William Cassidy, and Susan L. Schwartz
2001   *Religions of Star Trek* (Boulder, CO: Westview Press).

Lawrence, John Shelton and Robert Jewett
2002   *The Myth of the American Superhero* (Grand Rapids: Eerdmans).

Lentz, Susan A.
2003   "Where No Woman Has Gone Before': Feminist Perspectives on Star
        Trek', in Chaires and Chilton 2003: 136-59.

Mandel, Geoffrey
2002   *Star Trek Charts: The Complete Atlas of Star Trek* (New York: Pocket
        Books).

McLaren, Darcee L.
1999   'On the Edge of Forever: Understanding the Star Trek Phenomenon as
        Myth', in Porter and McLaren 1999: 231-43.

McLaren, Darcee L., and Jennifer E. Porter
1999   '(Re)Covering Sacred Ground: New Age Spirituality in *Star Trek:
        Voyager* in *Star Trek and Sacred Ground: Explorations of Star Trek,
        Religion, and American Culture*', in Porter and McLaren 1999: 101-15.

Okuda, Michael, and Denise Okuda
1996   *Star Trek Chronology: The History of the Future* (New York: Pocket
        Books, 2nd edn [1993]).

Okuda, Michael, Denise Okuda and Debbie Mirek
1999   *The Star Trek Encyclopedia: A Reference Guide to the Future* (New York:
        Pocket Books, 3rd expanded edn [1994]).

Philips, Ethan, and William J. Birnes
1999   *The Star Trek Cookbook* (New York: Pocket Books).

Plasketes, George
1997   *Images of Elvis Presley in American Culture, 1977–1997: The Mystery
        Terrain* (New York: Haworth Press).

Porter, Jennifer E.
1999   'To Boldly Go: *Star Trek* Convention Attendance as Pilgrimage', in
        Porter and McLaren 1999: 245-70.

Porter, Jennifer E., and Darcee L. McLaren (eds.)
1999   *Star Trek and Sacred Ground: Explorations of Star Trek, Religion and
        American Culture* (New York: State University of New York Press).

Porter, John M.
2003   *The Tao of Star Wars* ([n.c.]: Humanics Publishing Group).

Pullen, Kirsten
2006   'The Lord of the Rings Online Blockbuster Fandom: Pleasure and
        Commerce', in Ernest Mathijs (ed.), *The Lord of the Rings: Popular
        Culture in Global Context* (London: Wallflower Press): 172-88.

Ravenwolf, Silver
1998   *TeenWitch: Wicca for a New Generation* (Woodbury, MN: Llewellyn).

Riess, Jane
    2004   *What Would Buffy Do? The Vampire Slayer as Spiritual Guide* (San Francisco: Jossey-Bass).
Kraemer, Ross S., William Cassidy and Susan L. Schwartz
    2001   *Religions of Star Trek* (Boulder, CO: Westview Press).
Schofield Clark, Lynn
    2003   *From Angels to Aliens: Teenagers, the Media, and the Supernatural* (Oxford: Oxford University Press).
Shatner, William
    1999   *Get a Life* (New York: Atria).
Staub, Dick
    2005   *Christian Wisdom of the Jedi Masters* (San Francisco: Jossey–Bass).
Van Hise, James
    1990   *Trek Fan's Handbook* (n.p.: Movie Publisher Services).
West, Kate
    2001   *The Real Witch's Handbook: A Complete Instruction to the Craft for Both Young and Old Alike* (New York: Thorsons).
Winslade, J. Lawton
    n.d.   'Teen Witches, and "Wanna-Blessed-Be's": Pop Culture Magic in Buffy the Vampire Slayer' (http://www.slayageonline.com/essays/slayage1/Winslade.htm)

Internet References
'The Force is with Everyone' (http://www.beliefnet.com/story/105/story_10570_5.html).
'Gay League—Gay Star Trek Timeline' (http://www.gayleague.com/forums/display.php?id=76).
'Gay, Lesbian and Bisexual Characters on Star Trek: A 12-Year Saga of Deceit, Lies, Excuses, and Broken Promises' (http://www.webspan.com/dsinclair/trek.html).
'The Gospel according to Luke (Skywalker)' (http://news.bbc.co.uk/2/hi/entertainment/1204829.stm).
'Jedi Makes the Census List' (http://news.bbc.co.uk/1/hi/uk/1589133.stm).
'Jedi "Religion" Grows in Australia' (http://news.bbc.co.uk/1/hi/entertainment/film/2218456.stm).
'Pagan Today' (http://www.pagantoday.com/wicca_faq.htm).

Websites (All web addresses cited in this study were accessed 2 June 2008.)
'The International Star Trek Fan Association' (http://www.sfi.org).
'The International Federation of Trekkers' (http://www.iftcommand.com).
'The Jedi Creed' (http://www.jedicreed.org).
'The Klingon Assault Groups (KAG)' (http://www.kag.org).
'Slayage. The Online International Journal of Buffy Studies' (http://www.slayageonline.com).
http://www.trekkies.dk

Films
Trekkies (Roger Nygard 1997).
Trekkies 2 (Roger Nygard 2004).

INDEXES

INDEX OF REFERENCES

INDEX OF AUTHORS

INDEX OF FILMS

Book no. 27 in the series *Religion in the 21st Century, University of Copenhagen*, www.ku.dk/satsning/religion

Books published in the series:

1. *Gudstro i Danmark (Faith in God in Denmark).* Ed. by Morten Thomsen Højsgaard and Hans Raun Iversen, 2005
2. *Gudebilleder. Ytringsfrihed og religion i en globaliseret verden (Pictures of God. Freedom of Expression and Religion in a Globalized World).* Ed. by Lisbet Christoffersen, 2006
3. *Tro på teatret. Essays om religion og teater (Faith at the Theatre. Essays on Religion and Theatre).* Ed by Bent Holm, 2006
4. *Vendepunkter. Religion mellem konflikt og forsoning (Turning Points. Religion between Conflict and Reconciliation).* Ed. by Lene Sjørup, 2007
5. *Tørre tal om troen. Religionsdemografi i det 21. århundrede (Dry Numbers on Faith. Demography of Religion in the 21st Century).* Ed. by Margit Warburg and Brian Jacobsen, 2007
6. *Nye muslimer i Danmark (New Muslims in Denmark).* By Tina G. Jensen and Kate Østergaard, 2007
7. *Indvandrerne i Danmarks historie. Kultur- og religionsmøder (Immigrants in the History of Denmark. Cultural and Religious Encounters).* By Bent Østergaard, 2007
8. *Dansk konversionsforskning (Danish Research on Conversion).* Ed. by Mogens S. Mogensen and John H.M. Damsager, 2007
9. *Scener for samvær. Ny antropologi om ritualer, performance og socialitet (Scenes for Being Together. New Anthropology about Rituals, Performance and Sociality).* Ed. by Inger Sjørslev, 2007
10. *Pinochet: frelser og forsoner - og de fattiges teologiske modstand (Pinochet: Savior and Reconciler – and the Theological Resistance of the Poor).* By Lene Sjørup, 2008
11. *Bateson. A Precursor for Biosemiotics.* Ed. by Jesper Hoffmeyer, 2008
12. *Biosemiotics. Signs of Life and the Life of Signs.* By Jesper Hoffmeyer, 2008
13. *The Religious in Response to Mass Atrocity: Interdisciplinary Perspectives.* Ed. by Thomas Brudholm and Thomas Cushman, 2008
14. *Integration og retsudvikling (Integration and Development of Legislation).* Ed. by Rubya Mehdi, 2007
15. *Unveiling the Hidden. Contemporary Approaches to the Study of Divination* Ed. by Anders Lisdorf and Kirstine Munk, 2008
16. *Abrahams spor. Abrahamfiguren i religion, filosofi og kunst (Traces by Abraham. The Abraham Figure in Religion, Philosophy and Arts).* By K. Bruun, Finnn Danmgaard, Thomas Hoffmann, Søren Holst and Jesper Skau, 2007
22. *I hjertet af Danmark. Institutioner og mentaliteter (At the heart of Denmark. Institutions and mentalities).* By Peter Gundelach, Hans Raun Iver sen and Margit Warburg. 2008
23. *Law and Religion in Multicultural Societies.* Ed. by Rubya Mehdi et al., 2008

Printed in the United Kingdom
by Lightning Source UK Ltd.
133204UK00001B/97-99/P

9 781906 055363